ST MARTIN'S

TRUE CRIME
CLASSICS

# ALWAYS IN OUR HEARTS

## THE STORY OF AMY GROSSBERG, BRIAN PETERSON, AND THE BABY THEY DIDN'T WANT

## DOUG MOST

St. Martin's Paperbacks

Published by arrangement with Record Books

ALWAYS IN OUR HEARTS

Library of Congress Catalog Card Number: 98-32047

ISBN: 0-312-97309-8
EAN: 80312-97309-4

Printed in the United States of America

Record Books hardcover edition published 1999
St. Martin's Paperbacks edition / April 2000

St. Martin's Paperbacks are published by St. Martin's Press, 175 Fifth Avenue, New York, NY 10010.

10   9   8   7   6   5   4

# AUTHOR'S NOTE

This book is an account of the events leading up to, and subsequent to, the birth and death of a baby boy on a night in November 1996. No names have been changed in the book.

The author acknowledges that some of the facts in the case were disputed and will continue to be in dispute. Some of these disputed facts cannot be verified. The author has presented what he believes is the most plausible version of events based on court records, police reports, transcripts of interviews, and nearly one hundred personal interviews with people involved in the case and those who followed it in the news.

When the two teenagers offered different accounts of a single episode, the author chose the version that seemed most likely to have occurred, and that could be proven.

The dialogue in this work was created, based on reported conversations, transcripts, correspondence, the recollections of the parties involved, and official records in which words were paraphrased and not quoted directly. Both families denied repeated requests for interviews. The author's intent is to give a factual account of the people, places, and events surrounding the baby's birth and death.

# ACKNOWLEDGMENTS

Above everyone else, I must first thank my parents and brother for their constant encouragement throughout my career. No one could ask for a more supportive family.

From the entire family of *The Record*, from Malcolm A. Borg on down, I owe tremendous gratitude, particularly to my editor for two years on this story, Matt Purcell. Also, thanks must go to editor-in-chief Vivian Waixel and to assistant managing editor Mike Semel for keeping me on the story from the start when they barely knew me and giving me the time to write this book.

This book would never have happened so smoothly without the energy and enthusiasm of Marc Watrel at Record Books, the subtle but firm hand of my editor for the project, Bill Thompson, and the go-ahead from Lois Di Tommaso, director of new products at *The Record*.

Special appreciation goes to three friends at the paper: Peter Sampson, for backing me up and offering advice; Paul Rogers, for being the sounding board every reporter craves and providing me contacts in Wyckoff; Ruth Padawer, for her guidance on critical women's issues. Thanks also to the entire photography staff, particularly Mel Evans, who was with me so many times in Delaware, and to the librarians at *The Record*, who never tired of my questions.

Mike Kelly and David Blomquist dispensed their wisdom freely and frequently and I welcomed it more and more each time. Their constant encouragement pushed me forward.

Sara Weissman, a reference librarian at the Morris County Library, has no idea how valuable she was to me as a friend, a reader, and a researcher. Her children are lucky to have her. Similar gratitude to Mercy Villacampa, a best friend who always had an objective ear for me and understood why my life disappeared. At University of Delaware, Leo Shane III handed over back issues of the student newspaper and made my job simple in the most hectic of weeks.

As often happens when a person works so long on one project, new friends are made along the way. Warren Trent at WPVI-TV in Philadelphia; Alexis Andrianopoulos, formerly with the Delaware Department of Health and Human Services; and Jim Nolan at the *Philadelphia Daily News* made my visits to Delaware worthwhile. To the entire staff in the prothonotary's office of Wilmington Superior Court, especially Linda Jablonski and Carolyn Sherr, you went above and beyond the call of duty while being swamped with so many requests. I owe an immense debt of gratitude to Steve Fox, the police detective who was consumed by this case for its duration, and to the prosecutor, Peter Letang, and his wife, Debbie, for letting me into the case and into their frenetic lives.

There is no way I could thank everyone who made this book possible, but I hope those people know how much their support meant.

# CONTENTS

# PROLOGUE

**December 9, 1995**

It was a magical night for the Ramapo High School Class of 1996, their Senior Holiday Ball. A light snow fell outside, the wind gusts blowing the flakes sideways past the tall windows of the plain-looking brick school. The drab cafeteria was disguised as a grand ballroom strung with silver balloons and little stars sparkling everywhere.

As the students walked inside, a poster board sign resting on an easel greeted them. "Stars, Moons, and Good Times," it read. And that's what it was for the two hundred teenagers from the high school in Franklin Lakes, New Jersey.

They arrived in bunches on this Saturday night, a few in their parents' cars, many in their own, Hondas, Jeep Cherokees, Mustangs, most of them gifts from their parents for performances at school, for simply being wonderfully trustworthy and bright, or for simply being. This was the best of the next generation of leaders, power brokers, lawyers, whatever they wanted to be. Most of their parents were not born into money, but earned their keep with good grades, good jobs, and good work habits. The parents provided their children with all the tools to make it, and make it big, and all these kids had to do now was simply what was expected of them: succeed just as their parents did.

The ball was a smashing hit. Giggling, hugging, singing,

eating. These were the memories they would take with them to college, huddling with their best friends at the school dance, no parents around, no pressures, only the watchful eyes of the teachers. A three-course meal was served and, of course, nearly everyone danced the electric slide. The girls wore short velvet and silk slinky dresses, their dates were dressed in snappy blazers and ties. Unlike the prom that would follow six months later, the Holiday Ball was not an all-out tuxedo-and-gown affair with beaming students pouring out of limousines. The fall term was about over, and winter vacation was coming; then followed a lazy second semester waiting for the thin or thick college letters of rejection or acceptance, then graduation, summer, and finally college and the start of the future.

Among the couples at the Holiday Ball was one of the cutest and most recognized pairs at school. Inseparable, they danced fast to the hard songs and held tight for the slow ones, her head resting on his chest. They had dated on and off since tenth grade, the fall of 1993, and everyone knew theirs was as serious as high school relationships got. Individually they were well liked and sweet, though hardly the most popular seniors in school. But everyone knew them. They held hands and shared the occasional hallway kiss, and when he had an important soccer game, she was there, cheering as loudly as anyone. They were a couple.

To memorialize the images from the winter dance, a roving photographer strolled the dance floor and the tables that lined it, snapping the pictures that would appear in the 1995–96 yearbook, *Ad Astra*, Latin for "to the stars." When he came to the table where the adorable couple was sitting, he couldn't resist asking them to lean in tight. The boy, in a white dress shirt and blue tie, smiled wide, displaying the blue eyes and dimples that had helped him land modeling spots as a child. His brown hair was almost military length, too short to be parted to one side or the other, and his no-muss bangs were combed straight down. A small bit of acne had broken out on his chin. The girl, in a black dress that showed off her petite figure and was cut with a conservatively high neckline, leaned forward, her left cheek an inch away from his, her long, straight brown hair hanging down the side of her face. Her smile turned to a giggle as the photographer got ready to click, her white teeth framed by bright red lipstick, her high cheekbones flushed pink. Her brown eyes looked straight into the camera.

When the yearbook came out in the spring of 1996, its theme, "Game for Anything," the posed senior pictures of these two blended in among those of their classmates. He was a class clown of sorts, and the quote underneath his photo read "Beef. It's what's for dinner." She, like most of the girls, took the more conventional approach by putting a gentler sentiment under her name: "Friends may come and go, but those who truly love you will never leave you." With parents who were high school sweethearts themselves, she had often hoped she was on the same path with her one and only beside her.

Toward the front of the book, on the bottom of one of the two pages dedicated to the Senior Holiday Ball, the two were shown together in the cheek-to-cheek photo.

"Amy Grossberg and Brian Peterson will treasure memories of the ball," the caption read.

It was just a picture of two teenagers, two bright, good-looking, promising, yet unremarkable members of the college class of 2000. They were a couple.

# THE CALL

**November 12, 1996**

Huddled under his winter comforter, Brian Peterson just stared at the ceiling as his clock passed midnight. He should have been sleeping, like most of his classmates. He knew it. He was exhausted. But none of them had his problems, his fears, his nightmares haunting them. The piercing ring from his telephone was so unexpected, it startled not only Brian, but also Mark Pollak, his roommate at Gettysburg College, a small, coed Lutheran school along the southern edge of Pennsylvania.

Outside, a biting wind whipped through the pretty tree-lined campus and the empty, well-lit streets. The classroom buildings, each of them cut from the same red brick and white trim mold, were all dark. The Safety and Security Office was open, but the radios of the officers on patrol were silent. Inside one dormitory, Hanson Hall, a few lights were still on, but most of the room windows were dark, the students asleep, gearing up for their Tuesday classes. A light frost was forming on the huge lawn between the dormitory and the towering Christ Chapel on North Washington Street.

Sleeping, thinking, even eating, had been difficult for Brian lately. He didn't know what tomorrow would bring. Every day, every night, was filled with cold sweats and thoughts of what might have been. And what might be. He looked at the clock. 12:23 A.M. He knew who had to be calling. No one else would dial him at this hour tonight. He had just seen her over the weekend at the University of Delaware, and although she was nauseated and had vomited on Sunday, she had told him on Monday that she felt fine other than being a little tired and sick. But the voice Brian heard on the telephone was not fine. Amy Grossberg was in a panic.

"I think my water broke." She sounded close to crying.

"What happened? Tell me what happened." Brian tried to soothe her, but he could tell it was useless.

"It feels like I peed in my pants," she said softly. She was whispering, almost embarrassed to say the crude words, but she didn't know how else to describe what she was feeling.

Brian had class in a few hours. And soccer practice. He was tired. He was terrified. He was good-looking and eighteen, away at college for the first time, surrounded by cute new girls, and his girlfriend from high school was a hundred miles away. Everything about this phone call told him to stay in bed. Tell her to relax, it was probably nothing. Call her first thing in the morning and continue to visit her on weekends and be her support system. Brian's split-second decision on this night, and the series of choices he would make in the next five hours, would say as much about his good heart and his devout loyalty to Amy as it would about his immaturity and his unwillingness to take charge.

"Okay, just wait there," Brian said. "I'll come down and get you. I'll be right there."

"No, don't come. I don't think you should drive all the way here now. Maybe it's nothing. I don't know what's going on."

"I want to come. Just to make sure everything is okay. I won't stay. If it's nothing, I'll just drive back."

They talked for twenty minutes. It was 12:45 A.M. when they hung up. Brian dressed quickly. His roommate stirred but said nothing. Brian grabbed his wallet and keys and dialed Amy back.

"Okay, I'm leaving now. I'll be there by three."

Those who knew Amy and Brian knew them as a couple. He loved her and would do anything to make her happy. She loved him, she needed him. He was her rock, her most loyal friend who, she was absolutely certain, would never walk away from her. They were a somewhat odd pairing, but they didn't care what others thought, including their parents. They were in love, they had been since high school.

After hustling downstairs, Brian ran across North Washington Street toward his black two-door Toyota Celica, a gift from his parents. He ran with the quick feet he usually reserved for the soccer field, where his slick moves and slight frame allowed him to dart between defenders like a waterbug among lily pads. At every level he played, Brian had never been the best, but he had always been fearlessly competitive. Aside from his family and Amy, he loved nothing as much as sports, from the intense sweat he worked up playing soccer to the steely nerves he needed on the golf course.

His car was a mess. On the floor of the passenger front seat was a loose-leaf binder filled with papers, diagrams of the plays he had to learn for the Gettysburg freshman soccer team. Gum, Chap Stick, his cellular telephone, and a pack of Tums all littered the front seat. Amy's stomach wasn't the only one rumbling these days. Also on the front seat was a map of the Pennsylvania and Delaware region, with the route he usually took from Gettysburg to Newark, Delaware, highlighted in yellow.

As Brian pulled out of the parking lot to the four-way intersection next to his dormitory, the glow was gone from the red neon sign of the tiny Pizza House where he and his friends grabbed many of their lunches and dinners and played video games endlessly. His steering wheel was freezing, but he couldn't wait for the heat to kick in. Amy needed him. He could see each puff of his breath in the dark of the car as he tore out for the drive east he'd taken more than a dozen times this fall. It was 1:01 A.M. when he

stopped for gas at the Sunoco Mart on Route 30 just outside Gettysburg.

Amy was pregnant. There was no use pretending she
wasn't. They had done that for months, and nothing had
changed. But Brian was anything but an excited, expec-
tant father. This was a baby he didn't want to see, to hold,
to hear, to smell, or to feed. This was a baby that could, in
a heartbeat, forever rewrite the scenario their parents, their
friends, their neighbors, and most of the people in their
small New Jersey hometown had come to expect children
like them to follow. This was a baby he and Amy had been
wishing and wishing and wishing for months would just
disappear. Poof. Amy had told no one she was pregnant.
At her insistence, neither had he.

The drive between Gettysburg and Newark is frustrat-
ingly slow and boring. The closest highway to Gettysburg
is Route 83, but it runs north and south, connecting Baltimore with Harrisburg. No highways come close to linking
the two small college towns, so Brian had to improvise his
own route every time he visited Amy, which was most
weekends. Winding his way south and east on a variety of
narrow, one- and two-lane country roads, never going too
far without encountering a stoplight or small town, he
crossed the Susquehanna River into Maryland around
2:15 A.M.

The trees along the roads were all bare. And the roads
were dark. At just about every intersection, Brian's headlights were alone. He passed the occasional truck or car,
but he drove in a daze, oblivious of his surroundings. The
heat blasting in his face and the music blaring from the
radio could not take his attention away from Amy. His
mind was racing as he drove. He just wanted her to be
okay, to be the cute, spunky girl he had grown to love and
not the scared, panicked, and maybe even suicidal girl she
had become. If only . . .

It was late October when Amy dropped Brian a note.
She sent him at least one a week, sometimes two or three.
There's a greeting card for every occasion and Amy had

been sending them all to Brian in the last few months. The cards were a reflection of Amy. On the outside, cheerful, happy, no sign of any trouble. On the inside, pain, tears, fear.

> *Dear BriBabes*
> *What's going on cute boy? Nothing much here. Just a little Halloween card to tell you how sad I am when you're not around. I know I've been stressing lately. . . . I just don't know what to do. . . . Every part of my body is swollen and aching. I can't handle the pressure. This has ruined my life, it's making me miserable & therefore I'm making you miserable & and I'm sorry for that. But seriously I'm going out of my mind. I've never been so scared in my entire life. I don't know what to do. I don't even know what's going on in my own body.*

His dorm room was filled with her cards, many of them signed the same way.

> *Let's hope and pray we get through this. Sorry. I love you lots. Love—Me.*

Speeding toward Delaware, Brian focused solely on the girl he loved and all they had been through in the last year.

*I'm late.* The words every teenage girl dreads uttering and every teenage boy dreads hearing.

*Just make it go away.* In letter after letter Amy begged him to help her, to make the pregnancy, the whole situation, disappear, as if he had some mysterious power. Didn't she understand that he was as petrified as she was, and that if he could have snapped his fingers and turned back the clock, he would have?

*We can't tell my mother.* It had become Amy's mantra. Brian had agreed never to betray his girlfriend, never to abandon her. So many times he had wanted to tell her parents what she could not. But Amy's wishes came first. Her mother never did find out, but this was not the plan either of them had envisioned unfolding as the alternative.

From the day they'd both accepted she was pregnant, way back in the late spring, Brian had always assumed it would never reach this point. First, they both had hoped it would pass, maybe the pregnancy would just terminate on its own, a miscarriage. Then he'd thought Amy would get an abortion. He had the money and certainly was more than willing to pay for it. It just had never happened. As time passed, he'd finally assumed they would go home for Thanksgiving, her family would take one look at her, and she would have to confess. Then he would tell his family, everyone would help her through the delivery, and the baby would either be given up for adoption or whatever. He'd never really got that far in his mind.

Not once during Amy's pregnancy had either of them actually envisioned holding a screaming and crying newborn, their child. They'd never looked into the future beyond the events of a single day. "Just make it go away," Amy had begged of Brian so many times. Their plan, if you could call it that, was to get through each hour, each day, each week, pretending everything was normal.

It was 2:30 A.M. when Brian reached Route 95 North. He pushed toward seventy miles per hour, and in twenty minutes he came to the green sign on 95 for the University of Delaware and exited on to South College Avenue.

Maybe Amy's water hadn't broken. Maybe nothing was wrong. Maybe the Thanksgiving plan was still a possibility.

Amy wasn't positive that Brian really was driving to her, but she was praying that he was. She needed him. He was her Bri-Babes, her Sweetness, her Baby Dumps. No one else could help her now. No one else would understand. She didn't want anyone to think less of her and was sure they would if she had a baby. She couldn't doze off. Her head throbbed. Her stomach churned. Every limb was sore. She lay on her bed in sweatpants and a sweatshirt, tears welling in her eyes, listening to the silence and watching her roommate sleep. Every few minutes a sharp pain jabbed below her stomach, a new pain in addition to all her other aches. The glowing numbers on her bedside digital clock seemed to take forever to change: 2:34 . . . 2:35 . . . 2:36 . . .

*Hurry, Brian.*

It's not a pretty strip, South College Avenue. It's an assortment of the quick and cheap, where travelers rest to break up a long drive, maybe to New York or Florida, and where truckers pull off Route 95 to pass the night in one of the $50-a-night motels. Late at night, the Boston Market, Friendly's ice-cream shop, Dunkin' Donuts, Discount Liquor Store, McDonald's, Ground Round, Pepper's Pizza, and the car wash are all closed on the strip. The roar of the cars and trucks from the highway is steady. Of the drivers that do exit, most don't even stop, taking the back roads to detour around a toll on Route 95. Except for the occasional car cruising back to campus, weary traveler heading for a room, or garbage truck on its route to empty trash bins before the next business day begins, the strip is dark at night, the road quiet, the traffic lights changing pointlessly over the empty intersections.

But just a mile past all the neon lights and congestion, a small rise in the road near a huge Chrysler Corporation parts distribution plant leads to a bridge about three hundred yards long. On the opposite side lies another world. The streets are lined with trees and colonial homes and the red-brick, white-trimmed, ivy-covered buildings of what's known in town simply as UD.

The students, more than fifteen thousand of them, and most of them white, upper middle class, hail from New Jersey, Pennsylvania, Maryland, and Delaware. They stroll the sidewalks and paths with backpacks over their shoulders, their worries limited largely to their studies and whether to party at a fraternity house or in drab Newark, where the bars are sparse.

Brian zipped through South College Avenue and drove on to the UD campus at three A.M., parking in front of Thompson Hall on Academy Street across from the tennis and basketball courts and next to the university bookstore. Thompson looked like every other building on campus, red brick with white trim around the windows. A quad area behind the dorm attracted students during the daytime for reading, Frisbee, basketball, and football. A bulletin board there is constantly covered with flyers advertising local bands playing nearby and health and pregnancy services provided by the university. Thompson, like most UD dorms, was coed. Not by floor. By alternating room. Boys, girls, boys, girls.

Like his own campus, which Brian had left two hours earlier, UD was eerily still. Amy, who had been watching for the headlights from his car from a hallway window, met him in bare feet, standing on the stairway inside the side door. She was leaning against the wall, shivering. Brian walked up to her and hugged her tight, kissing her lightly on her cold right cheek. Together they walked to his car. It was freezing outside, but her shaking was as much from the fear coursing through her as it was from the cold.

"I don't know what's going on," she said softly.

"Do you want to go back to your room?" he asked.

"No, we can't. Holly's there."

Holly was Holly Shooman, Amy's roommate and, like her, a freshman from New Jersey. They got along in their first two months together but were hardly best friends. Shooman resented how much time Amy spent on the telephone, most of it with Brian. Like most of her floormates, Shooman suspected, was positive, that Amy was pregnant. It was a taboo subject, though. Don't ask, don't tell. Her body, her business. Amy's silence prevented any real intimacy between her and Shooman.

Amy and Brian were about to leave when he saw that she had nothing on her feet. He ran up to her room for her shoes, tiptoeing around so as not to wake Shooman. The room was a cluttered mess. A footlocker and two pieces of luggage lay under Amy's bed, a pile of clothes and a bean-bag chair covered the floor near her desk. At the foot of her bed was a plastic toolbox filled with the art supplies she would use late at night. Next to the minirefrigerator was a trash can overflowing with garbage. With a bottle of water, her slip-on sandals, and a blanket in his arms, Brian scurried back to his car, pulled a U-turn on Academy Street, and sped off.

He drove slowly along Academy Street, then turned right at the light at East Park Place and left onto South College Avenue, heading back toward town and Route 95, opposite the way he had arrived a few minutes earlier.

"Where are we going?" Amy asked him.

"I don't know. Somewhere."

"I just need a place to lie down. I'm so tired."

She was shaking, her teeth chattering as she wrapped her arms around herself in the passenger seat and pulled her knees toward her chest, curling up into a little ball.

Contractions? Brian wondered. Was this baby really going to be born tonight?

Inside, he knew the answer.

He held her left hand gently as he drove slowly along South College Avenue. Every few minutes Amy's hand tensed and squeezed his even tighter until it almost hurt. Her face muscles clenched each time she squeezed. Cross-ing the bridge back toward town, Brian drove past the football stadium on the left. As he approached the inter-section of Route 4, a left turn and a five minute drive north would take them to the driveway of Christiana Hospital. To doctors who would know what to do. How to help them. Amy said nothing. Brian went straight. They were a couple.

# A SUBURB FOR THE
# NINETIES

As one exits off Route 208 into Wyckoff, across the short stone bridge on Russell Avenue and past the mayor's century-old white Victorian with the circular driveway and stained-glass windows, the trees are a striking sight. White birches punctuate the top-heavy willows surrounding broad oaks standing firm and tall. Impressive at any time, they are spectacular in the fall, a brilliant and dense blanket protecting the sleepy town in northern New Jersey where Amy and Brian grew close.

New York City's skyline, a scant twenty-five miles away, is an improbable backdrop. From the high points in Wyckoff, the rolling hills of the Ramapo Mountains, the sharp point of the Empire State Building looks near enough to touch. As close as it is, the big city does not intrude on life in this postcard community. Urban woes are of little concern here. Murders? That's there, not here. Drugs? Their street corners, not ours. Teenagers having babies? That's a problem of the poor, minority neighborhoods. Besides, our children know better.

Like hundreds of suburban towns across America, Wyckoff rejected the lifestyle of a city in favor of the idealized one pursued by its residents. Neighborly people. Working hard, earning good money, to insulate their children from the dangers written up in the daily newspapers or chronicled on the evening news. Those are city kids, with no support system, no one to tell them what's right, what's expected of them. Not our kids.

"If you have kids, you want the absolute best for them, and you could have that in Wyckoff," said Tom Kernan, a former principal of Ramapo High School. "There's a high degree of well-educated people in the community, and that pushes the expectations even higher."

Welcome to the 1990s upper-middle-class suburbs, where new money rules, both parents work, the streets are safe, the schools are high-tech, the fashion-conscious students are college bound, the churches and temples are crowded, and the teenagers are trying to look older as their parents are trying to look younger. This is Wyckoff, but it could easily be Greenwich, Connecticut; Chevy Chase, Maryland; Shaker Heights outside Cleveland; or any town where image is preeminent, where the pursuit of success is what matters most, and where "crime" and "failure" are dirty words.

In these towns where the address and car let the neighbors know who's making it, children are perhaps the greatest status symbol, which is why many of the parents want to make absolutely certain their children know how important it is that they succeed. The children know. When the high school's annual class rankings are released, the hallways are dripping with tension. It is the one number the students know their parents are counting on more than any other. One student recalled a friend whose class ranking was sixth out of a total of 223 students. Sixth. Yet he was petrified about telling his parents.

"They expected him to be top five," his friend said.

As hard as the parents work for what they earn, they are eager to hand over the rewards of their labor, maybe to provide their children with the luxuries they lacked growing up. The per capita income in Wyckoff is more than $42,000, almost twice the national average. It is one reason why success in school begets rewards. Many of the children are paid for good grades, sometimes with cash, sometimes with cars, something the experts agree sends a dangerous message.

"The kid hasn't worked for it, hasn't earned it, hasn't made the vital connection between hard work and success," said Harriet Porton, who co-edited the book *Adolescent Behavior and Society: A Book of Readings* (McGraw-Hill, 1998) and is an education professor at Goucher College outside of Baltimore.

So why do some parents today do things that they know their own parents would never have even considered?

Raising her daughter in Wyckoff, Sonye Grossberg fell into the trap that experts in adolescent psychiatry say has swallowed up her entire generation of successful, professional parents. Growing up in the rebellious 1960s and 1970s, most of them became determined to be different from their own boring, conservative, uptight 1950s parents. They want to drive sexier cars than their parents drove. They want to be cooler, more permissive, than their parents were. They want to dress sharper than their parents dressed. They convince themselves they will not age as their parents aged and that if their children think they are hip to the times, they will view them as a friend and not hesitate to come to them with trouble.

The problem is it doesn't work that way. Their children don't want their friendship, they need their leadership. Their children don't need their own pagers and their parents' cellular phone numbers. They need their time, their attention.

Elyse Frishman, the rabbi at Barnert Temple in Wyckoff, said that every day she is amazed at the poor communication she sees between parents and their children in her congregation.

"We tend to see children as little adults," she said. "There's a reason they're called adolescents. They're children."

Parents today become angry with their children, she

said, not because of what they do, but because their children's behavior, their performance, is a direct reflection on their parenting skills. Rather than seek help, like counseling, they prefer to keep their troubles within the walls of their homes. Is it any wonder, Frishman asked, that their children don't seek help when faced with their own trouble?

"Parents are never their children's best friend," advised Dr. Bennett Leventhal, the head of child and adolescent psychiatry at University of Chicago. "It doesn't mean you can't have an intimate, open relationship with them, but you're not their friend. Parents set limits, make rules, act as role models."

Part of the problem, he said, is that the boundary between adults and children has been blurred by culture. Children today dress like adults and look like adults, and it makes their parents feel older.

"It doesn't mean you can't be friendly with your child, but you can't be their friend," Leventhal said. "Being your daughter's friend makes you feel younger. It's a false attempt and it can be embarrassing."

The parents don't see it as embarrassing, and they are quick to act at the first sign of trouble. They want only to protect their children from anything bad. Sometimes they're overprotective.

Some parents, like Amy Grossberg's, are with their children every step. Literally. Amy's mother did everything with her, right up to taking her eighteen-year-old daughter to the doctor's office, to a pediatrician, and sitting with her in the examination room throughout the appointment.

But when do those children ever make an important decision by themselves or learn what it's like to make a mistake? Other parents, like Brian's, let their children grow up largely on their own, to fend for themselves, their baby-sitters often spending as much time with their children as they do. Do these children grow up knowing that when a crisis arises, their parents are the first people they should seek out?

It's a fine line. If a child truly believes that her parents think she can do no wrong, as Amy did, and she has never made an important decision on her own, what happens when she does misstep? Keeping it a secret suddenly seems an attractive alternative, maybe the only alternative, to having to see the hurt and disappointment on your parents' faces. But what if a child grows up, as Brian did, used to not having Mom and Dad around? Maybe he learns to accept that he can, that he has to, face his problems alone.

Finding the middle ground is the ultimate challenge for parents. Those who find that place are more likely to raise children who know that no matter how badly they might mess up, their parents will be more disappointed if they don't come to them for help than if they do.

"Sometimes you have to let the kid touch the hot stove or else he won't know it's hot," said Neil Kaye, a Delaware psychiatrist who would later become involved in Amy and Brian's case. "Parents today don't want their kids to experience any pain."

When a child brings home a C on a report card, his parents react by calling the teacher to fight for a higher grade or hiring a tutor instead of giving the child a chance to repair the trouble on his own. A number of teachers in Wyckoff said they have lost count of how many times they had reprimanded a student for something she was caught doing, only to have one of her parents march in and make up some excuse for why it happened.

When a 1997 study revealed that half of all violent juvenile crimes take place between two and eight P.M. on school days, experts in suburban life were not surprised.

"The middle-class and upper-middle-class residential suburb was designed with a certain concept of the family, with the mother being home all the time," said Robert Fishman, author of *Bourgeois Utopias: The Rise and Fall of Suburbia* (Basic Books, 1987) and a history professor at Rutgers University. "That was the whole purpose of the suburb, to remove women and children from the evil city so that the mother's influence would dominate."

But when financing that suburban lifestyle became so expensive that both parents had to work to afford it, the houses were suddenly empty all day and the children were alone. That is especially true in places like Bergen County, one of the country's ten richest counties. In towns like Wyckoff, the children have time to burn and money and a car to burn it with until their parents come home. In Wyckoff, six out of every ten children between the ages of six and seventeen come from a home where both parents work.

That was one factor that led Wyckoff Police Chief John Ydo to the town council in late 1995 after a dozen complaints were lodged by shoppers and store owners about teenagers loitering at shopping centers in town. They were bored. The council and police both agreed to work together to stop teenagers from loitering. They could stop them from loitering, but not from being teenagers. The following week the police arrested two students with beer in their car, which they said came from a party in town. Those were Wyckoff's troubles, at least the ones people read about and talked about openly. Isolated incidents of bright and bored, mischievous teenagers. More sensitive and serious subjects, like pregnant girls and boys with drugs, were brushed aside. Not my kid.

On their own, the children aren't necessarily looking for trouble, but they are seeking attention.

"Money is left for them, and they are on their own," Professor Porton said. "When moms went back to work, that changed parenting styles. I'm not suggesting women go back to the kitchen, but everything has a tradeoff. If parents are going to work and not be home in the evenings or on weekends when their kids are home, and they're sending the kids to camp in the summer, look at how frayed the family has become."

For many, daytime parental responsibilities are farmed out to nannies, sports coaches, music instructors, and neighbors who happen to be home when they're not. And the children notice. Parents may believe that because they work so hard, their children will see that they have provided them with every possible ingredient to make it and make it big and follow their lead. But to Porton, children sometimes see things differently. They may see their parents working so hard as a sign that nothing else matters, that work comes before family.

"Children are brilliant observers and lousy interpreters," Porton said. "You have to be home to know what your kids are doing. That's nothing new. But the lack of time parents are spending with their children, that's new."

To learn a little about how children in towns like Wyckoff are raised and what they are feeling inside, all you have to do is listen to someone like Jeff Boucher for an hour. No one in town tries to get as close to the teenagers as the young and spirited youth minister at Wyckoff Baptist Church. With its tall red steeple and four front pillars, it stands as a landmark in town, greeting the drivers who exit off Route 208 onto Russell Avenue and stop at the busy corner of Wyckoff Avenue before turning left toward the center of town. The sign in front displays in big black words the times of Bible school and services.

When Boucher asked his youth group—comprising teenagers of all religions and backgrounds, some from the town's strongest families—to write him letters about the troubles they are facing, he was stunned at the sampling he received. One child said his parents fight all the time and he can't stand it. Another said no one took the time to understand him, and he had no one to talk to. One sixteen-year-old girl said she "wants to go to heaven because I'm going crazy with this pressure."

Sixteen and going crazy with pressure. Not all that unique in Wyckoff.

Boucher, stocky and athletic looking, with a crew cut

and a visible passion for his preaching, said his youth group teaches him something new every week about the pressures teenagers face in town. At a seminar he organized, parents listened to anonymous students, who were speaking from behind a screen, confess that three out of every four of them had tried drugs, and more than 50 percent were sexually active.

"The parents' mouths dropped open," Boucher said afterward. "They thought their children were perfect. You could almost see their faces hoping that their children were in the twenty-five percent who had not tried drugs."

In Bergen County the police almost chuckle when they hear parents and principals minimize the problem of drugs in the schools. An average of five hundred teenagers are arrested each year on drug possession or distribution charges, and their parents are always shocked. They had no idea, because many of them don't know how to ask about drugs, sex, or anything else. They just assume. They provide their children with a car to get around, money for them to buy whatever they need, and a first-rate education with the promise of paying for college, and they expect in return only one thing: Not my kid. My kid wouldn't do drugs, my kid wouldn't cheat, my kid wouldn't get pregnant. My kid wouldn't keep any big secrets from me.

But the police know better. They say they could follow every week the students who leave school at three P.M., drive across the George Washington Bridge into Manhattan with the few hundred dollars their parents had given them or that they took from a parent's wallet, and return an hour later with a supply for themselves and their friends. Wyckoff students say nearby Paterson, and not New York, is the first dope destination.

"A white kid doing laps on certain blocks in Paterson in a shiny car is not a big mystery," one student said. Students estimate that at least five in every ten at Ramapo had smoked marijuana.

The town is, as one student wrote in the high school newspaper, "in its own glass bubble," secure in its belief that its families, its teenagers, are immune from the temptations and troubles that strike elsewhere. Occasionally a pebble nicks that glass, like the time police had to break up a party just outside town that attracted hundreds of teenagers and ended with one from Wyckoff being arrested for distributing alcohol to a minor. But parents and school officials responded quickly, holding town meetings to air worries that their children might be organizing too many secret drinking bashes. Wyckoff rarely got worse than that.

It is not by chance that some of Wyckoff's streets are named after the Ivy League colleges of Dartmouth, Cornell, Harvard, and Yale. Those are the schools many of the parents in town attended, and nothing would make them happier than to see their children follow their example. On those streets in town are the split-levels, Cape Cods, and ranches, the modest and affordable homes for $200,000 and $300,000. In the center of town many of the eighteenth-century stone houses remain from Wyckoff's original days as a Dutch settlement. To the west, near the border of Franklin Lakes, million-dollar Tudors and faux English cottages with brooks running through the lawns sit on half-acre lots along Russell and Sicomac Avenues. The lawns are perfect, many of them manicured by professionals.

Though impressive from the outside, some of the most spectacular homes in both Wyckoff and Franklin Lakes are sparsely decorated inside because the owners had overextended themselves financially simply to live in the town. The typical home owner pays a monthly mortgage of nearly $1,800 in Wyckoff, more than double the national average. But it's worth it.

To keep the residents from streaming away to the growing number of crowded shopping malls within a short drive, Wyckoff built up a triangle-shaped business district, from Franklin Avenue to Wyckoff Avenue to Main Street. At the busiest intersection in town, where Franklin and Wyckoff Avenues meet, the old and the new come together.

Bicyclists, joggers, BMWs, eighteen-wheel trucks, and especially shiny new Range Rovers all pass through the crossing with regularity. At one corner is a red-shingled Revolutionary barn converted into the Brown Stone Inn Bar & Grill, a symbol of the town's history. But on the other three corners stand signs of its present: Coldwell Banker; Wyckoff Ford; and Cabinet Corner. Jewelry stores and banks are seemingly at every corner.

Despite the growth and the population boom, police officers in town rarely find themselves investigating anything more serious than a burglary or the occasional fire. In a twelve-hour stretch on November 12, 1996, the same morning Brian rushed to be with Amy, New York City police shot and arrested a thirty-five-year-old man for assaulting an officer, charged a foster mother with burning her child, jailed a high school senior for punching a classmate to rob him of $1.50, and investigated the shooting death of an unidentified man. At the same time, the police in Wyckoff were not quite as busy. At 3:00 P.M. they responded to a house alarm that went off, at 3:53 P.M. a street light was reported out, at 4:15 P.M. a man applied to register his gun, at 5:00 P.M. a woman reported her mailbox had been damaged, at 8:36 P.M. an officer made a traffic stop, and two more alarms went off shortly after 9:00 P.M.

Built around a dozen ponds linked by meandering streams and brooks, Wyckoff, which means "water" in the language of the Leni Lenape Indians, who lived in the region during precolonial times, covers seven square miles of sheer beauty that was originally farmland before its incorporation in 1926. It's a town, the Wyckoff Chamber of Commerce likes to boast, "where you know your neighbors," all seventeen thousand of them.

On the surface Wyckoff is serene, relaxed, religious, the perfect picture of suburban life in the shadows of the big city. The volunteer spirit in Wyckoff is remarkably strong. When three young mothers wanted a place for their children to play, they organized fund-raisers and recruited volunteers to build a $150,000 playground. It would become the most popular children's spot in town.

"Kids have great relationships with their peers," said Henry Shotmeyer, the mayor of Wyckoff, who grew up in the town and whose family is one of the largest property owners in the area. "Parents seem able to build neighborhoods by themselves."

But there is also a tension here, a competitiveness, particularly among the top students at Ramapo High School, of which many of the parents are largely oblivious, but that the children, particularly the teenagers, are keenly aware. Ask the parents their child's grade point average, extracurricular list, career path, and class rank, and there is no hesitation. But what about their son's five best friends? Their daughter's sexual curiosities? Is she on the Pill? Is he buying condoms? Do they smoke?

"They expect their kids to do well at everything," one mother in town said. "They don't expect their kids to get knocked up."

No child wants to disappoint his parents, but when expectations have been set so high, so soon in life, a child's greatest fear is not simply failure. His greatest fear becomes bringing shame and embarrassment to his family.

"I'm not sure parents are capable of changing anything," said Jonathan Braunstein, the president of Ramapo High School's class of 1997. "Parents need to take a step back, and they need to learn who their kids are. The lines of communication are not good because a lot of the parents don't want to know."

Some of the parents even acknowledge the problem.

"So many of our kids walk around in a kind of cocoon— of course, we create it for them," one mother said.

"This is a town of high achievers," said Valerie Morrissey, whose son was two years behind Brian and Amy in high school. "There is so much competition. They want their kids to excel, to succeed under pressure. To the kids, that means: 'If I fail, my parents will kill me.'"

Her son, Michael, agreed.

"Some parents, if you get a C, they treat it like it's the end of the world. I think it goes overboard, and some of the kids get scared."

Parents in Wyckoff provide so much for their children, far more than they had as children, that they see no reason why their children should not match, and exceed, their own achievements.

"Parents want to fix everything right away," said Nancy Eisenhower, who runs a teenager counseling program at Indian Hills High School in Oakland, New Jersey, a similar Bergen County town. "'Omigod. My kid got a C. I've got to fix it now.' If you've never learned how to make a personal decision, you won't be able to when the time comes."

Frank Grosso has two sons who attended high school with Amy and Brian, one graduating the year before them, one the year after. He owns the popular eatery the Wyckoff Delicatessen, just off the busiest intersection in town, Wyckoff and Franklin Avenues. He recalled finding condoms in one son's bedroom during high school and being stunned. He wished his son had waited, he said, but was relieved to see he was at least being careful. His slight Italian accent barely noticeable, Grosso spoke passionately about parenting and how parents in a town like Wyckoff sometimes are so intent on making money and providing an impressive lifestyle for their children that they don't spend enough time talking to them, demanding that dinner be spent together, knowing their friends, their patterns, their lives.

"If you think your kids are angels," he said, "you're lying to yourself to make yourself feel better."

Young working couples earning good money, who are willing to pay huge tax bills, look at the reputation of the school system before they even start house hunting. In Wyckoff the schools are the featured selling point. By the third grade students are typing, and by high school graduation better than nine of every ten Wyckoff teenagers are preparing for a four-year college.

And students don't just study at Ramapo. After-school clubs they can list on their college applications are too numerous to count. There are clubs for writing, art, skiing, Rotary, debate, the environment, science, academic decathlon, Students Against Drunk Driving, and foreign-language clubs from German to French to Spanish. There is also Teens Need Teens, a roundtable group where students try to confront social pressures, and the Interact Club, a camp program for the privileged students of Wyckoff and Franklin Lakes to work with the less privileged children in the city of Paterson. At Ramapo the clubs are respected and popular, and, just as important, they help students get into their preferred college.

When trouble arises, in the classroom, on the ball field, anywhere that a blotch on the transcript might derail that plan, the parents jump in to keep things on track.

"Easy money, easy life, easy solutions," Professor Porton said. "Life isn't easy. There are no easy solutions, which is why when a crisis hits, these kids are totally unprepared."

# "SWEETFACE"

That first serious kiss. Holding hands in the hallways at school. Talking every night on the telephone. Sneaking around for privacy to explore those curious urges. On your best behavior in front of her parents. Flowers and stuffed animals. Slipping notes into his locker. The senior prom. It's love. You're sure of it. He is the only one. She is all you can think about. Everyone remembers their high school sweethearts, but only a few marry them. Usually graduation and college push high school memories into the past faster than those dreaded calculus equations. New friends and new interests surface.

Some sweethearts do survive, though, and their photo albums are filled with pictures of only one boy, one girl, one love.

Sonye Dorf was a cute and petite brunette at Fair Lawn High School in Bergen County in 1966, her hair flipped up at the bottom and a bow holding her bangs off her face, a member of the prom committee, student council, and, just like her older sister, the Future Teachers Club. Alan Grossberg was her handsome, clean-cut, athletic boyfriend, active in the Key Club and, like Sonye, the student council and prom committee. They fell in love. They attended their senior prom together, held hands at graduation in June 1967, and didn't stop until they reached the altar.

Sonye was born in the Bronx in 1949 to Joseph Dorf, a veteran of World War II who was awarded a Purple Heart and managed a door manufacturing business, and Carolyn Edelstein Dorf, a secretary to the high school guidance counselor. She was raised with her older sister, Andrea, and brother, Mitchell. Her parents' marriage was solid.

Alan Bruce Grossberg was born in Brooklyn in 1948 to Leo Grossberg and Sylvia Bernstein. Growing up on 27th Street in Fair Lawn, a street lined with pretty colonials and split-levels, he was one of three brothers. Their father was a sales representative for furniture manufacturers and earned a good living before retiring with his wife to Florida.

Alan, after a brief stint at Northern Michigan University and enrolling in the army reserves, returned home to Sonye and enrolled at Rockland Community College. He worked briefly for Oscar Meyer Inc. before his father encouraged him to follow him into home furnishing sales. While Alan was launching his career as a salesman, Sonye studied at Fairleigh Dickinson University, working toward a degree in elementary education.

The late 1960s and early 1970s was a simultaneously thrilling and terrifying time to be reaching adulthood. Blacks and whites coming together while finding out how far they had been apart, the Vietnam War pulling people in opposite directions, the threshold of space energizing the country. Young men and women who fell in love endured the most turbulent era of the second half of the century together, and some found that it strengthened their bond. In 1970, while still living with her parents, Sonye Cheryl Dorf, a white lace veil over her head, married her high school sweetheart on Christmas Eve in a beautiful Jewish ceremony half an hour south of Fair Lawn in the town of Millburn. He was twenty-two with brown hair and a thin mustache, soft-spoken and career minded. She was twenty-one, feisty, proud, and ambitious.

After they married, to save money for their first home, they lived with Alan's parents in the house he grew up in on 27th Street in Fair Lawn. He continued in the furniture business while his wife started teaching grade school in town. In 1972 they bought the house from his parents for $35,000. It gave them the first taste of the life they would hope to one day provide for their children.

On July 26, 1975, Sonye gave birth to a six-pound baby boy, Jason Richard, at Hackensack Hospital. She immediately left teaching and became a full-time mother. When she became pregnant again three years later, they knew they were going to need more space.

It was 1977 when, like so many young couples in the New York City metropolitan area in search of their second home, a place to raise their children and educate them in the best schools, Alan and Sonye Grossberg found themselves on the highway, exiting off Route 208 into Wyckoff.

As they drove through the streets that spring, they instantly felt at home. For the both of them it would be difficult to leave behind Fair Lawn, where they were raised, where they met, where they first lived together. But they could do it, for Jason and their expected second baby.

It was all of these qualities that led Alan and Sonye Grossberg to sell their house in Fair Lawn for almost twice what they had paid and, in the fall of 1977, move into a four-bedroom, brown-shingled contemporary on Karen Place in Wyckoff that had sold for a little less than $100,000. It was a pretty and modest neighborhood of narrow, winding streets, away from the growing downtown district, where the people mow their own lawns and the garages hold one or two cars. They had been there just six months when Sonye, twenty-eight years old, went to Hackensack Hospital and, at 1:43 A.M. on July 10, 1978, delivered Amy Suzanne. She was called "sweetface" by her grandparents, "angelic" by her uncle.

Life was set. A son, a daughter, a strong marriage, a beautiful house in a quiet town with an outstanding school system. All that was left was to settle in and watch their children blossom.

\* \* \*

"The Grossbergs weren't born with silver spoons in their mouths," said Diane Dobrow, a longtime family friend of theirs and a teacher at Ramapo High School. "They're hardworking people who've earned every penny. All they've ever wanted is to give their children a good life."[1]

And they did. Jason, like most boys in town, became involved in sports, playing baseball in the youth leagues. Amy took a liking to arts and crafts and games of stickball and softball in her neighborhood. Her mother introduced her to museums at a young age, and it had an impact. She was a spirited girl with a short, boyish haircut, a neat freak who loved to draw. Her dream as a child was to be a fashion designer. She would play tag with friends in her backyard on Karen Place and dress up her dolls in all sorts of stylish looks.

No one wanted to be Amy's friend more than her mother. Sonye, always conscious of her own appearance and that of her daughter, passed on her affinity for clothes to Amy. Shopping together became a pastime for them, and as Amy approached adolescence she had a wardrobe her friends envied, filled with top-of-the-line labels. Like so many children raised in towns like Wyckoff, she learned she could have what she wanted. When she wanted it. As long as she did what her mom wanted.

"They were the most involved parents, concerned about everything from family values and education right down to one of the kids' sporting events," Sonye's brother, Mitchell, would recall later. "Nothing ever got missed, and we always did it as a family."[2]

As Amy grew, Sonye, with her girlish, tightly curled blond hair and her fashionable wire-rimmed glasses, maintained a youthful look. She wore knee-length skirts to show off her still-shapely legs. Alan, with thick, graying hair combed straight back and a bushy silver mustache, was an equally sharp dresser, wearing simple suits and brightly colored ties. From her mom, Amy learned how to piece together the outfits they bought, from her shoes, to her belts, to her slacks, to her jewelry. Elegant, not flashy.

Like so many mothers, Sonye looked at her daughter as a miniature version of herself. And her daughter knew it. Slightly pudgy as a child, Amy thinned as she reached her teen years and made every effort to stay that way.

Amy's relationship with her mother was tight. Some would say later they were inseparable, best friends, maybe so close that Amy never learned how to make a decision on her own. But others would wonder just how close they could have been given the secret Amy would keep from her mother.

"Sonye and her daughter are close," said Barry Grossberg, Amy's uncle. "Whatever troubles one troubles the other."[3]

Amy's parents were hardworking. They were not the most visible couple in town. They were occasionally active in school functions or town activities, devoting their attention to their work, their home, and their children. Sonye joined Alan in the furniture business, working for a different company as an independent furniture sales representative. With both of them selling in the New York metropolitan region for some of the largest furniture distributors from North Carolina, money was good.

Through her childhood, first at Sicomac Elementary School and then at Franklin Avenue Middle School, Amy could do no wrong in her parents' eyes. She had blossomed into a hardworking girl with no shortage of friends and activities to keep her busy.

"She was a young girl who loved school," Amy's kindergarten teacher, Audrey Fournier, remembered. "She was always polite, well mannered, eager to learn."[4]

Another of her teachers, Adrienne Panico, recalled a happy and giving child who always offered to stay after school and help clean up. Amy was nine when she began taking weekly art classes with a local instructor, Mary Guidetti. It became her favorite way to pass time, drawing in her room, in the kitchen, in the living room, usually with her pad resting on her lap.

Alan's income, and Sonye's, like so many during the early days of the Wall Street boom, had taken off by the late 1980s. He became the youngest president of the New Jersey Metropolitan Furniture Association. His commissions soared as the furniture business thrived.

Amy was twelve and her brother was fifteen when their parents sold their modest house on Karen Place for four times what they had paid for it and moved five miles west into a $750,000 brick Tudor in Franklin Lakes, with a circular driveway and arched front doorway. At the corner of High Woods Drive and Arapaho Terrace, the home stood in a neighborhood of palaces. The houses on High Woods Drive have columns in front, enormous windows, cobblestone driveways, professionally manicured rolling lawns, gated security systems in the driveways. No one on this street mowed their own grass, and the Grossbergs, like their new neighbors, hired a maid.

The schools in Franklin Lakes, like those in Wyckoff, are technologically advanced. They have their own computer staffs and impressively equipped computer laboratories where students can log on to the Internet. Learning is advanced in the towns, and so are the students. At Franklin Avenue Middle School, Amy started studying French and became active in the student council. She also joined the town recreation cheerleading squad, her pint-size build always landing her on top of the cheerleading pyramids. She was more soft-spoken than most of the cheerleaders at the youth football games and fun to be around.

"She had a lot of friends, she was a sweet girl," said Leslie Anderson, who was a year older than Amy and cheered with her on the town recreation squad.

Twice a week after school, Sonye picked up Amy outside the school, hopped onto Route 208 eastbound for two minutes, and exited onto Russell Avenue in Wyckoff. Just off the highway, Temple Beth Rishon sits on a hill with a vast parking lot big enough to accommodate its thousand-member congregation. Amy, now a button-cute thirteen-year-old with chubby cheeks and wide eyes, would sit with Rabbi Arnold Mark Belzer for an hour, sometimes two, and read from the Torah in preparation for her bat mitzvah. For her parents, religion had always been important but not vital. They were conservatively religious, celebrating the major holidays and not much else, but making sure their children respected their Jewish heritage from an early age.

Amy was in the seventh grade when she developed irritable bowel syndrome, a condition that would flare on and off without warning throughout her teenage years and require her to take medication to control the stomach pains and excruciating cramps that accompanied it. Her mother suffered from the same ailment, and they would often share medication when one of them ran out.

As Amy started the eighth grade, she fit right in among her classmates and friends. Outside the school in the morning, many of the thirteen-year-old girls arrive looking more ready for a Friday night date than a day in class, skirts above their knees, silk blouses, subtly competing with each other for the best look. The boys look like boys. Blue jeans, baseball caps, untucked shirts, sneakers, and the signs of peach fuzz around their chins. Around each other, though, the boys and girls are still awkward. They want to be noticed, to be liked, but when they are, they are unsure how to handle it.

Each morning the children go to school, their parents go to work, listening on their commute to the New York stories about the dead bodies in Central Park and bricks falling off crumbling buildings onto unsuspecting victims below. But when their evening news ends, they know that on their side of the Hudson River they can leave their car doors unlocked in their driveways, leave the convertible top down, take a walk alone without a worry, and put their children on school buses each morning confident that their classmates won't be packing a handgun or switchblade in their backpack.

On June 15, 1991, just before her thirteenth birthday, Amy's extended family and best friends gathered at Temple Beth Rishon for her bat mitzvah. With her innocent smile, she read from the Torah as her parents sat in the front row, beaming with pride. It became even more memorable when Amy broke her arm playing with her friends afterward.

"Amy and her brother, Jason, demonstrated through their respectful and most appropriate demeanors the high standards that were set for them by their parents," Rabbi Belzer would say later.[5]

# "PEEWEE"

Even as a tot, Brian Peterson exhibited a certain irre-sistible charm, cuteness, and then some. Maybe it was his hair. Sandy brown, always more blond in the summer, shaped in that Beatles cut, long bangs hanging straight down over his eyebrows and snipped evenly across his face. It was as if the barber had placed a cereal bowl over his head and trimmed whatever hung out. As he grew older, he cut his hair shorter, giving it a spiked look. Or maybe it was his slight gap-toothed smile and pinchable dimples. It might also simply have been the way he could have fun, indoors, outdoors, by himself, in a group, any place, any time.

"I thought he was adorable," said Sharon Cohen, who baby-sat Brian from 1984 to 1987. "He was a cutie-pie. The perfect kid. An effervescent personality."

He was born on Long Island on June 10, 1978, exactly one month before his eventual high school girlfriend. But unlike Amy, Brian Carl Peterson Jr. had no siblings. He was raised Catholic, an only child in a quaint red-brick, brown-shingled ranch, with a pool in back, on Marlin Street in the town of Dix Hills on Long Island, fifty miles east of New York City. Unlike the marriage between Amy's parents, Brian Peterson Sr., a handsome, soft-spo-ken man with sandy brown hair, and Barbara Peterson, a beautiful woman with jet black hair, struggled in theirs.

When Brian came along, instead of spending more time together, they gradually drifted apart. Brian was alone. A lot.

A community largely of farms until the 1960s, Dix Hills, though not as affluent as Wyckoff, is not so different from the New Jersey suburb. Both attract New York commuters, both are appealing because of outstanding school systems, both have a busy highway cutting through, Route 208 in Wyckoff, the Long Island Expressway in Dix Hills, and the people who live there expect their children to attend college.

Over time, Brian more and more resembled his father, even in how they walked, head down, shy looking, shoulders slumped slightly forward. But Brian was a bundle of uncontrollable energy.

With his mother teaching math at junior high school and traveling to New Jersey, where she was helping to start up a video distribution business with a friend, and his father working long hours as a computer programmer, Brian returned from Otsego Elementary School every day to a baby-sitter. He played with his dozens of Nintendo games and various toys and learned to be independent. He made friends playing sports, attending religious classes, and just being out in his neighborhood. And he loved his dog, Cindy, feeding her, walking her, his companion when no one else was around.

"His childhood was good because of us," said one of his boyhood friends.

But he missed his parents. He would step off his school bus at three P.M. every afternoon and be greeted by a baby-sitter. His mother often called from New Jersey late in the afternoon to hear how he was, and he came to love the calls and understand that was her life. But when he would hear a door to the house open in the early evening, he would run to it, hoping to see his father or mother. It was usually his father, who would ask him about school, about his friends. Their relationship was good. But the house was generally untidy, the cupboards filled mostly with junk food, sweets, and canned foods, all of which Brian generously shared with his friends. Dinner for Brian was sometimes a can of SpaghettiOs with his latest baby-sitter.

"He was always frustrated," Cohen, his baby-sitter, said. "I think he missed his mother, her presence."

In three years, Cohen said she saw Barbara Peterson half a dozen times at the most. Still, Brian seemed happy, a well-adjusted latchkey child. Without his parents there, his life revolved around his neighborhood gang, a fun bunch of athletic, smart, and mischievous kids, from John Daley, to Hal Danziger, to Brian Fuentes, to Craig Michel.

Michel first met Brian at their morning school bus stop right in front of Michel's house on Marlin Street. They would grow up together, along with the other neighborhood boys who attended schools within the Half Hollow Hills Central School District. Michel was always the tall and lanky one; Brian, the short jitterbug with the blond hair and gap-toothed smile who always looked younger than his age.

Brian and his friends played the occasional game of Ring and Run, ringing a doorbell and sprinting away before being seen. They came from all different backgrounds and religions, but their link was sports: watching sports, reading about sports, and, like all young boys, fantasizing about sports, the big play in the big game in front of the big crowd. Brian was always the leader, never the follower, teasing his friends about how they couldn't catch him, couldn't stop him. And with his toys and snacks he was always openhanded.

"Brian always knew how to have a good time," Michel recalled. "And he always had the girls."

Girls weren't the only ones taken with his sparkling blue eyes and his adorable smile. When he was four, Brian appeared in several television commercials and magazine advertisements, hawking brownies, cookies, cheese snacks, and toys. A framed picture from one of his commercials was hung in the house.

One of Brian's idols was the great Denver Broncos

quarterback, John Elway, and he wore his orange Elway number 7 jersey everywhere. He also loved the speedy Rickey Henderson, major league baseball's greatest base stealer, and Keith Hernandez, the popular first baseman of the New York Mets, his favorite team. Football, baseball, whiffleball, basketball, street hockey: he and his friends played them all, and Brian was always the quickest and usually the smallest, earning the nickname "Peewee." He loved soccer more than any sport, the running, the freedom, the aggressiveness. He started wearing a rope chain with a soccer ball on it when he was nine.

On the outside Brian was a happy kid, an average student who stayed clear of trouble, made lots of friends, did what his parents asked, and obeyed his baby-sitters. But what seemed like an easy childhood was really a period of mixed emotions for him. At home his parents' marriage was dissolving.

When he was ten his mother moved out, leaving him alone with his father so that he could stay in the schools he liked, with the friends he needed, until his mother was settled in New Jersey, where she had moved. While attending Candlewood Middle School, Brian picked up two new sports: wrestling and golf, which he started playing with his father at the nine holes of the Dix Hills Golf Club. It would become his second passion.

In 1990 his parents divorced, and by 1992 both had remarried. When Brian finished eighth grade in Dix Hills in June 1992, he moved to be with his mother and her new husband, John Zuchowski. They had just traded in a modest home in the northernmost Bergen County town of Mahwah for a spectacular $750,000 brick Tudor in Wyckoff. Lavelle Court, a dead-end street with a cul-de-sac, has seven houses, all immense, all built after 1970. The house Brian lived in had a three-car garage to the left, a basketball hoop to the right, and deep woods and a swimming pool behind it. Brian added his touch: he posted small golf course signs around the lawn.

As in Dix Hills, Brian was forced to be independent in Wyckoff. His mother and stepfather were running Prime Time Video Inc. in the town of Ridgefield. A service distributorship—not a video store—that they had started in 1984, the company became innovators by aggressively pushing for video rental programs in supermarkets and chain stores.

In addition to providing rental programs to more than one hundred supermarkets, Prime Time began allowing the stores to own and operate their own video departments. Barbara became president, her husband handled marketing and sales, and the business, with fourteen employees, surpassed $7 million in annual sales. Brian was put on the payroll as a utility worker, earning $8 an hour.

In Wyckoff their lifestyle was a perfect match. The town's population of six thousand before 1950 exploded after 1960 to almost seventeen thousand. Though taxes are heavy, averaging $5,500 on most homes, the median household income of more than $80,000 is double the national average and makes for comfortable living. Their home was lavishly furnished, and John Zuchowski named his thirty-eight-foot power boat *Prime Time*.

From his relatively modest lifestyle as a toddler, Brian was suddenly thrust into a community of money, lots of it. It would be in his new home, and in Amy's five miles away in Franklin Lakes, that Brian and Amy would ultimately spend much of their time together over the next three years, watching rented movies, fooling around when no one was home, falling asleep on the couch in Brian's basement. For both of them, those would be their best times.

# KEYS TO THE KINGDOM

It sits on fifty acres at the top of George Street in Franklin Lakes, a brick, putty-colored, one-level school surrounded by woods, at the end of a residential road lined with pretty, unassuming ranch homes and perfectly cut lawns. With all of Wyckoff's beauty and charm, safe streets, and bustling shopping districts, its heart and soul is its school system. That's why young families move there. For the parents of teenagers in Wyckoff, and for some parents in Franklin Lakes, that means Ramapo High School.

A cute new face arrived at the school in 1992. Most of the students, Amy among them, grew up in town and had brothers and sisters who had preceded them through the schools. The students all knew each other from earlier grades. The teachers knew their names because their faces often had that sibling resemblance to a previous student. When Amy was a freshman at the high school, her brother was a senior. Brian had no such recognition.

He wore number 6 on the freshman soccer team, and by his sophomore year in the fall of 1993 he was playing on the varsity soccer and golf teams and beginning to show the qualities of a leader.

Through mutual friends, Brian and Amy met in their sophomore year, Brian with his hair still so short that it spiked up on top and Amy, cute, with her chipmunk cheeks. Brian was a midfielder on the soccer team, a hard worker in class some days, lazy the next. Amy, along with volunteering in the Department of Special Education, was into her drawing and her friends. She was a star student in French, algebra, English, and especially art.

"Her work displayed patience and technical expertise as well as thoughtfulness," recalled Janice Nelson, who taught Amy in advanced placement art.[6]

Brian and Amy seemed an odd match to their friends. They had so many differences. Amy was more shy, insecure, difficult to get close to. Friendly and well liked in her tight-knit circle of pretty friends, she was protective of herself, her image, and her relationships. Brian was a prankster, more popular and confident, eager to make new friends. He was athletic and an average student, but not the standout hard worker that Amy was. She was Jewish, he was Catholic. He was an only child. She had an older brother. Her parents were high school sweethearts, happily married for more than twenty years. His parents were divorced, and both had remarried. He had grown up on Long Island, where his father still lived. She had grown up in Wyckoff.

But their differences were what helped draw them together. Amy was attracted to Brian's outgoing and animated nature, his athleticism, his popularity, and, most of all, the polite attention he paid to her. Brian was pulled in by Amy's close, loving, and structured home and her constant affection for him, both of which he had missed out on as a child.

Amy, he could see, had no shortage of love at home. They had a family dinner at least two or three times a week, and Amy and her mother seemed to do everything together. But while her relationship with her mother was tight, one subject they never discussed was the one the experts say all parents struggle to broach with their children: sex. As Amy and Brian became more serious, she never confided in her mother about it, and her mother never questioned her about it. Sonye Grossberg would admit later it never occurred to her to even think about whether her daughter was sexually active. "Sweetface" would not have sex. She wasn't ready.

At the end of each school day at Ramapo, some nine hundred students stream out of the classrooms and into the buses out front or their own cars in the back parking lot by the football field. The girls are giggling, dressed mostly in skirts and sweaters, with the occasional blue jeans and cropped shirt revealing a belly button. The boys are pushing and joking. It's not a diverse student body: more than 90 percent are white, with only a handful of blacks and two handfuls of Asians.

Students at Ramapo get a taste early in life of what it's like to have money in their pockets, of the lifestyle they are expected to achieve. Lunch money in high school takes on a new meaning here, where it's not unusual for a high schooler to have $50 or even $100 or more in his wallet and the steering wheel of a new car under his fingertips. The student parking lot at the high school is a showroom, packed each morning with cars more impressive than the teachers' lot, from Acuras and Jeeps to the occasional BMW and Porsche. Teenagers and parents in town say it's not uncommon for cash and cars to be awarded to a student for a good grade or a straight A report card.

"We want to give kids more than we had," said Cherylin Roeser, president of the Ramapo–Indian Hills Education Association. "When you have kids, you want to give them everything you didn't have. A brand-new car, the keys to the kingdom."

But what message are those keys sending? While the teachers like Roeser are working to instill in their students a love of learning just for the sake of learning, at home the children are being taught that education is less about what they learn and more about what they get for it. *What's my reward?*

"That mixed message is so confusing," said Nancy Eisenhower, who has taught for thirty years at Indian Hills

High School, the second high school in the Wyckoff and Franklin Lakes school district.

Mike Moran thought so, too. In the 1970s, a metal whistle around his neck, Moran was the gym teacher and head football coach at Ramapo. But it was never satisfying enough. He enjoyed coaching, he loved the sweat, the competition, the strategy, but he found it difficult to get close to his players off the field, to learn about them as young adults, not just as athletes in pads and helmets.

In 1982 he saw the opportunity. He knew students drank at Ramapo, and he knew there were drugs, not just marijuana, but cocaine. Several students had mentioned it to him. But he also knew it would be a hard problem to tackle, particularly in towns like Wyckoff and Franklin Lakes where image was everything. He thought if he could organize the students, get them to come to regular, informal rap sessions, they might do it. And maybe some of their problems and pressures would come out. First, though, he had to get permission from the Board of Education and the school administrators.

"The board wasn't reluctant, they were behind it," he recalled of the confrontation. "But the administration was somewhat reluctant. It made it appear as if we had a problem. It was hard for them to swallow."

While the administrators did nothing to discourage Moran, they hardly encouraged him. The parents were the same. Their children didn't need the help, they believed. Pressure? What pressure?

"A lot of parents resented the program," Moran said. "It was presenting a negative image in the schools."

It took persistence, and it took begging, but he finally raised $7,500 on his own from bake sales and Lions Club donations, and he launched a program he called TNT—Teens Need Teens. It caught on quickly. Soon he was meeting with three hundred students a week, just listening to them talk about their drug and alcohol concerns, pressures they felt from their parents and their peers, and anything else on their minds. The meetings were voluntary, yet the students showed up. In droves. A day after Moran had a recovering addict speak with his group, three students told Moran they had a problem with cocaine.

"I guess I was naive. I didn't think they were pure kids, but I never thought we had drug addicts walking around the school."

Students would come to him, he said, sometimes in tears, overwhelmed with pressure to live up to their parents' expectations and their own. He set up a twenty-four-hour phone line and found it ringing at two A.M. with panicked students pleading for his help and panicked parents wondering where their children were.

For the first three years of TNT, Moran handled both high schools in the Ramapo–Indian Hills Regional School District, Ramapo High School and Indian Hills High School. When this became too much work, he set up separate programs at both schools. He handled Ramapo, and Nancy Eisenhower took Indian Hills.

In September 1993 a pretty and petite fifteen-year-old sophomore showed up at one of his weekly TNT meetings. She immediately jumped in on the conversations.

"She was just delightful, one of the sweetest girls I've ever known," Moran remembered. "Within the group she was active, outspoken, savvy, very sophisticated."

Amy was just starting to gain confidence as a young woman when she attended those few TNT meetings. When Moran saw her picture on television the first time three years later, he didn't recognize the girl who had joined him and dozens of other students all those afternoons in high school. Then he heard her name and took a second look.

"I was blown away," he said.

So were parents in town. Pressure? What pressure?

When the high school newspaper, the *Rampage*, conducted a survey asking how many students smoked cigarettes, they found almost one in three did. Again, many parents were shocked. One student said a friend of his who had a car smoked while driving, but when confronted by his parents about the smell in the car, he told them he let his friends smoke but he did not.

"His parents didn't say a word," the friend said.

The survey on smoking made the school newspaper. But other stories on more delicate subjects sometimes do not, or at least not before a battle between students and the staff, who would prefer to censor them rather than risk potential damage to the school's sparkling reputation.

When a student said he wanted to put together an article on drug and alcohol use by teenagers and conduct what would have been a random survey, he had to argue for weeks before finally getting it in. And when a senior in the high school became pregnant and gave birth, she granted a candid interview with the *Rampage* about taking responsibility for her actions. It never appeared.

With those standards comes an intensity, a competitiveness, at Ramapo that peaks each spring when those chilling letters start arriving in mailboxes with the news of who got accepted to what college and who got rejected from where. An acceptance letter from Harvard, Duke, Yale, or Princeton is the ultimate high.

"Our class, and those in the last three or four years, have been cutthroat," said Patrick Crosetto, a 1998 Ramapo graduate who went on to Harvard University. "The students wanted to be the best in everything, play as many sports as possible, join as many clubs as possible. Getting into Ivy League schools is expected. And if not Ivy League, then Tufts or the other top schools, like Stanford."

At Ramapo, the pushing works. The students are bright, aggressive, career minded, ambitious, all the things parents want to see. More than a third of the average graduating class at Ramapo, approximately 90 out of 230 students a year, make the National Honor Society. One, maybe two, students a year opt against continuing their education after high school. A visitor to town need look no further than the rear windshields of the cars to know how bright the children are and how proud the parents are of them. Many of the seniors want to get into the elite schools as much, if not more, for their parents as for themselves. Certainly not all the students attend elite colleges. Brian and Amy would not. But students say it's one example of the message they have been given that failure is unacceptable, in school and in life. Parents with little faith in their students' guidance counselors hire independent college advisers for as much as $2,000 to coach their children through the application process.

One student recalled how a friend of his, a decent student but hardly a star, had applied to all eight Ivy League schools at the urging of his parents, and as a safety school, he'd applied to Rutgers University, the respected but hardly prestigious state school. Eight rejection letters later, and he headed off that fall for Rutgers's New Brunswick campus ninety minutes south of Wyckoff.

"His parents outshot him," his friend recalled. "He was hurt. Students look down at Rutgers."

# A COUPLE

For Amy and Brian, any awkwardness from their early days of dating had long faded by their senior year. They were serious. Everything clicked. Amy looked at her parents and how their relationship had started, and she envisioned a similar ending for her and Brian. Brian did, too. He saw how his parents' marriage had failed and how much fun it was to be with Amy, to take classes with her, to go to the movies with her. They talked about their future, even about a family, but they accepted that if they were to wind up together, it would have to wait until after college.

Nothing defines a childhood growing up in towns like Wyckoff more than how a student caps his public school education, how he finishes out his senior year. For seventeen years children have been groomed for college, for success, for adulthood, and to botch everything as a high school senior would be like a baseball team blowing a 10–0 lead in the last inning. Inexcusable. And the students know it. Their parents are ready and eager to pay for college. The checkbooks are out.

"Not just *a* college, but *the* college," said Moran, the phys ed teacher who ran the Teens Need Teens program until he retired in 1994. "God forbid you were a kid from Ramapo not going to college. Those kids were just remorseful. They couldn't be a part of the cafeteria talks."

They knew getting into Rutgers University wasn't good enough, he said.

"I think it's bragging rights for the parents," Moran said from his home in Maine. "I even used to do it. I would say, 'My daughter went to Cornell, my son went to college.'" (His son attended Syracuse.) "It's an ego thing for parents."

For Amy and Brian, the start of the 1995–96 school year meant a resumption of their relationship. During the summers between their sophomore and junior years and junior and senior years, they took a break from dating. Between his travels with his family and soccer club and her busy schedule working with children at the local YMCA or earning $8.25 an hour at the Market Basket, a gourmet food shop in Franklin Lakes whose yellow delivery vans are seen all over town, they had little time for each other. They stayed close. She wrote him letters and called frequently, and he called her and dropped her the occasional flowers or stuffed bear. Every stuffed animal he gave her went straight on her bed.

By their senior year, Amy's parents were welcoming Brian into their home, though he was never completely comfortable there. When he would visit to pick her up or simply hang out with her, Alan and Sonye would insist he join them for dinner if they were eating. When they ordered out for pizza or Chinese food, they ordered for him. In their daughter's eyes, they saw the same love, the same attachment, they had felt for each other when they'd started dating at Fair Lawn High School in 1966.

"He was a nice boy," Sonye would say later. "They went to all the dances together, we have all the pictures. For us, it was very special. Being high school sweethearts ourselves, I looked at them the way I remember Alan and I doing things, and it was very special and very nice."[7]

What she didn't know was that her daughter and Brian had graduated from infatuation to a serious relationship.

"We started to discuss sex during our junior year," Amy would say later. "We talked about it a lot. We loved each other very much, were very close, and respected each other. We both wondered if we were ready. Brian never pressured me and always made me feel comfortable."[8]

They were seventeen, and on Christmas break from high school, when they found themselves alone at Brian's house. Their first time was both awkward and, at the same time, loving and safe. Brian used a condom. But sex after that became a regular thing, once or twice a month whenever they could find the privacy. Of course, their parents never knew.

Like most of their Ramapo classmates who were sexually active, birth control was more of an inconvenience than a necessity, a nuisance that took the fun and spontaneity out of making love. Buying condoms was embarrassing and dangerous if they were spotted by someone who knew them or their parents. If condoms were handy, they used them. If they weren't, well, what was the worst that could happen? If it was a day or two after Amy's period, they used nothing. That was the "safe" time. For Amy, the Pill was out of the question. She could have gone to any health clinic and, after receiving the standard lecture about other options, such as celibacy, been handed the contraceptive. Girls at Ramapo know where to get the Pill. Five dollars a month is all they cost. But Amy wouldn't. She couldn't. She might gain weight on her tiny frame, as some girls do who go on the Pill, and she feared that her mother would grow suspicious immediately.

After climbing steadily for two decades, the proportion of sexually active high school students in the United States has fallen 11 percent during the 1990s. A federal study found that 1997 was the first year this decade when fewer than half of the nation's high school students said they had sexual intercourse. However, while there has also been a decline in teen pregnancies in recent years, one million teenage girls still become pregnant each year— 2,750 a day, 114 each hour, and 2 every minute.

Amy certainly would not have been the first Ramapo girl using the Pill to avoid getting pregnant. In their senior year, the first issue of the *Rampage* contained an editorial cartoon of a girl and a boy with the words "AIDS," "Abstinence," "Pregnancy," "Sex," and "Condom" floating above their heads, along with a question mark. An editorial criticized students for being indifferent about sexual practices.

"After all of the sex education classes, with teachers trying to get information across to students, the only thing that shakes anyone up is when a fellow student becomes pregnant," the article read. "But a pregnant student is not to be scorned; she is no different from many of Ramapo's sexually active students. The only difference is that most of the others who have unprotected sex are lucky enough to not get pregnant, or do not continue the pregnancy."

The article went on to remind students that the bubble in which they live is not indestructible. As aggressive as the school's mainstream curriculum is, Ramapo students are taught cautiously and conservatively about sex, and most of the parents seem to like it that way. As one mother said, "If we don't expose them to it, maybe they won't try it." But as Jeff Boucher, the Baptist minister, pointed out to the parents, and as studies show, their children are trying it, in overwhelming numbers.

Students at Ramapo spend more time learning about how to put on a condom, something most of them probably know as much about as their teachers, and less time on the consequences of sex, what it's like to be pregnant, and what to do in case of a pregnancy. Abortion, adoption, and counseling options are almost never mentioned. Abstinence is brushed over and not taken seriously by the students. In the 1995–96 yearbook, number two in a student list of the "Top 10 Ways to Be Politically Correct" was, "Do not ask your health teacher what form of birth control she prefers." The joke is right there for the parents, the teachers, the principals, to see, and some wonder if anyone is paying attention.

"What happens when you get pregnant, what are their options?" said Kernan, the former principal at Ramapo High. "They are learning a great deal about the physiological part of sex, but what happens when you are pregnant?"

Sex education, or "family living," as it's called, is not even offered at Ramapo High for most students until their senior year, by which time they are seventeen and eighteen years old and, in many cases, sexually active. As juniors their health class is first aid, and as sophomores it's driver's education.

"I felt the teachers expected the students to have already engaged in sex, and although they said to stay abstinent, it seems as though they are saying it halfheartedly and not enthusiastically or authoritatively," said Patrick Crosetto, the 1998 Ramapo graduate.

"They were into abstinence training rather than what happens if we actually had a child," said Jeremy Rosenberg, who graduated Ramapo with Brian and Amy and attends Rutgers University. "The class really dealt with how to use a condom and ways of abstaining. It was meant to scare us. They also told us about sexually transmitted diseases and other risks, but in terms of what to do if any of that happened, they didn't say anything."

Other students said they recalled at least several incidents where their teacher in health class was talking about the birth control pill, only to be distracted by a girl pulling out her round birth control pill holder and whispering: "Like this?"

Amy and Brian took health class, or sex ed, as the students dubbed it, in the fall. Guest speakers helped break up the monotony of the daily lessons, which covered sexually transmitted diseases, how to put on a condom, ways of abstaining, and the occasional reference to unwed mothers. But rarely did teacher Magda Karpati get through a class without a hearing a giggle or whisper. Unlike the rest of the school's subjects, which were taught to classes of between fifteen and twenty-five students, the health class typically had thirty or more students. The highlight was flour babies.

The aim of having students carry around an ordinary

five-pound bag of flour or, as Amy and Brian did, a Cabbage Patch doll as if it were their infant, was to teach them how much work motherhood and fatherhood is. There is no break, no time off. Every second of every day you must know where your baby is. If you drop it, you hurt it. If you leave it alone, you risk losing it.

It was not mandatory, but those students who participated increased their chances of getting an A and those who ignored it were more likely bound for a B. A few students took it seriously, toting the five-pound bag of flour around with them every minute of the day or instead using a doll they could dress up. But, inevitably, a bag of flour would get dropped during the semester, flour would be spilled in the hallways, and the project became more of a running joke than a lesson.

"The flour baby project was not taken seriously by the students, the administration, or the teacher," one student said. "Most of the kids just fooled around. Flour was all over the school, because many of the kids kicked around their babies or their friends' babies."

What could be more devastating to an image-conscious family than a teenage pregnancy, an unwanted baby? Some 1.2 million legal abortions are performed nationally each year. Students and teachers in town say they know of at least two or three that happen each year, some secretly, some with the parents' knowledge and consent. But a high schooler having a baby carries a stigma. The children see it in their parents' eyes. When a girl in the high school becomes pregnant, it is talked about in whispers. The other parents breathe a sigh of relief that it wasn't their daughter. Then the girl disappears for a month or two without a trace. Mononucleosis is a common excuse because it lasts so long. And when she returns, her classmates and teachers know not to talk about it unless she brings it up. Eventually the girl emerges from her shell, smiling and proud, sometimes even bringing her baby to graduation. But it's not easy. It's not the plan.

The senior year for Amy and Brian had just started in

September 1995 when a column appeared in the town's weekly newspaper, the *Wyckoff Gazette,* titled "Just Before the Catastrophe Hits: Don't Worry, Mom, I Can Handle It." In her column, Margaret Craig wrote: "Who says that reaching the age of 18 automatically makes a person capable of reaching mature, informed opinions and decisions?"

Margaret Craig is the sixty-four-year-old mother of four sons; with her glasses and light brown curly hair, she resembles the fourth-grade teacher who would praise you one minute and chide you the next. In her *Gazette* article, Craig wrote that eighteen-year-olds are able to vote, fight for their country, be charged with a crime as an adult, and get married without their parents' permission, but none of that makes them adults. Parents in Wyckoff, she wrote, provide their children all they need to succeed. They raise them to study hard and appreciate culture, with the museums and theaters of New York so nearby. But those same children, she wrote, will still put the red sock in with the white load of laundry, then ask their mother how to fix their pink underwear. They are too dependent.

"We've tried to explain various problems which may arise as they set out on the road to independence," she wrote in the column in the fall of 1995. "But until that independence is in jeopardy, the words a parent most often hears are: 'Don't worry, Mom, I can handle it.' Generally, that is said just before some major catastrophe hits!"

Craig remembered one conversation she had with a school official when she was winding down her ten-year stint on the Ramapo–Indian Hills Board of Education in 1990. She had heard about a program some schools were using to educate students about pregnancy. The "Empathy Belly," which slipped over the body like a vest, showed students what it felt like to be pregnant, to gain thirty pounds, feel constant pressure on the abdomen, suffer backaches and shortness of breath and a need to urinate frequently.

Brochure in hand, Craig went to Tom Kernan one afternoon in 1990 when he was principal at Ramapo High. She suggested the school consider trying the "Empathy Belly." Kernan said he did not recall the conversation. Craig said he simply gave her an honest answer.

"I thought if anything will teach them how uncomfortable a situation it is, this is it," she said. "He laughed because he said the school board and the parents would never allow it in the school."

An annual summary of student performance at Ramapo High reads, "The parents of the students are employed in professional, managerial, and executive positions in northern New Jersey and the New York metropolitan area." There is no wiggle room, no doubt as to what's expected of the graduates. Your parents made it, in many cases because both of them worked long hours to provide everything you have. You will make it, too. Period.

When a child's parents disagree with a grade their child has received, one that threatens to keep her off the National Honor Society and out of the Ivy League, or Duke, or MIT, they sometimes storm into the school and demand a change. When Amy's mother disagreed with a B grade her daughter received in her senior year art class, she wrote a letter to the school administrator, seeking a change to an A. She got it.

"The stress to have an impressive class rank is so absurd that students are willing to compromise their morals in order to get good grades," read an editorial in the school paper. It described the competition among students as "cutthroat."

The students put the word out there, and no one blinked. No one, not the parents, not the school officials, saw cutthroat competition among the students as a problem. No one wondered how a student would handle failure in the midst of that cutthroat atmosphere.

To try to maintain their success, some Ramapo students take huge risks. More than a dozen students and parents interviewed said, without even being asked, that cheating at Ramapo is commonplace—more, they said, than at other high schools because of the intense pressure to succeed. Students recalled seeing classmates peeking into the brim of their baseball cap, or at a tiny crib sheet, anything to avoid possible failure. One student remembered two classmates cheating on a French IV final and skewing the grading curve. When they showed up the next year for French V, the teacher, who had learned of their deceit, threw them out.

And the most cheating occurs not among the few struggling students, but among the elite.

"There is so much more cheating in the honors classes because that's where all the pressure is," one honors student said.

That's who feels the most pressure. Students say they know of tests stolen straight from teachers' desks and of students using their advanced Texas Instruments calculators to store information that they simply re-call with the push of a button during a test. Douglas Anderson, who served on the Ramapo–Indian Hills Regional School Board, said he sees the tension in the parents as much as the students.

"There's an edge, a tightness, to some parents who are so driven," he said. "You can see it in their faces. Some parents go off the deep end."

For Brian, the fall of 1995 meant soccer, a sport he thrived in even more than golf. He had played for the Ramapo Green Raiders since his sophomore year, and now, as a senior, he was chosen co-captain, along with Sam Graziano and Artie McConnell, by their coaches Aldo Cascio and Evan Baumgarten.

"There are kids that you forge great relationships with over a lifetime, and he's one of them," Baumgarten would say later of Brian.

The 1995 season was supposed to be mediocre at best for the Green Raiders following the graduation of three all-county players the previous year. With McConnell out with a broken wrist, the team struggled early, winning just five of its first twelve games. When McConnell returned, though, and teamed with Brian who was playing the critical midfield position, the Raiders went on a tear, winning seven straight and reaching the state sectional finals before losing to the top-seeded team, Sparta, 2–1 in overtime.

"We started playing together because we were all having fun," McConnell said. "There was no pressure on us—seeing that no one expected us to go anywhere."

For Amy, senior year meant schoolwork and her friends. She was a star student in her French and physics classes and was working almost nightly on a new drawing, sketching in charcoal various faces and landscapes in her oversize pad until all hours of the night. She didn't play sports or join any clubs. Her life revolved around her classes, her artwork, her tight circle of girlfriends, and, of course, Brian.

The beginning of the school year was a roller coaster of emotions for officials at Ramapo. On the sports field, Chris Simms, the son of local celebrity and former New York Giants star quarterback Phil Simms, was starting at quarterback as a freshman on the Ramapo football team. Inside the building, a week after officials were elated about working with neighboring high schools in a regional interactive television project, a Ramapo custodian was fired after being charged with harassment for allegedly touching the stomach and leg of a student as they talked in the locker room.

But there were good times. Ramapo Spirit Week in early October showed the students' creativity as they competed with each other for the craziest hat, ugliest tie, and best college sweatshirt. The week ended with pep rallies in the gym and the Raiders marching band working the students into a frenzy.

As bright as Amy and Brian both were, they were

hardly among the brightest in their class of 223, all of whom would graduate on schedule. Five of their classmates would go on to become National Merit Scholars, twenty-four would be named Garden State Scholars, and the Ramapo Academic Decathlon Team would place third in the state. Team members won thirty-four individual awards, and a banner was placed outside the school heralding their efforts.

The soccer season for Brian ended in late November, right before Thanksgiving. The 1995 Thanksgiving weekend marked the first football game in five years between crosstown rivals Ramapo and Indian Hills High Schools. Before an overflow crowd at Hank Boggio Field in the town of Oakland on November 23, Ramapo beat Indian Hills, 21–0. Brian and Amy watched with friends, huddled close in the chilly fall weather, cheering on their Raiders.

Two weeks later, December 9, was the night Brian picked up Amy at her house for the Senior Holiday Ball. They danced and kissed and hugged all night long. They were as in love as any high school sweethearts. Winter vacation had ended, and snowfall from the January blizzard of 1996 had almost melted away, when Amy and Brian found themselves alone in late February. For Hanukkah, Brian had given Amy a necklace with a diamond heart. She showed it to all her friends and wore it everywhere, especially around Brian.

"She looked up to him because he was more popular and made himself known—she was very proud to be his girlfriend," said Marc Veli, Brian's friend and soccer teammate.[9]

The stressful final deadline for most college applications had passed by late winter, and senioritis had settled in for the two of them and their classmates. Amy had applied to ten colleges, all with strong art programs. The motivation for studying was gone for Ramapo seniors.

Exactly when and where Amy and Brian had sex on this occasion, neither of them would remember months later. There were no parents around, and no condoms, either.

# A SECRET

Most mothers know when her daughter has her period. She knows the signs. She knows what feminine products her daughter uses and how often she needs more, because Mom is usually the one doing the shopping. Once a month the daughter is more cranky and irritable, her appetite changes; it's usually obvious. To a mother. Amy's period had never been perfectly regular. Some months she spotted lightly, some months she was a week late, other months she was as normal as any teenage girl. Her mother knew this.

Several times Amy had been late and begun to panic, even writing Brian a letter about it once, swearing she had learned "a valuable lesson." When her period finally came, she wrote him another letter, expressing her relief and apologizing for putting him through any grief. Then they resumed their unsafe sex. They would discuss her cycle only casually, just so he knew all was well and there was nothing to worry about. But in March there was no cycle. Amy told Brian, but neither of them panicked right away. It wasn't a first. They assumed it was, willed it to be, her normal irregularity.

April was a crazed month at Ramapo, as always. College acceptance and rejection letters began arriving, and the hallways were buzzing with competitive anticipation. Brian got his acceptance letter from Gettysburg College, a small liberal arts school in southern Pennsylvania, and he was thrilled. He had met with the soccer coach there, Dave Wright, and was optimistic he'd make the team as a walk-on.

But he also got a letter from Amy. She had written him dozens of letters over the course of their relationship. But this one was different.

*I don't know how it happened. This is the one disappointment my parents wouldn't understand. I'm not ready for this.*

She was pregnant.

Amy's own acceptance letter from University of Delaware was the one she had most wanted. When she and her parents had visited UD, they'd fallen in love with its campus, the small town of Newark, and the friendly students. The art department was strong, the UD campus was beautiful, and the university was only two hours from home and two hours from Gettysburg and Brian. Everything about it was perfect.

Just as Brian associated fall with soccer, spring meant golf. The previous year the Ramapo golf team had won its division championship, and as a senior captain, Brian, along with his friends and classmates Jeff Larson, Chris Langbein, and Justin Lipton, led another successful season. The season opened on April 2 against Saddle River at the team's home course, the High Mountain Golf Club in Wyckoff. No one—not his classmates, his coach, Leo Donnelly, anyone—suspected the anxiety beginning to build up within him.

May passed with Amy again not getting her period. Whenever they saw each other and discussed it, the conversation was usually brief and always the same.

*I don't know if I'm just late or pregnant.*

*How late are you?*

She would tell him how many months it had been. Then she would say maybe it was nothing and that they should just wait.

*My mom could never imagine her little angel letting anything like this happen to her.*

Telling someone was not an option so soon. Denying it was much easier. Amy begged Brian not to tell anyone, and he swore he wouldn't. He promised. It was as if he were eight years old again and he and his friends were stomping through the neighborhood in Dix Hills, playing Ring and Run and swearing to each other to keep it their little secret.

*I promise. I won't tell if you don't.*

"It's about shame; these kids were ashamed," said Neil Kaye, the Delaware psychiatrist who would join the case. "Shame is one of the most painful emotions there is." He said they were not just worried about shaming themselves, they were also concerned about embarrassing their parents in a community where so many knew them.

"The expectations for achievement were so huge, and kids are really worried they won't live up to their parents' expectations and lose the only unconditional love there is."

One weekend in late May, Sonye Grossberg was straightening up her house when she saw something in an upstairs trash can that was hardly unusual: a sanitary napkin wrapper. It was Amy's, probably the result of some light first-trimester spotting, a common occurrence in young women particularly in first pregnancies. Maybe Amy thought her bleeding meant she wasn't pregnant anymore. If she did, she said nothing to Brian.

As spring passed, Brian didn't have to ask anymore about Amy's period because he knew if she got it, she would call him. During her classes Amy wrote Brian letters, dozens of them, apologizing for causing so much pain in their relationship, wishing their troubles away, praying for that bloated feeling, the tender breasts, those signs every girl attaches to her period.

Their senior prom was approaching when they started discussing their options. One thing they agreed on: they didn't want this baby, they really didn't want this baby. Amy told Brian she could not tell her mother, and Brian agreed he would say nothing if that's what she wanted.

His loyalty to her would come above everyone and everything, no matter the price. Brian wasn't exactly eager for the conversation with his parents, either. Friends. Teachers. No one. They kept up their act, smiling in the hallways, talking about college and how they were determined to keep their love alive. Their friends never suspected.

"I can't get caught," Amy told Brian over and over. It became her mantra, but it would not keep her from her work, from putting on a happy face.

In late May a pointillist ink portrait Amy had done was chosen along with ten other art pieces by students at Ramapo High to represent the school at the Bergen County Teen Arts Festival at Bergen County Community College. The next week, Sonye, like most mothers in town, took her daughter shopping for a prom dress. The gowns the girls would wear cost anywhere from $200 to $500, and Sonye certainly wanted her daughter to maintain her status as one of the best dressed in school. After trying on gown after gown, and making no attempt to hide her size one figure from her mother in her underwear, they finally settled on a burgundy dress that managed to show off her attractive shape, which had not yet been affected by her pregnancy.

Harlan Giles, a gynecologist and perinatologist who would later interview Amy and Brian at length, said they were so focused on keeping the secret, they never considered the consequences of an actual baby. And as sophisticated and nominally educated as they were, Giles said they were clueless as to how to handle a pregnancy.

"They are both individually bright, but equally medically naive," he said. "It points out the paradox between intellect and medical naïveté. Some parents say that by withholding contraception for our daughter, she won't be encouraged to have intercourse. The exact opposite occurs. The intercourse still occurs, and they are unprotected."

Amy's parents, he said, never imagined their daughter

could be pregnant, because they, like so many suburban parents, never imagined she was sexually active.

"Parents' expectations can be too high, too lofty," Giles said. "They overlook the basic body reflexes that kids go through."

Giles and other experts said the refusal by Amy and Brian to discuss the pregnancy in terms of a coming infant was typical of teenagers in distress. By begging Brian to make "it" go away so many times, as she would do throughout her pregnancy, Amy was displaying the most common form of denial seen in pregnant teens.

"If you deny it and don't want it, it's a thing," said Dr. Kaye, the Delaware psychiatrist. "You don't bond to it. It's just a foreign object passing through."

On Saturday, June 1, Amy and Brian arrived as almost every student did—by limousine—at the elegant Woodcliff Lake Hilton just off the Garden State Parkway in a park of corporate office buildings. They were a dashing couple, Brian in his tuxedo and Amy in her gown. They ate the four-course meal, they danced close on the floor of the Grand Ballroom, they kissed when the teachers weren't looking. They forgot about their problem for one memorable Saturday night.

Brian's eighteenth birthday was June 10, and five days later, an overcast day, was Ramapo High's graduation inside the school gymnasium. Amy, with a 4.19 grade point average out of a possible 5.0, graduated 106th in her class of 223, an indication of the competitiveness at the school for top honors. Brian was fifty spots lower. Brian in his black cap and gown, Amy in her white, smiled throughout the ceremony. As they paraded toward their families hand in hand, their proud parents took pictures of them holding each other close, oblivious of the fear eating them up inside.

After the ceremony Amy and Brian joined their classmates for a bus ride into Manhattan and boat cruise around the island. Students danced, smoked cigars, and ate, and for most of the trip Amy and Brian sat at their table and talked quietly.

They had begun discussing how to make the pregnancy go away. Adoption was out of the question, because that would mean telling their parents. They could marry, but they knew their parents would never allow it. Brian offered to make an appointment for an abortion, to pay for it, and to stay with Amy throughout it. She agreed reluctantly, and Brian looked into setting it up. He was just getting started when he received a card from Amy. Inside was a picture of them smiling, taken the morning after the prom.

"What are we going to do?" she wrote.

As the summer began, Amy's image in her mother's eyes could not have been more wholesome and virtuous. She had just graduated high school with terrific grades. In the fall she would leave for a good college without straying too far from home. She had never had detention or a speeding ticket. She was that rare child who had found a skill she loved at an early age—art. And she loved working with children. Parents could not ask for more.

What Sonye didn't know was that Amy saw how her mother looked at her, and it terrified her. Suddenly she wasn't the perfect child. Not only wasn't she a virgin, she was pregnant. At least during school, Amy had Brian to lean on every day. His smile, his hugs, always relaxed her. But as the summer began, their daily contact diminished. Amy worked, and Brian spent his days and evenings playing soccer and golf and helping out at the family video business. Amy was a mess inside, writing Brian letter after letter explaining how sorry she was for hurting their relationship and causing him so much pain.

Her parents were distracted as they began house hunting. With Amy on her way to college in the fall, and Jason already out of the house, they had no need for their spacious Franklin Lakes Tudor. They turned back to Wyckoff, where they had grown as a family, and started looking at smaller houses and upscale town houses.

Fifteen miles south of Wyckoff, at St. Joseph's Hospital and Medical Center in Paterson, a blue-collar city with a heavy Hispanic population, Linda Locke sees 250 teen pregnancies a year. She manages the midwifery and teen obstetrical programs and said it no longer surprises her when a girl comes in with her mother, complains of stomach pains, and walks out a mother herself.

"It's quite a shock to bring a daughter to the emergency room for what you thought was appendicitis, only to learn she's going to have a baby in a few hours," Locke said. She said the girls keep believing it will simply go away, never envisioning the consequences of what will happen if it doesn't. "Parents are the important people to please, and to destroy that means destroying the image of yourself," she said. "This wasn't supposed to be a part of the picture."

That's especially true in the affluent towns. In Paterson, though, where smokestacks and apartment buildings are visible from Route 80 and there are as many broken families as there are tight-knit ones, when a teenage girl becomes pregnant, the schools hardly notice. It's not expected, but it's not surprising, either. Classmates of a girl won't hesitate to ask if she's pregnant. They've seen it happen enough times. So have their parents.

Just outside the center of Wyckoff was the Wyckoff Family YMCA, a model YMCA in every sense, with the smell of chlorine and the look of a wood cabin. Parents had been taking their children there for forty-five years, for Tiny Tot Gym, judo, karate, gymnastics, swimming lessons, and day care. The summer day camp, Wydaca, keeps children busy with water sports, arts and crafts, and playground games. That summer Amy was hired as one of the dozens of counselors for Wydaca, assigned to supervise five-year-old girls, to teach them art, help them at the playground and pool, and watch them at nap time. As camp began in late June, she was a natural, dropping to her knees to play with her tots and talking to them at their level.

"Amy was very good with the kids," said Sean McInnes, a senior counselor at the YMCA.

Amy met two other counselors, Jennifer Tighe and Francesca Montalto, who were also heading to the University of Delaware in the fall. She would talk to them about Brian and how they were determined to keep their relationship going at college. But it wasn't long before other counselors began to notice something odd about Amy. She wasn't going in the pool. She had always had an adorable figure and had never been afraid to show it, but now, even with eighty- or ninety-degree summer days and most of the staff stripping to skimpy shorts and bathing suits, Amy was almost never seen out of her jeans and baggy shirts. Some counselors would say later they were curious why they saw her in a bathing suit only once or twice. But at the time, with the distractions of children running around and the chaos of summer, no one said anything to her.

Dr. Robert Blum, a professor of pediatrics at University of Minnesota who has studied teen pregnancies for more than twenty years, said when a girl is pregnant and in public, her mother and father are not the only ones at fault for missing the signs or at least asking the key question.

"It's not just that the parents don't realize it," Blum said. "But nobody does. It's not just two people, but a whole community is conspiring. That's what's so extraordinary."

Wyckoff was hardly conspiring. But in a town where it's simply assumed that every child will graduate high school and leave for college, no one wants to confront a possible problem. Experts say that secretly the girl is hoping, praying, that someone does figure out she's pregnant, to take the burden off her.

Neil Kaye, the Delaware psychiatrist, calls it the "conspiracy of silence."

"Both sides essentially are conspiring not to talk about things as if they don't exist," he said. "Ask these parents if they know what their kids are doing. They don't want to believe it, and they look for things to support that. They just assume their kid would tell them if they were in trouble."

While Amy had to hide her belly, Brian had to hide only his emotions. Like many of his contemporaries, he didn't have to work over the summer, and his hours at the family video business were flexible, to say the least. Those who did work did so more for the experience, the business education, than for the money. Brian hid his stress doing what he loved, playing soccer and golf. He'd play golf with neighbors, friends, whoever was available for a round. And on the soccer field with the Torpedoes, the local youth team he had played with for years, he could burn off his frustrations.

Together, Amy and Brian kept up their front, going out on Brian's stepfather's boat and attending an occasional party at the Indian Trail Club, a spectacular country club in Franklin Lakes across the street from the gourmet food shop where Amy had worked. Her parents were members.

In late June Amy went to Delaware for freshman orientation. Hundreds of eighteen-year-old men and women wandered the campus with visions of freedom dancing in their heads. Amy was almost four months pregnant, but no one could tell. She talked to Holly Shooman, her future roommate at Delaware, to discuss who would bring what, from furniture to a stereo to a television to an answering machine. She naturally said nothing about her condition.

As it became obvious to Brian that Amy was never going to tell her mother of the pregnancy, he had to make his own decision. Nothing prevented him from telling his parents or hers. He could have had a friend make an anonymous call to her parents to tell them their daughter was pregnant. He could have written them a letter, unsigned. He could have taken an action. But he didn't.

He wouldn't betray her. If she wasn't going to tell, he would respect that.

"What could I have done?" Brian would say later to a counselor. "I felt so bad for her. It's her body. She's the woman. It's her body."

Her baby, her body, her choice. It was the liberal man's position that he backed into, one that the pro-choice movement preaches when arguing why abortion rights are so important. Just as Amy had her way of wishing away her pregnancy, this was Brian's. He wasn't denying there was a pregnancy, only that it was in his control. He was a boy having to make a man's decision. It was her baby and her body. But it was *their* decision as to whether to keep it a secret. Both agreed to try to have the abortion before Brian left for Europe in mid-July on a soccer trip with his local club team.

New Jersey is one of the few remaining states that does not have a parental permission law for abortions. Any girl, any age, can get an abortion without her parents' permission, though most clinics and doctors will encourage patients to tell their parents first. Amy turned eighteen on July 10. She was approximately five months pregnant, but neither she nor Brian was certain of that. Because Amy was so irregular, and late frequently, they just didn't know when she had become pregnant, whether it was March, April, or maybe May. Brian thought she was two months, three months at the most.

On July 11 Amy left work at the YMCA and met Brian at the Cedar Hill Shopping Center. Brian drove them onto the Garden State Parkway south for about thirty minutes, where he got off at Exit 131 in the town of Iselin. He turned left, drove a mile alongside the Amtrak train tracks, and made two right turns onto Middlesex/Essex Turnpike, a busy street with small contemporary homes on the left and businesses on the right adjacent to the railroad tracks. As he passed the Iselin Post Office and approached the modern three-story office building on the right, Amy began shaking her head. A Quick-Chek convenience store was across the street.

"I don't like this neighborhood," she said. "I can't do this. What if I get an infection?"

In truth, her fear was simple. She had never been to a doctor without her mother, never been to an OB/GYN even though she had been sexually active for more than a year, never made an important decision without consulting her parents. There was no way she could do this.

Brian pulled into the parking lot anyway. Inside the air-conditioned building, a security guard sat by the elevators next to the board listing a host of businesses, from tax consultants to lawyers to a dating service to a temporary service. On the third floor was a business simply called Options, an abortion clinic. Brian and Amy never made it there. They sat in the parking lot and talked. And cried. They drove back to Wyckoff, found their privacy, and made love.

The next day Brian and his soccer buddies, along with the high school coach, Evan Baumgarten, left on their thirteen-day trip to Italy and then Holland to play in the Verona Cup. They would eventually lose in the championship game, but Brian would play well and hide his emotions. Thousands of miles away from Amy, surrounded by his best friends in a foreign land, he would keep their secret. What else could he do?

Students attending the University of Delaware in the fall were not required to have a physical, but they did have to produce a document that certified they had had their immunizations, including those for Hepatitis B and tuberculosis. The new vaccine for chickenpox was recommended for any who had not had the illness, but it was not required.

No internal examination was needed for Amy. Still, it meant a visit to the doctor, the last person she wanted to see. After Amy had received a bright pink envelope in the mail from the college with the required medical forms for incoming students, her mother pestered her for weeks about making an appointment, only to hear Amy tell her she was having her period and needed more time. Finally her mother simply made an appointment at Bergen West Pediatric Center, where Amy had gone for her checkups since she was a little girl.

Just before Brian left for Europe on July 12, Amy told him about her upcoming doctor's appointment. She didn't know what to do because she needed the physical for college, and she was panicked that the doctor would figure out she was pregnant.

On the morning of July 16 Amy dressed to go to her doctor's appointment. Just before leaving, she put in a sanitary pad, and then she and her mother drove to the Cedar Hill Medical Center in Wyckoff. On busy Cedar Hill Avenue just off Route 208, the doctor's office was in a building that looks like a college dormitory, red brick with columns in front. The Bergen West Pediatric Center was the first door inside on the left. With her mother seated beside her in the waiting room, Amy filled out the requisite forms about her medical history and then was called in to meet with Dr. Douglas Fenkart. It was Fenkart's first time seeing Amy.

Her mother went with her, right into the examination room, as she always did when Amy went to a doctor.

"Mom's trying to keep this child a baby," said Professor Harriet Porton, the expert in adolescent behavior. "No eighteen-year-old should be going to a pediatrician. This is an adult body. This is not a body that requires pediatric care. Mommy's keeping this kid a baby. Parents need to recognize this kid is emerging as an adult."

She said the doctor is as much to blame for fostering that attitude. A pediatrician should tell an eighteen-year-old girl it's time to see a gynecologist, and it's time to go alone and leave Mom in the waiting room. Better yet, at home. Amy could never do that, which was why her mother was standing there right next to her as she changed out of her clothes into a paper-thin white gown. She left

on her underwear. First in to see Amy was one of the
nurses in the office, Marlene Lynch, who was late in her
own pregnancy. She measured Amy's blood pressure at a
normal 123/58.

"When was your last period?" Lynch asked Amy.

"I'm having it right now," Amy said.

Lynch wrote it down, that Amy was menstruating, and
then asked her to stand on the scale. Amy knew her height
and weight. She was always a tiny thing: five feet one and
between 100 and 110 pounds, except for a brief period at
age thirteen when she struggled to shed some baby fat and
climbed to 120 pounds. In April 1995, her last physical,
she had weighed 109 pounds. But that was then. The scale
now showed 123 pounds. Amy looked at the bar balancing
in front of her and started to sniffle and then cry. She had
never weighed close to that in high school, when her
petite figure was so important to her. Her mother walked
over to her and stroked her hair, and then Lynch followed.
Instead of being curious as to an eighteen-year-old girl's
sudden and dramatic weight gain, everyone reassured her
nothing was wrong. Any teenage girl would be upset, they
thought. The nurse pulled out a chart that showed that for
her height, Amy's weight was in the normal range. Fifteen
pounds heavier, but still normal.

Amy calmed down, and then she and her mother
waited for the doctor. Sonye wanted a complete checkup
of her daughter because the year before, Amy had come
down with mononucleosis, which can lead to an inflamed
liver or spleen. Sonye wanted to make sure there were no
lasting effects. Fenkart walked in a few minutes later and
asked Amy to lie flat on the table. As she did, she crinkled
up the tissue paper on top of it. The slight bulge in her
underwear from the pad was noticeable. There would be
no internal examination.

Amy closed her eyes as Fenkart's cold hands felt
around her. He palpated her abdomen and felt around her
diaphragm. Poking, pushing, prodding.

This was it. Amy knew it. Her mother stood off to the

side. The doctor was going to feel something. He had to. Amy was sure of it. There was silence. Fenkart continued to poke, giving a more thorough examination than he normally would have because of Amy's earlier mono. But then his hands stopped. He asked Amy to sit up. She looked at her mother, and the doctor, and had to hide her disbelief. *He'd missed it!* She thought she was free. She forgot about her shots.

It's called Varivax, the live vaccine for preventing chickenpox. Amy had never had chickenpox, so she and her mother had agreed she should get the shot. The American Association of Pediatrics recommends that Varivax be given to all healthy children between twelve months and eighteen years. However, pregnant women do not get it. Its pregnancy risk factor in the *Physicians' Desk Reference* is level C, which means as follows: "Either studies in animals have revealed adverse effects on the fetus and there are no controlled studies in women, or studies in women and animals are not available. Drugs should be given only if the potential benefits justify the potential risk to the fetus."

Amy knew none of that when she first walked into the doctor's office. But suddenly Fenkart was explaining it to her.

"Amy, are you pregnant? If you're pregnant, you cannot get the vaccine." The question sent Amy's heart racing. Her mother was standing beside her. A hesitation would imply guilt. She didn't hesitate.

"No. I'm menstruating now."

She closed her eyes, turned her head, and took the shot. When she relaxed a few minutes later, Fenkart said the last thing he needed was a urine sample, to check her blood sugar and test for diabetes.

"I don't think I can go, I just went before I came here," Amy said.

She was afraid Fenkart would test the sample for pregnancy. Fenkart gave her a small plastic take-home bottle for a sample and told her to bring it back as soon as possible. She would return three weeks later for a second dose of the vaccine and repeat her claim that she was not pregnant. But she wouldn't bring back the urine sample. Ever.

What happened inside that tiny room would eventually lie at the heart of Amy's criminal case. It would also raise questions about how the forty-one-year-old pediatrician with a solid reputation could miss a pregnancy in its fifth month, no matter how routine an examination he did, how little Amy was showing, and what she told him.

Fenkart finished his paperwork, noting on his chart that Amy was menstruating and "not pregnant" and that she had no concerns. That simple notation would provide an opening for Amy's lawyers later, when she would be asked when she knew she was pregnant.

Her mother paid the $165 bill with a check, and they left the office. Amy could not wait to call Brian in Europe. She reached him in Italy and told him what happened.

"The doctor felt my stomach and didn't say anything to me. I didn't know why he didn't say something," Amy told him. "My mother didn't say anything. I guess they didn't find out."

When she mentioned the chickenpox vaccine and said she'd had to take the shot because her mother was right there, Brian wasn't sure how to react. He asked what the shot would do to the baby.

"I don't know, but there was no way I could not have it because my mother was sitting right there," she said.

Brian returned from Europe on July 26 and found his girlfriend worse off than when he'd left her. She complained to him of headaches and abdominal pains, as well as the first signs of swelling.

What she didn't know, and what a doctor would have told her if she had sought prenatal care, was that those were all early symptoms of a pregnancy illness called preeclampsia, or toxemia. It strikes in roughly one of every ten pregnancies and most often with women thirty-five and older, teenagers, and women carrying their first pregnancy. It originates in the placenta, which requires a consistent blood supply from the mother to sustain the growing baby. If a woman's arteries do not enlarge as they should during the first half of a pregnancy, the cause of preeclampsia, her baby may develop more slowly because it gets less oxygen and blood than most. The only treatment for preeclampsia is bed rest, and if a woman is suffering from it, her doctor will often try to deliver the baby as early as possible without endangering the fetus or the mother.

Amy knew none of this because she never saw a doctor. They'd discussed it, and Brian had encouraged it, but the fear that her mother would find out always won out. When Brian returned home, he quickly set up another abortion appointment.

In the Bergen County Yellow Pages under "Abortion Services," the quarter-page advertisement for Metropolitan Medical Associates says that it terminates pregnancies up to twenty-four weeks. Brian and Amy were not sure what week she was, but both knew it had to be close to that. The ad promised "privacy and confidentiality" at a "reasonable cost" and with "general or local anesthesia." Cost was not a concern for them. Neither was the anesthesia. All they wanted was privacy and confidentiality.

Brian made the appointment for August 6, under the name Maria Vasquez. That morning, after withdrawing $500 from his savings account, he drove with Amy to Metropolitan, fifteen minutes east of Wyckoff along the always congested Route 4 toward New York City. One-way traffic moved slowly along Engle Street into the main shopping district of Englewood, past the Mercedes-Benz dealership on the left. Across the street from the modern Englewood Library and Lexus of Englewood, and sandwiched between First Union Bank and the Smoke Chophouse and Cigar Emporium, was an inconspicuous three-story, red-brick building. The heavy, black, windowless doors provided no clue as to its inhabitants. Only a tiny sign in a first-floor window, beneath a videocamera that watches the front doors, identified the business as Metropolitan Medical Associates.

Brian parked his Celica on the street, fed the meter, and walked with Amy toward the front doors. They are doors that have been the site of dozens of pickets and arrests in recent years because of Metropolitan's willingness to perform so-called late-term abortions. Police have had to drag men and women antiabortion demonstrators away by their hands and feet as they shouted at women walking into and out of the clinic. Those protests were usually hyped in advance by the demonstrators and covered by the media. But on this day Engle Street was calm except for the heavy car and foot traffic through the bustling downtown shopping area.

As they neared the front door of 40 Engle Street, Amy stopped, turned, and kept walking past the building. Brian followed her, confused. Together they walked around the corner onto narrow Bergen Street, where Amy sat on the curb and cried, pounding her fists on Brian's chest.

"I can't do it!"

"It's okay," Brian said, comforting her.

"What if I get sick? My mother will find out."

All Brian could do was encourage her and tell her how unlikely it was that her mother would ever know. But nothing worked. Amy was terrified. They left.

The summer was ending. On August 25 Brian left for Gettysburg, for the start of the soccer season. An abortion was out. A baby was coming, but neither of them was thinking that far ahead.

"They just avoided it and kept thinking it would go away," said Dr. Kaye, the Delaware psychiatrist who would later interview Brian and who has studied dozens of cases of hidden pregnancies that ended tragically. "They just thought it would resolve itself in some way. If there is one idea that is so hard for people to recognize, this is it."

The last week of August the Grossbergs moved out of their Franklin Lakes house into a slate gray town house in the Cedar Hills development of Wyckoff, across the street from the office where Amy had her July doctor's appointment. It was less space, but hardly less luxurious or beautiful than their Franklin Lakes home. The unit came with an elevator from the two-car garage to the den, a marble fireplace, a deck in back, three bedrooms, and three bathrooms.

Less space would make it that much more difficult for Amy to keep her secret, to hide from Mom. But she wouldn't have to hide for long. On August 31, six days after Brian left town, Amy's parents drove her to Delaware and helped her unpack everything from her clothes, to her stereo, to her art supplies, to her prescription of Donnatal pills, the muscle relaxant that eased her pain during her bouts with her bowel problem. Actually, it was her mother's prescription. She wanted to be sure Amy knew what was in the bottle.

# "DEAR GOD"

## September 4, 1996

Seated before David Roselle today are 3,364 freshmen, the Class of 2000 at the University of Delaware. They range in age from sixteen to forty-eight, though most are just like Amy, eighteen years old, three months out of high school, days out of their parents' grip. In each of the students, Roselle, the university president, said he saw unlimited potential, and he wanted them to know that how they performed, how they behaved, over the next four years would play a huge role in determining their future.

"I'm going to fast-forward to say to seize the opportunities that lie before you here today," Roselle told the students. "Make it your challenge to make a difference."

For every freshman, college was the chance to explore, to start a new chapter, to make new friends, find new interests, survive without nagging parents. For Amy, Roselle's words about making a difference barely registered. Turning that page to a new chapter was impossible. Her past wouldn't let her. She woke up smiling every morning, chatting with the friends she was making in Thompson Hall and with her classmates, trying to be one of them. She rarely complained to them about her headaches and nausea and never mentioned her increasingly sore wrists and ankles.

Amy's only challenge was keeping her secret. She

would find out quickly just how hard it would be. On the second day of classes, Amy and her classmates in her drawing class had to bring in five personal objects. Sitting next to Amy was Christian Jackson, a twenty-one-year-old single mother and part-time student. Class was about to begin when Jackson leaned over to Amy.

"When is your due date?" she asked.

Jackson thought nothing of the question. She remembered her pregnancy, her son, Cody, and how young and scared she'd been when she'd given birth, and thought Amy might like a comforting voice, maybe a friend to talk to who knew what she was going through.

"I'm not pregnant," Amy answered her.

Jackson almost laughed in disbelief. It was so obvious to her; the signs were all there, from the slight swelling to the belly. But she left Amy alone and turned to whisper to another student.

Jackson had been bold enough to come right out and ask. No one else had done that. But Amy could see them stare and hear them whisper. She hated that she was the focus of their gossip. She hated pretending. She hated lying. She hated looking like someone other than herself. It was just her third day of classes when, in her morning three-dimensional design class, she opened her loose-leaf binder and turned a deaf ear to the teacher for five minutes.

*Hey Baby Dumps—*
*Hope everything becomes peachy keen for us soon. I hope nobody hurts me forever. This is just eating me up inside & out. I can't go on much longer like this. I'm going insane. I wish I could take everything I did back, but that's not how life goes. You must pay the consequences. I guess that's what I'm doing. I hope the God above is listening. I need help big time. Oh well, love you lots, always forever. Miss you more than ever. Wish we were with each other right now. I love you lots. Me.*

Brian was trying to act normally at Gettysburg. The freshman soccer season had started, and he had made the team. He was busy with a schedule of classes geared toward a business major, heavy in accounting. But concentrating was impossible—on the field, in the classroom, in his dorm room. There was no relief, certainly no fun. Not as long as he was talking to Amy three and four times a day.

At Gettysburg Brian's classmates found him moody and quiet. Had they known him, they would have suspected something was deeply wrong. But the freshmen were all new to each other. Maybe that was just Brian, his dorm mates thought.

One week into their classes, Brian drove to Delaware and picked Amy up to drive home with her for the weekend of September 8. The stress was clearly getting to her, and her slim and pretty figure was a thing of the past. It was something she missed desperately.

But for a girl who was so desperate to keep this secret from her parents, Amy was not hiding from them. Why go home knowing you are starting to look pregnant? She wanted to see them. It was curious behavior, yet experts say it was not surprising. Somewhere deep inside of Amy, far beyond her most basic fear and shame and embarrassment, she wanted to get caught. She wanted her mother to know. She just couldn't bring herself to tell her. As each day passed, Amy became more embarrassed not only about her pregnancy, but about keeping it from her parents. The longer she carried on her act, the harder it became to put an end to it.

"Oftentimes people do things with the hope that they will get caught," said Dr. Carol Tavani, chief of staff of Christiana Care Health Services, who interviewed Amy numerous times after her arrest and grew close to her family. "She's got this humongous secret, and she's terrified of disappointing them, but she knows she desperately needs their help."

She also needed Brian, and she was afraid of losing

him. By mid-September Amy started to worry that he was embarrassed to be with her, that he might lose his attraction for her and find someone else. Someone without a problem. Someone who had a cute figure. The truth was that Brian had opportunities to date at Gettysburg right away, with friends offering to set him up. But he wouldn't. He didn't. His mind was on Amy. He gave her a teddy bear in mid-September, and she immediately placed it on her bed next to the puppy dog stuffed animal he had given her over that summer.

"Now I'm surrounded by you," she told Brian on the phone.

He first visited her on the weekend of September 15, and they barely saw daylight. He had his car at college, but Amy did not have hers. Freshmen at UD had to park so far away from the main campus that it was as much of a hassle as a convenience to have a car. They spent the weekend huddled inside her room and cried endlessly together. It was there where Amy released her pain, in the arms of her boyfriend. Her roommate had suspected Amy was pregnant almost as soon as they met, but she never asked her about it. When Brian visited, Shooman left them alone as much as she could except to sleep.

When Brian was not visiting, Amy took comfort in her sketchpad. She had dreamed of being a fashion designer since she was a girl. Drawing was her escape from life. In her first weeks at UD she would sit in her bed for hours, her oversize drawing pad on her lap, sketching whatever struck her.

Most of her dorm friends knew what she wouldn't tell them. Aside from the few students who first met Amy and thought nothing other than that she was slightly chubby, most could tell she was pregnant. And they didn't care. They figured she would make it through the semester, have her baby over winter break, and then either return for spring session or drop out. Whatever her plan, to her classmates Amy was just one of them.

Only freshmen lived in the coed Thompson Hall. More

than four hundred eighteen-year-olds under one roof, their music and televisions blaring, window fans keeping their cramped rooms cool. Directly next to the Perkins Student Center and the cafeteria where most of the freshmen ate, Thompson also overlooked a quad where students relaxed in the warm weather, playing sports, reading, and chatting. A bulletin board outside the dorm was always a hodgepodge of tattered announcements: students looking for rides home; used cars for sale; local bands hyping their bar concerts; Student Health Services reminding freshmen girls that if they are pregnant, late, or merely worried, counselors, pregnancy tests, and contraception are all available.

Amy and her mother had been inseparable when she was growing up, and now, away at college, they were talking every day, two or three times on some days. About her classes, her teachers, her new friends, her health. Everything except her pregnancy, which by late September was in its seventh month. For that, Amy talked only to Brian, calling him from all over campus throughout each day, sometimes just to hear his voice. She wrote him letters, some on her notebook paper, others on dozens of Shoebox cards she bought. Frightened and insecure, she would apologize for pestering him, for putting him in a bind, for her constant mood swings. But Brian wasn't looking for an apology. He wasn't angry at her. She was scared and alone. He was, too. He needed her as much as she needed him.

Amy's counselor had always been her mother, and when Rosh Hashanah came in late September, so did Mom. Alan and Sonye had never been apart from Amy for the Jewish New Year, so on the Saturday of the holiday weekend they drove south to be with her. Amy sat with her mother and father in her dorm room, dipping apples in honey as the holiday calls for, a tradition to help bring in a sweet and good new year. It was an intimate family moment for Amy and her parents, a perfect chance for her to break the news to them. But she didn't. Instead, they talked about classes, Brian, the new town house her parents were living in, everything else.

Four weeks into the semester, Amy was terrified and homesick. Like every freshman. At the beginning of her pregnancy Brian had been by her side every day, always there with a shoulder to cry on, to hold her and tell her everything was going to work out. College had taken him from her, and she was lonely. Her boyfriend was cute. And she was pregnant. Was he going to forget about that and abandon her when she most needed him? Wouldn't most guys? Was he dating, cheating on her?

They talked every day, usually three or four times on a set schedule, and left messages for each other constantly. On September 17 Amy called Brian eighteen times, sometimes reaching him, other times getting his answering machine, and a few times just hanging up.

Two days later Dr. Ruth Westheimer, the spunky and diminutive sex doctor, spoke to UD students to hype a new book she had written with Ben Yagoda, a journalism professor there. A crowd of more than one hundred at the Trabant University Center listened, but she could have been talking to Amy directly when she said: "People need significant others around them. They need unconditional support." That was all Amy wanted from Brian.

> *. . . . I don't mean to scare you & upset you when I say that I'm going, but I just feel like it's my only hope because honestly I can't go on like this. . . . I'm repulsive and not only that, it's dangerous because I don't feel good. Not that I want to leave, because trust me, I don't. But I just feel like giving up sometimes. This is killing me physically, mentally, and emotionally. . . . I would do anything in the entire world if it just went away. It would be a dream come true. I and you would be happy again. We did this to ourselves, maybe that's why nobody is helping us. But I think we've suffered enough, at least I know I have.*

Talking to Brian, she would never use the word "suicide," but Brian knew what she meant when she talked about "going." And it scared him. She never sounded serious, but in her letters to him she would talk about disappearing, just going, and freeing him of all the worries she had caused him. Brian kept shrugging off her suicide talk as just that. Talk.

But then one night in late September she told Brian on the telephone she loved him and that he would not have to worry about her anymore. She was crying as she talked. As she hung up, Brian shouted at her, upset at her veiled threat. He called back, and she didn't pick up right away. When she finally did, he was reduced to tears as he begged her to keep talking to him. She did. She didn't want to hurt herself. She wanted only to not be pregnant.

Brian became panicked that if he broke his promise to her and told someone, she would hurt herself, maybe even take her life. He stayed true to her. Amy knew that he would, and in every letter she reminded him with one line, always at the end, right before she said good-bye: "*I need you now more than ever.*"

In early October the state announced that its infant mortality rate had declined by 10 percent. Alexis Andrianopoulos, the spokeswoman for the Delaware Department of Health and Human Services, a department that would soon be under a barrage of attention, attributed the drop to the state's efforts to reduce teen pregnancies.

"For instance, teens may not know they are pregnant or wish to tell their parents," Andrianopoulos said on the day the new figures were released. "As a result, they may not get the proper prenatal care."

Little did she know how prophetic her words would be. Amy was seven months pregnant. She had told no one about her pregnancy. And she had sought no prenatal care. Laurel Hall, home of UD's Student Health Services office and a gynecological clinic, was a block away, a two-minute walk from Thompson Hall. Amy never went. A block farther was a small house, Planned Parenthood. The girls who walk inside the front door often peek around, maybe to see if anyone is watching them. Amy never even made it to the front door.

In her dormitory Amy was cheerful and helpful, studying hard, helping others, and drawing in her pad while sitting on her bed at night. No one asked about her condition.

"You knew, but you didn't know, and you didn't ask," said Seth Chorba, a freshman who lived five doors down from Amy. "Every time you saw her, she was smiling. She always got up on the right side of the bed. No one disliked her."

In public, she was smiling. In private, she was moody, with almost hourly swings from one emotion to another. She would snap at Brian one minute and apologize profusely the next. She hated looking at herself in the mirror. She knew something was going to happen soon, but she had no idea what. She told Brian she needed to see a doctor but could not bring herself to walk to either of the services so close to her dorm. The longer she had kept her secret, the harder it became to reveal it.

In early October an article appeared in the student newspaper, the *Review,* discussing "the freshman fifteen," when college freshmen put on weight after leaving home for the first time by snacking late into the night and rarely exercising. The article talked about how girls in particular fall victim to it. But to those in Thompson Hall, and even among students in her art classes, Amy was clearly not a victim of the freshman fifteen.

Walking through campus on October 3, Amy tripped on the sidewalk and twisted her ankle. Grimacing, she made it to class and then back to her dormitory. The ankle swelled, as she expected, but she did not expect her other ankle to start swelling. Two badly swollen ankles all of a sudden. She knew something was wrong, but rather than stroll over to the Student Health Services building a block away, she ignored her pain. Her toxemia was worsening.

A week later, on October 10, Amy boarded a bus with her classmates for a field trip to the Philadelphia Museum of Art. When she reached up to put her backpack in the overhead rack, her sweater stretched up above her belly button, exposing her condition.

"She didn't look pregnant to me until I saw her on the bus," said Shannon McGinley, who was a freshman art major from Maine studying with Amy. "She was wearing a short sweater—and when she stretched, I saw her stomach."

But McGinley said nothing to Amy. She assumed she knew she was pregnant and that she would be having the baby soon, since she looked too far along to have an abortion. Whether she would leave college to raise her baby or put the baby up for adoption, no one knew. And no one asked.

> *October 15, 1996:*
> *Dear God—*
> *Why does it seem like I just do everything wrong. I mean why can't I just get a break, once in a while. Everybody hurts me. I can't take it anymore. I feel so hopeless. I mean nothing is going my way. Why do I always get hurt. What I need is so important, though. I know it was my fault, but it's me I'm always pleasing. Others and I should have been more responsible, but I realize how stupid I am and I regret it. Please help me. My life is ruined, don't do this to me. I don't deserve such harsh treatment. Granted I deserve what has happened, but I've learned my lesson. Don't let it go any further, please. I beg you. This would mean the world to me. I will never ever do anything like this ever again. Trust me. Don't hurt me like this. Haven't I gone through enough. Gosh, all I ask is for a little help for a big mistake I realize. But I'm so good otherwise. Please don't ruin my life any further. I can't apologize enough. I'll do anything. Everything always goes wrong for me. Am I that bad? Do I deserve it all? Please, I'm down on my knees, help*

*me. Don't hurt me. I need you to come through for*
*me now more than ever. I can't handle it. I've defi-*
*nitely learned a huge lesson. Please. I beg you.*

*Thanks. I appreciate it more than I'll ever be*
*able to express. I beg you, soon as possible. Love*
*and thanks a million.*
*Amy S. Grossberg*

*Whenever is better than never. Please, now more*
*than ever. It's not fair. I can't handle this. I'm not*
*strong enough. I'm sorry that I did what I did, but*
*don't hurt me anymore. I can't do it. I've learned*
*the biggest lesson of a lifetime. I'm trying to be*
*strong, but it's hard. I'm begging you don't need to*
*hurt me. Please—help me—I need you.*

She never mailed it anywhere. She just kept it in her
loose-leaf binder, written on a single sheet of blue-lined
paper during her morning art class. She was a tortured
girl, not a young woman, but a girl beaten down physically and emotionally by a pregnancy she desperately did
not want. She told God she had learned her lesson. But she
had said that before after false alarms and nothing had
changed. It was too late for God, Brian, or anyone to make
it go away.

By late October Amy's body was swollen and aching all
over. She couldn't complain to anyone but Brian. She
couldn't sleep. She wasn't hungry. Every weekend Amy
had a visitor. Brian would arrive Friday night or Saturday
morning and they would huddle in her room, crying and
talking. Amy wanted to go home, she missed her parents.
Brian had done the math. He suspected Amy had become
pregnant in April or May, which would have put her seven
months along by late November. But Amy told him there
was no way she could go home for Thanksgiving because
she looked too pregnant to hide it from her parents any
more. She told Brian not to worry, that her stomach was

hurting a lot and that something was going to happen soon.

> *Hey Babes*
> *What's going on baby? I want a big hug from you right now. . . . I know lately I've been really, really, really emotional. It's really not me talking. It's my wacky body, but I'm still sorry. Thanks for always listening. . . . This mess we got ourselves into is a total disaster, if I've ever seen one. . . . I mean, what did we do to deserve this. . . . My body is doing things it's never done before. I'm so scared. All I want is for it to go away. I can't get caught. I mean I really can't. Can't.*

Thanksgiving was a month away when the UD students cleaned up their rooms, did their laundry, and organized their books. Parents Weekend was coming, the chance for the children to show they have survived on their own and the parents to see whether their fears were justified about their children's eating, bathing, and studying habits.

When Sonye and Alan arrived on Saturday, October 26, to see their angelic daughter, she looked nothing like the girl who had left their home two months ago. She always wore clothes well. Slacks, long skirts, blouses, she could make any outfit, no matter how tight fitting, work on her slim frame. And she had a closet full of Donna Karan and Calvin Klein, every style for every occasion. She loved clothes, and clothes loved her. But those outfits were tailored for her tiny 105-pound build. That had disappeared over the summer in her second trimester and was long gone by the time Parents Weekend arrived. By the last weekend in October Amy weighed more than 130 pounds. Some of it was from too many midnight snacks, but most of it was her pregnancy. And that had to be hidden.

Instead of greeting her mom and dad in one of the dozens of outfits she had bought with her mother, Amy spent the weekend dressed like a member of a grunge rock band. Baggy jeans, baggy shirts, baggy sweaters. For most college students it was a typical hippie look, but for Amy it was out of style and out of character. Her face was noticeably heavier, with the hint of a double chin showing. For someone who always had been rail thin, this was an obvious change, and her parents couldn't help but worry.

Privately Alan and Sonye talked about Amy. They were not happy with how their daughter, their sweetface, looked. They looked at her weight and blamed it on the "freshman fifteen," her first two months away from home, midnight snacks and pizza deliveries, no exercise. She had always been a terrific student, so they thought her studies were keeping her up late.

Instead of sleeping in her dorm room with her parents in town, Amy stayed with them Friday night in their room at the Christiana Hilton a few miles north of the campus off Route 95. She was swollen everywhere. Her body was so tired. She wanted to tell them. She wanted this charade to end.

*Mom, Dad, I have to tell you something, but I'm afraid of how you'll react. I'm in trouble. I'm so scared. I'm pregnant.*

Before they went to bed, Amy and her mother talked briefly.

"Are you feeling okay?" Sonye asked her daughter.

"I'm okay. I've been really tired. I haven't felt so good lately, but I'm sure it's nothing."

And that was it. She chickened out, and Mom had nothing else to ask. No questions about Amy's weight gain, no suggestion that she see a doctor, no suspicion that something was wrong.

"The only thing she complained of was that she was a little tired, and she wasn't feeling great," Sonye would say later in a televised interview. "College in the beginning is difficult. And the kids go to sleep at two or three in the morning, or whatever, and it's not like your own bedroom."

The next morning Amy's parents took her to breakfast and then food shopping, and then they left. Immediately Amy called Brian. And kept calling. Once, twice, three times. She got his answering machine eight times. They talked twice. The secret was safe.

In early November Amy's condition worsened quickly. Her preeclampsia was in full effect, the headaches and nausea constant reminders of her trouble. She said nothing, went to class, studied, and talked to Brian. She complained to him that along with her stomach pains, she could feel the baby moving. Her swelling was out of control, every finger, every toe constantly aching. Her days were long, trying to study and keep up with her art projects to stay distracted. But the baby was coming faster than she anticipated.

On November 2 Brian took Amy home with him to Wyckoff. His mother and stepfather were away, so the house was empty. Amy felt so sick that she didn't want her parents to know she was in town, but she still went on Saturday afternoon to watch Brian play soccer with his old high school friends. She sat in the bleachers, huddled in a baggy winter coat. His friends saw her and waved, but no one could tell what she was hiding beneath her layers. When Amy went home to Brian's house that night, they slept close. Very close.

Amy had been worried for months that Brian might leave her when she needed him the most. She wanted to have sex so badly, she missed him. But she couldn't. It was too painful for her. She apologized all night, and Brian held her tight, telling her not to worry. As he drove her back to Delaware Sunday, she promised him they would make up for lost time when their future was clear.

*Baby Dumps,*
*Hey babes, what's going on? Kisses, kisses, kisses. I had so much fun with you this weekend. You make every second of my day happy. . . . You are absolutely the greatest boy ever. Thank you for tak-*

*ing me home with you. Being with you is the only*
*thing I want. Your snuggles and cuddles are the*
*greatest. . . . I'm sorry that I couldn't give you what*
*I really wanted to Saturday night because it hurt too*
*much, but I hope you enjoyed it anyway. . . . I love*
*you lots. I miss you so much. Can't wait to see you*
*real soon. I love you.*

The weekend of November 9 Amy had two visitors:
her best girlfriend from high school, Tara Lermond, and,
of course, Brian. Lermond would later tell police she had
no idea Amy had been pregnant. Saturday night Amy
stayed in with Brian, just hugging and crying, and when
she woke up Sunday morning she threw up. Brian had
never seen her so distraught. She looked pregnant. Anyone could tell just by looking at her legs. Normally pen-
cils, they were obviously swollen right down to her
ankles. The couple discussed Thanksgiving. Amy said
there was no way she could go home looking the way she
did. But she told Brian not to worry. Something was going
to happen before then. She sensed it. She felt it. This pregnancy was not going to last until Thanksgiving. On Monday morning, after Lermond left, Amy started feeling sick
to her stomach again and called her mother.

"I've been throwing up, Mom, I feel horrible," Amy
told her.

"It's probably just a virus," Sonye told her. She had
spoken with her son over the weekend in Boston, and his
roommate was throwing up, too, so Sonye told Amy a bug
was probably going around.

"Brian was here, he took care of me," Amy said.

Amy was fighting, refusing to give in to her sickness.
She made all her classes.

Monday afternoon she called two friends on campus
whom she had met while working at the Wyckoff YMCA,
Francesca Montalto and Jennifer Tighe, and the three of
them made plans to meet for dinner shortly after five P.M.
Dinner was an hour of gossiping and laughing, Amy try-

ing her hardest to keep up her routine despite feeling sick
to her stomach.

"Nothing that night seemed strange, unusual, or out of
the ordinary," Montalto remembered later.[10]

"There was no distress in her eyes or concern in her
voice to warn me of any kind of problem," Tighe would
also recall.[11]

Amy went back to her room after dinner and called her
mother again. She still felt nauseated, but the conversation
was short. Amy had classwork to do. She worked until
midnight on her art project, when her stomach started to
rumble and a strange, wet sensation invaded her sweatpants. She reached for her phone again, but not to call
Mom.

# "GET RID OF IT!"

Despite seeing how sick Amy was, and despite hearing her say something was going to happen soon, Brian was still confident Thanksgiving would be their savior. If Amy went home, her parents would find out. If she tried to stay away, as she vowed to do, her parents would grow suspicious. Either way, Thanksgiving was on his mind when Amy called him after midnight on Tuesday and he raced to be with her.

As they left her campus a few minutes after three A.M., driving over the short bridge and past the football stadium on the left, Brian saw a motel on the right. Sleep Inn. He had never heard of it before, never even noticed it in all his trips in and out of Newark. But there it was. Privacy. He turned into the driveway and pulled under the awning in front of the office.

"Just wait, I'll get a room and be right back."

He walked quickly up to the front glass door, but to get inside at such a late hour he had to ring a bell. The front desk was empty, so he rang. Once. Twice. No one appeared.

"No one there," Brian explained as he jumped back in his car and pulled away. "Maybe we should go to a hospital."

"We can't," Amy said. "You know we can't. I'll get sick. They'll have to call my parents."

He turned right back onto South College Avenue. Their future was in his hands as he held his steering wheel with his left and Amy's trembling hand with his right. He could drive straight home to Wyckoff, to her parents. He could drive to the nearest hospital. The road was desolate as they passed the car wash, the Dunkin' Donuts, and the Mobil station, approaching the highway. Out of the corner of his right eye, he could see Amy, and he could feel her hand. Every few minutes her body would quiver and tense up. He had never seen a woman in labor before, but he knew what a contraction was, and that's what it seemed Amy was having. He knew right then this baby was coming out tonight. Just before the ramp to 95 South, Brian saw a Comfort Inn on the right. He didn't hesitate. He pulled in, parked, and walked into the lobby, leaving Amy in the car.

Underneath an unsightly orange A-shaped roof, and unattached from the 102 guest rooms, the office at the Comfort Inn was small and simple. A television played off to the right of the front desk as Brian walked in, and to the left sat a rack of maps and a coffee maker, as well as two glass jars filled with cold cereal for the morning continental breakfast. A rack of religious pamphlets stood near the desk. One was titled "Must Nice People Repent?"

This was hardly the first time the motel had an early morning arrival. Truckers came in at all hours, frequently with prostitutes in tow. And with the college just down the street, where privacy wasn't always easy to find in a dormitory room, students occasionally sought out a motel room. Brian put on his best smile and asked the night clerk, Deborah Shephard, for a room.

Never without cash, usually $100 or more, he paid the $52 after filling out the slip for the room. Like most of his friends, he had a fake driver's license to get him into bars and help him buy beer. If ever there was a time to use it, this was it. It never occurred to him. He printed his correct license plate number, his correct name and address, and signed his name. He wasn't a criminal. He hadn't done anything wrong. Why should he sign a false name or write a fake license plate? He took the key to room 220, went back to his car, and walked with Amy to the left of the office, up the stairs, and to the left. Walking the outdoor corridor, with the rooms on their right and South College Avenue below to their left, Amy and Brian were no longer just college students in love. They were two teenagers in a crisis. And without a plan.

But they were a couple.

Together. It defined their relationship more than any word. For three years they had taken every major step in their young lives arm in arm. Their junior prom. Their awkward first sexual experience. Their senior prom. High school graduation photos. And their secret that had taken them to the door of room 220 at a roadside motel in Newark, Delaware, at 3:10 A.M. on a bitter Tuesday morning.

The room was a relief from the cold, despite its drab beige wallpaper and floral bedspreads. The one window faced out onto the street, a clear view of the roof of the motel office and the Howard Johnson and Friendly's across the street. The television remote lay on the table between the two double beds against the right wall. A table, dresser, and the television lined the left wall, and the bathroom was in the rear. They were alone. Whatever happened was their secret if they wanted to keep it. Amy's pains worsened, and Brian knew that this was really going to happen. Amy was going to have their baby, and he would have to play doctor.

Amy went straight to the bed closest to the bathroom. She lay down and rolled on her side. Brian crouched on the floor between the beds. He felt helpless. He needed her as much as she needed him. She looked so uncomfortable, shivering, crying softly.

"Do you want to pull your pants down?"

"No, leave them on. I'll just tell you when it's going to happen."

"How do you feel? Are you okay?"

"I'm fine. Just scared."

"Me too."

Almost an hour passed. The room was silent, except for the occasional rumble of a car or truck on the nearby highway or the whistle of the wind outside the window. Brian was lying still beside Amy when she rolled over on her back and he helped pull off her gray sweatpants. He stood up, went to the foot of the bed, and tugged them off her right leg. He reached for the left pants leg, but Amy stopped him.

"Just leave it," she said.

She pulled down her own underwear. Brian stood up and walked to the bathroom. He thought he might need towels, so he grabbed the stack above the toilet and the washcloths. Lying alone on the bed, Amy seemed to be having more frequent contractions now than she'd had in the car. Finally, just after four-thirty, she slowly spread her legs. Neither of them knew about the preeclampsia Amy had been suffering and how it would impact the delivery. It had left her swollen all over, from her fingertips to her toes. Her vision was blurry. Her head throbbed. The bedside light was shining in her eyes, so she took a washcloth and shielded them. She wasn't pushing, she wasn't sobbing, when suddenly a bulge appeared at her vagina, the head forcing its way out. A doctor would have shouted, "The head is crowning!"

Brian stared, dumbfounded.

As the next contraction came, Amy felt strange. Most women about to give birth for the first time speak with friends ad nauseam about the agony, the ecstasy, the painkilling drugs, all of the curiosities about childbirth so they can go in prepared. Amy had spoken to no one about how it might feel to have a baby force its way out of her body. If she had, she would not have been completely terrified about what she was feeling.

"It feels like it's coming out of my butt," she said in a panicked voice, the washcloth still covering her eyes.

Brian was absolutely lost. Near hysterics. He turned away and started to hyperventilate. He closed his eyes and tried to catch his breath as sweat dripped off his forehead. He had been intimate with Amy many times, but he had never seen her like this. So open. So vulnerable.

"What's the matter?" Amy asked him.

"I'm scared. We shouldn't be doing this. We don't know what to do. We should go to a hospital. Amy, we should really go to a hospital."

He hoped that now, at last, she would forget her mother, forget her father, forget what would happen if they found out, and listen to him. They could be there in five minutes, Brian thought. A doctor could deliver this baby instead of him.

"You know we can't now," Amy said, trying to soothe him. "My mom will find out. We can't do that."

She saw how scared Brian was and called for him to come to her. She hugged him and kissed him.

"It will be okay. I love you."

"I love you, too," he answered as he stroked her back.

"We will get through this together," she promised him. She didn't know how, she just hoped she was right. "Don't worry. Don't worry. We'll help each other through this. It's okay, it's okay."

Her voice relaxed him. But her position did not. He sat at the end of the bed and took a deep breath. His sweat was a cold sweat, not the type that he worked up playing midfield for the Ramapo Raiders. Nothing in Magda Karpati's health class had covered this. The flour baby exercise wasn't going to help him now. His girlfriend was lying on this bed, and a baby, his baby, was on its way.

He unfolded a towel beneath her legs and reached over to push up on Amy's abdomen toward her chest, trying to line up the baby for as smooth a delivery as possible. But he had no idea where to push, or how hard, and after two attempts he stopped. He stepped back. He was shaking as much as Amy. Breathing was hard all of a sudden. Amy was talking to him, but he could barely listen. She complained of some pain, but she wasn't screaming or writhing on the bed. There was only a little blood.

Brian was standing over Amy as she lay feet flat, her knees folded. It happened so fast. Amy would say later she felt a *squish* between her legs, as if a series of blobs were squeezing out from inside her. That *squish* would weigh more than six pounds and measure almost two feet in length.

The head peeked out, then the shoulders slid free, and in seconds the body slithered onto the bed facedown, the umbilical cord still attached, just as a doctor would want.

Curly black hair. Long eyelashes. And a penis. Brian had never seen a seconds-old newborn, but this one didn't look healthy. He thought the baby looked blue, not pink as he was expecting. A doctor's first move might have been to clip and tie off the umbilical cord and suction the baby's air passages with a vacuum, hoping to clear the airway of any mucus or other blockages possibly preventing him from breathing. Brian's first move was to ignore the baby, the few spots of blood and green slimy meconium on the baby's leg, and go to his girlfriend's side. She was hysterical, crying with her hands over her eyes.

There was no crying from the baby. Nothing like what he and Amy had seen so many times in the movies or on television. But that didn't matter. Brian would later tell police that even if the baby had come out kicking and screaming, he doubted the outcome would have been different. Two people had walked into that motel room. Two people were leaving it. On the bed, Amy was sobbing as Brian held her close.

"Get rid of it, get rid of it!" Her voice was hysterical. The washcloth had slipped off her eyes. She wasn't yelling out some premeditated, sinister plan they had scripted. They had no plan. They had never thought more than five minutes ahead each day of Amy's pregnancy. Brian stared at Amy. And then at the baby.

"I don't know what to do," Brian said. "It isn't crying. It isn't moving. What should I do?"

"Get rid of it."

Her voice calmed down, and Brian continued to rub her

back and neck. They ignored the baby lying a foot away on the bed and talked softly. For all these months they had somehow kept this secret, worrying more about themselves and not once about their coming baby. Amy's only concern had been her parents finding out. Brian's only concern had been not betraying Amy. Now their baby was here, and they couldn't tell if he was alive or dead. Not that it mattered to them.

Brian reached over for a towel and gently spread it on top of the baby, not to keep him warm, but to hide him from their sight. In the same motion, Brian could have reached the telephone on the desk next to the television. Dialing 9 for an outside line and 911 could have brought an ambulance to them in minutes, but he never even looked at the phone. They were just talking softly when Brian remembered he had a box of garbage bags in his car behind the passenger's seat.

"I'll be right back, don't move."

With the umbilical cord still attached to her, linking her with the baby, Amy was going nowhere. She was flat on her back, staring at the ceiling. As Brian ran out, Amy sat up and grabbed the cord to try to tear it, to separate herself from the baby. She yanked with all her strength, her fingernails digging into the cord. She had no idea how tough it was.

Outside, Brian bolted past the motel office and straight to his car, which was parked facing South College Avenue. The diner next to the motel was open, but quiet. He opened the passenger door, grabbed a bag from the box, and ran back to the room. It took all of ninety seconds.

That minute and a half would become the first of several crucial puzzles for investigators. Amy was alone with a baby she desperately did not want. She was physically drained and emotionally spent, but hardly unconscious. The baby was inches away from her legs, her feet. The room was quiet, the television black. Traffic outside was light. The clock read 4:40 A.M.

Suddenly the door opened and Brian was back. Amy was sitting up on her elbows, the baby still between her legs, the cord still attached.

"Are you okay?" he asked.

"I'm fine. Just tired. I'm really sore."

He grabbed the top of the bag and whipped it through the air to open it wide. Forgetting about the cord, he gently picked up the baby and the towel to slide them into the bag. But as he did, blood spurted out of a small tear in the cord, splattering the bed and Amy's leg. The baby may not have looked healthy, but blood spurting from the cord was a likely sign that the baby's heart was beating. Brian didn't think of that. He wiped the blood off Amy's leg with a fresh towel and put the baby back down so he could catch his breath. The blood formed a small puddle on the towel and spilled onto the mattress. He sat back on the bed, and they waited for the little bleeding to stop.

"Is it a boy or a girl?" Amy asked Brian.

But she cut him off before he could answer.

"Never mind."

The bleeding stopped a few minutes later, and Brian stood up to try the bag again. As he pulled the baby and towels toward him, the cord tore free and squirted a little more blood. With the baby in the bag, along with the towels caked with blood, he grabbed the yellow drawstrings and cinched them up tight. Bag in hand, he stood up and wiped the dried tears from his eyes.

"I'll be right back."

"Hurry up," Amy whispered at him as he left.

The door shut behind him, and a blast of cold air smacked him in the face. He turned right and then right again toward a stairway that led out back. As he held the weighted bag in his right hand in front of his body, he scampered down the one flight of outdoor concrete stairs into the dark parking lot behind the motel. He looked left, then right, and saw the Dumpster in the far corner. Darting between the few parked cars as though they were defenders on the soccer field, he ran toward the trash bin, tying the drawstrings on the bag as he ran. He closed within about twelve feet of the Dumpster and, without hesitating, stopped in his tracks and tossed the bag sidearm into the bin. He stood to watch as it banged off the far inside wall of the Dumpster like a basketball bank shot.

*Thump.*

The bag landed on a bed of empty cardboard boxes and overstuffed trash bags filled with cans of empty vegetables and other food remains. Exactly what type of trash would follow the baby into the Dumpster in the ensuing hours would become a second critical question.

Brian turned around, ran back up the stairs, his breathing becoming labored, and walked into the room. Amy was on the bed, a small piece of the cord still attached to her. Sex ed had taught them about the afterbirth, the placenta, but neither of them knew how it would come out, when it would come out, or even if it would come out. They sat and waited and talked about it, unsure if they should leave or stay, even if it meant waiting a few hours. Finally they decided to go. Brian felt thirsty. Amy was sore and exhausted. The sooner they could leave, the sooner they could put this behind them.

Not even two hours after she had pulled them off, Amy hiked up her sweatpants.

"Can you walk?" Brian asked her.

"Yeah, I'll be okay."

Leaving behind a mess on the bed, puddles of blood and fetal fluids, they left just as they had come in. Together. Using the banister to support her, Amy stepped slowly down the stairs with Brian beside her. He opened the passenger door, and she melted into the seat. Checking out of their room was the last thing on his mind. That could wait. Brian backed up his car when Amy asked about the baby.

"What did you do with it? Where did you put it?"

He pointed behind the motel, toward the Dumpster.

"Over there."

\* \* \*

The five-minute drive back to Thompson Hall was silent, and together they tiptoed back into Amy's room at five-thirty A.M. Shooman was asleep. As Amy undressed, she remembered she still had a piece of the umbilical cord to deal with. She asked Brian to go into her closet and get two feminine pads from her top shelf. Brian fetched them while Amy wiped a pair of cuticle scissors in rubbing alcohol. They went back into the hall and down to the men's bathroom. Brian got on his knees and clipped the cord as close as he could. He threw out her underwear and the small towel she had tucked into her underwear and walked with her back to her room.

They crept under the covers of Amy's twin bed, and Brian wrapped his arms around her and dozed off for about two hours. It was just before nine A.M. when Brian woke up first. He was already dressing, sidestepping her clothes strewn on the floor, when she stirred in the bed. Her head felt light, her entire body sore.

"Are you just going to rest today?" Brian said to Amy, assuming that she was.

"No, I have to go to class. I have to get up."

Brian looked dumbfounded at his girlfriend of the last three years, his high school sweetheart, a girl he loved, a girl he had talked with about marrying, and he saw a look of nausea and pain on her face that he had never seen before. She looked horrible. He begged her to stay in bed.

"What do you mean, you can't miss class?" Brian said. "You can miss class. Just stay here and rest."

So she did. She kissed Brian good-bye and slept through her first class of the day, something she had never done before. She didn't want to fall behind in her studies in her freshman year, not after being an A student throughout high school and making her parents so proud. Blowing off one class scared her, which made her all the more determined to make her twelve-thirty class.

When she finally did get up, she grabbed a towel, along with her soap and shampoo, and walked down the hall, past her floormates, to the showers.

Brian left the campus the same way he had six hours earlier when his pregnant girlfriend was beside him. In no hurry to return to Gettysburg, he pulled into a McDonald's. He ate and sat. And sat. For more than an hour. At eleven A.M. he left and drove over to the Comfort Inn parking lot, the same lot he had sprinted through six hours earlier, carrying a baby in a plastic bag. This time he was here to check out of his room. That done, Brian made one more stop. He drove to the White Glove Car Wash and let his car be pulled through the red and blue brushes.

He was long gone, on the roads back to Gettysburg, when a maid knocked on the door to room 220 at the Comfort Inn. Most of the guests there arrive late, leave early, and stay one night. When no one answered her knock, she let herself in. The mess she found inside would have floored most people, but all she did was retreat to her office to ask her manager how to handle it. Not the first time. Clean it up and move on, she was told.

The bed was soaked in fluids. The sheets were ruined, the foot of the mattress stained with blood. She followed her orders. She tossed the sheets in a plastic bag, threw them on her cart, flipped the mattress to conceal the red blotches, and made the bed with crisp, fresh sheets. Then she left. The soiled sheets were thrown out in a Dumpster behind the motel, not the one where Brian had tossed out a heavier bag hours earlier. No one knew who or what had left behind the bloodstained sheets. No one asked.

But in twelve hours the motel would be swarming with police. By then they would already know that Amy and Brian were responsible for the mess. Learning why would not be so simple.

# WHY?

It had been a night of mind-boggling decisions that would leave people in Wyckoff and around the country simply amazed. Nothing that Amy and Brian did made sense, from the summer when they hid her pregnancy, to the night they checked into the motel, to the morning after, when they pretended everything was normal.

Until the public had heard of Amy and Brian, the perception of mothers charged with killing their infants was that they tended to be young, poor, probably minority, alone, and uneducated girls. While that was an accurate portrayal for years, it no longer fits. The experts say more and more of the young women charged with killing their newborns are upwardly mobile, educated, and middle class, and their greatest fear is to have their good life derailed by a baby.

The U.S. Justice Department estimates that 250 newborns die at the hands of their mothers each year. While the availability of birth control and abortion have lowered that number since 1970, experts say there are likely dozens of infant corpses that are never found.

Half of all seventeen-year-old girls in the United States have had intercourse, and each year almost 500,000 teenagers give birth. Of the teen pregnancies, three in every four are unplanned. While the teen birthrate in America declined 8 percent from 1991 to 1995, teenage mothers are still much less likely than older women to receive timely prenatal care and are less likely to gain the recommended weight during their pregnancy.

Park Dietz is a longtime FBI consultant and widely renowned California psychiatrist who was hired by the Delaware prosecutors to study Amy's actions, but he never got to interview her. He said Amy and Brian will change how the public looks at the crime and mark the beginning of the "yuppification" of baby deaths.

" 'It's not time yet to have a baby,' " he said of the cute and promising cheerleader types charged with killing their infants. " 'I have so much to live for.' It's much clearer to have no loose ends."

But why? Every question about Amy and Brian on the streets of Wyckoff, every question in the hallways of their high school and at their respective colleges, every question on talk radio programs around the country, started with that word.

## Why couldn't Amy and Brian tell their parents? And if not a parent, why not a friend or a counselor?

This may be the easiest question to answer, but the most difficult to understand.

"She's trying not to shame their family's image," said Neil Kaye, the Delaware psychiatrist. "The whole family, in her mind, would be disgraced by this, not just her. Amy knew her parents saw her as perfect, and she just couldn't break that image for her mom."

Dr. Janice Ophoven, a pediatric forensic pathologist in Minnesota who assisted in Brian's defense and the mother of two twentysomething boys, said too many parents unknowingly send a dangerous message to their children.

"'You are my success story. You cannot fail because it is not you failing, it is me failing.'"

The public, and the media, latched on so strongly to the case because of the backgrounds of Amy and Brian, everything and everyone they had at their disposal that they ignored in favor of a trash Dumpster. But the experts

say what made Amy and Brian unique wasn't their upper-
middle-class opportunities, but the fact that Amy did not
go through her unwanted pregnancy alone. Brian stuck by
her side from conception to delivery, and that was most
unusual.

"The unique nature of the case was that the mother and
father were present," said Dr. Phillip Resnick, a psychiatry
resident at University Hospital of Cleveland and a professor at Case Western Reserve University School of Medi-
cine. When the defense lawyers went looking for an
authority to help them explain what had happened inside
room 220 of the Comfort Inn and why, Resnick was one
of the first they hired. "That's what made it extraordinary.
The affluence has been around. This was the twosome."

It was being a twosome that made keeping the secret
easier for Amy and Brian, because they had each other to
lean on. Amy wasn't alone. She wouldn't tell, and he
agreed not to tell, either, because that would betray her. It
was loyal and chivalrous up to a point. Then it became
stupid.

Until 1969 child murders had been lumped together as
infanticides. That year, at a meeting of the American Psychiatric Association in Miami Beach, Resnick coined a
new term: neonaticide, the killing of a newborn in the first
twenty-four hours of life.

"There is no crime more difficult to comprehend than
the murder of a child by his own parents," Resnick said at
that meeting.

Until Amy and Brian came along, the public had one
perception of neonaticide: "The majority of neonaticidal
mothers are unwed, poor, and have denied or concealed
the pregnancy, or both, since conception," Kaye wrote in a
psychiatric review of neonaticide in 1990. "They frequently give birth alone and dispose of the baby as if it
were an abortion that occurred 'too late.'"

The fathers, whether they knew their girlfriends were
pregnant or not, are nowhere in sight when the mothers
are charged. But Brian changed that. He was there to the

end, Amy's white knight, refusing to leave her side. Experts who researched two hundred years of records found not one case where mother and father conspired to kill their baby. Whether they actually conspired or not in that two-hour motel stay, this pair of educated and well-off teenagers from northern New Jersey changed the face of an entire crime.

"The cost of going to the parents is shame, loss of approval, disappointing the parents after all they've worked to achieve, shattering the dream of a family," said Dietz. "Those costs are perceived as high."

**Why would two bright teenagers with so much formal education, money, abortion clinics nearby, so many options at their fingertips, do nothing about an unwanted pregnancy?**

"What we consider to be options are not viewed as options to them," Ophoven said. "All the things Amy could have done would have exposed her to what she considered high risk."

That might explain why she had backed out of her abortion appointments.

"Street smarts" is a term often associated with inner-city children. Rarely is it used to describe children in towns like Wyckoff. Those children, it goes, are "book smart," though some are certainly more wise to the world than others. A year after Amy and Brian discarded their baby, a sixteen-year-old boy from the urban streets of Paterson, New Jersey, helped his fourteen-year-old girlfriend deliver their baby at home. Instead of panicking and discarding the baby, he wrapped the newborn girl in a blanket and took her to nearby Barnert Hospital. Even though he lied and told the nurse he had found the baby in a park a few blocks away, the baby was safe and was cared for. Less educated, but more street smart.

A pregnant teenager in New York City might not think twice about going for an abortion or visiting Planned Parenthood. That's life. There is no shame in it. But for Amy that would have meant making an important life-altering decision by herself, sneaking away, and looking over her shoulder constantly to make sure no one who knew her was in sight. And she would have had to do it without dis-. cussing it first with Mom and Dad. She had never done that. She couldn't.

Nancy Eisenhower, the teacher from Indian Hills High School, said she's lost track of how many students have come to her with family crises, upset about a fight their parents had or wondering why they feel alone, instead of going to their parents first, which is what she encourages.

"It's a good idea for parents to be explicit about what 'trouble' means," said Gloria Feldt, president of Planned Parenthood Federation of America. Is trouble flunking a test? A speeding ticket? Getting caught with a six-pack of beer? "If you drink, don't be afraid to call us to come pick you up," Feldt said. "The same is true when parents talk to kids about sex. We'd rather you wait for sex until you're older, but know that you can come to us for help."

But simply saying it is not enough anymore.

"It's more than just a line," Resnick said. "Parents need to create an ambiance at home where their children are comfortable coming to them."

**Why, once the baby was born, didn't they leave him on the steps of a church or anywhere so that he might have been found and maybe saved and cared for?**

To ask why Amy and Brian did not leave their baby somewhere to be found assumes that they saw a baby on that bed at all.

"If you deny it and don't want it, it's a thing, you don't form any bond to it," Kaye said. "It's just a foreign object passing through."

There was something there, an object, a "peach pit" that simply emerged from Amy's body one morning, as Resnick said. There was never a baby in their eyes.

"They are so much in denial that a baby will be born,

they don't believe they will produce a full-term live born child," added Ophoven.

Amy's letters to Brian support that. Not once does she mention her "pregnancy" or their "baby." She wrote over and over that "it has made my life miserable" and begged for Brian to "make it go away." The "it" she referred to so many times was not her baby, but her crisis.

The defense experts would say later that Brian did what he did because the baby looked blue, maybe even stillborn, to him. The public would be skeptical. It's the same argument that comes up in virtually every case of mothers charged with killing their babies. The cases boil down to who has the most convincing medical experts. The prosecutors say the baby was alive. The defense says dead. The public gets angry. Alive or dead is for a doctor to determine, not a terrified teenager giving birth in a motel room.

The word "dissociation" is often used to describe how a teenager giving birth goes on automatic pilot throughout the delivery.

"The way you get through such a thing is to bury the emotions, make the body do its job, do the mission, and do not let your emotions impede your actions," Dietz said. "You bury the maternal instinct to solve the dilemma."

Statistics are kept for the cause of almost every child death, from car crashes to gunshots to contagious diseases to collisions with soccer goal posts. But even with the homicide rate of children younger than four years old at a forty-year peak, little is known about the reasons behind the deaths. The most common causes of death in neonaticides, according to Resnick, are suffocation, strangulation, head trauma, drowning in a toilet, and exposure to cold weather. When a mother gives birth to a baby that she has kept secret from everyone close to her, "the need to stifle the baby's first cry makes suffocation the method of choice for mothers attempting to avoid detection," Resnick wrote in his landmark study.

In the study he broke down into two categories the

women who commit neonaticide: those who have strong "instinctual drives and little ethical restraint," who are usually older, more callous, and promiscuous; and "young, immature, passive women who do not initiate sexual relations and frequently deny their pregnancies. Rarely do those women plan the act."

The Greeks, Resnick found, were one of many early civilizations to abandon dying babies in the mountains rather than trying to save them. The Chinese, into the 1800s, sacrificed newborn girls because daughters could not carry on the family name and required the family to pay for a ceremony. Eskimos would kill one of most sets of twins, as well as babies with congenital defects.

Brian and Amy were none of those.

"They believed the baby was dead," Kaye said of Amy and Brian. "They wanted it to be dead, they perceived it to be dead, and then they disposed of it. There's not a whole lot of thought going on. These are panicked kids. Where is the thinking?"

Dietz said teenagers who throw away their babies don't see it as a crime. "Getting rid of it is perceived as a third-trimester abortion. Messy, difficult, but we can get away with it."

**Why didn't her parents ever detect her pregnancy, particularly when they visited her at college just two weeks before she would give birth to a full-term baby?**

Resnick put it simply. "Just as a teenager doesn't want to be pregnant, parents don't want their daughter to be pregnant."

Amy's mother had her best opportunity to confront her daughter in July 1996, when Amy was at least five months pregnant and already starting to panic. Sonye Grossberg stood by and watched as her daughter stepped on a scale in a doctor's office and was found to weigh fifteen pounds more than she had a year earlier. Amy's mother said nothing. She knew Amy had a serious boyfriend of three years, but did she ever accept that it had advanced beyond the "cute" stage? She knew Amy was heading off to college. Did she know Amy had been sexually active for more than a year? No. And she's hardly alone.

Amy's weight gain was hard to notice at first. That's typical of an eighteen-year-old girl with tight stomach muscles. But when her parents saw her in October 1996, she was clearly heavy. They said nothing to her that weekend and even bought her junk food, discussing her weight gain only in private and then brushing it off as the "freshman fifteen."

"Amy did not intend for them to find out," Kaye said. "The intention was to dupe everyone. The current dress code is to look silly and stupid. The inquiry process about how you look and what you're wearing is not politically correct. Parents don't want to see it. To accuse her of putting on even an ounce is a major affront to a teenager."

That approach, said Linda Locke, who sees more than two hundred teen pregnancies a year at St. Joseph's Hospital and Medical Center in Paterson, New Jersey, is what gets parents, and their children, in trouble.

" 'Not my child,' " Locke said of how many parents react. " 'My daughter wouldn't have sex, wouldn't get pregnant, and wouldn't keep it from me.' "

Kaye elaborated.

"Ask these parents if they know what their kids are doing," he said. "They don't want to believe it, and they look for things to support that. Parents have to take the blinders off. The conspiracy of silence has to go away."

In a town like Wyckoff, where the parents desperately want to believe that their children are not sexually active, a majority of the parents are more comfortable with the "less is more" approach. Abstinence is the preferred lesson, and the federal government is now distributing $50 million a year to the states to teach it. But study after study has shown this approach to be hopeless, and students say it's rarely taken seriously in class. In California, Governor Pete Wilson ended funding for abstinence teaching programs that he himself helped launch, after studies showed they had been ineffective.

Many parents fear that teaching their children about sex will make them curious to have sex. Teenagers have said in studies they want more information on birth control, but the simple truth is many of their parents are reluctant to give it to them. The result? A 1995 National Survey of Family Growth by the Alan Guttmacher Institute found that of women eighteen and nineteen years old, not even half, 46 percent, are using some method of birth control.

**Why should two panicked teenagers be punished for an act they committed in a moment of panic?**

Most experts favor leniency over long prison terms in these cases, while the public is generally less sympathetic. It comes down to determining the purpose of prison: to punish or to rehabilitate.

"The right way is to be condemned by the law, sanctioned, held accountable, but dealt with in a manner that is rehabilitative and allows [teenagers] to lead meaningful lives," Dietz said. "A more powerful deterrent than whether it's ten years or two is the shame of being publicly exposed as a baby killer and having everyone who knew you see you as a baby killer."

"Sending a message, that's nonsense," added Kaye. "If you believe a desperate teenage girl who finds herself in this situation will say, 'What happened to Amy might happen to me,' you're out of your mind. We need to teach responsibility, but I don't believe incarceration teaches responsibility."

Prosecutors, on the other hand, are determined to send a message that you cannot throw your baby out as if it were day-old trash and expect nothing more than a scolding, some community service, and a trip home to your parents.

In cases of neonaticide, prosecutors must overcome two challenges. They must prove that the infant breathed on its own, lived a life outside the mother's womb. It cannot be murder if there was no live baby. They must also prove that it was committed by a specific act, such as strangulation or suffocation. If those are not the cause of death, prosecutors must show that the defendant did nothing to save the infant and therefore caused its death.

An act of commission or an act of omission, a lesser crime, but a crime nevertheless. It had to be at least one of those to file charges. But even then, they are not easy cases to make, especially if the defendants are cute, smart, and every parent's perfect child, whose lawyers will argue they were under extreme emotional distress. Rarely do the young defendants, if convicted, serve more than five years; most serve less than three.

In England, even that's too much. In 1922 an infanticide law was passed there. Mothers who kill their infants less than one year old are now charged with manslaughter in England, never murder, and treated with psychiatric care instead of prison time.

In the days and weeks after Amy and Brian hit the news, they would become pawns for both sides in the debate over abortion rights. The pro-choice crowd would argue that Amy and Brian were the best evidence of how more sex education is needed and why more awareness about abortion clinics must be made available to teenagers. The antiabortionists fumed that America's consciousness toward death has been dulled by a million and a half abortions a year and that no one would have cared if Amy had aborted her baby, but the whole world cares when she and her boyfriend discard the baby.

# "WHERE IS YOUR BABY?"

Feeling refreshed from her shower but still wobbly, Amy slipped on one of her baggy winter sweaters and left for class, trudging down the stairs of Thompson Hall into the frigid fall air shortly before noon.

With her long straight brown hair, fair skin, and high cheekbones that made her look more sixteen than eighteen, she blended right in at the University of Delaware. Walking past the tennis and basketball courts along Academy Street and onto the brick path of the mall through the heart of the sprawling campus, she melded into the flow. Students at UD just like her, some still rubbing the sleep from their eyes, made their way to their classes in one of the dozens of red-brick university buildings.

Amy was carrying the cardboard three-dimensional building she had constructed for her design class when Christian Jackson, the single mother who had questioned Amy early in the semester about her due date, stopped her car and offered her a ride. Amy gladly accepted the chance to get off her feet. They were driving toward Recitation Hall when Jackson told Amy she thought she might be pregnant again and she was going to miss class to see her doctor. She asked Amy to tell the teacher.

"So is it hard raising a little boy and going to college and working at the same time?" Amy asked Jackson. Jackson was happy to share her experience.

"Yeah, I'm not going to lie to you or sugarcoat it for you. The absolute truth is that it is really hard raising a child and doing everything else."

Amy turned away and stared out the window as Jackson approached the art hall and eased to a stop. Amy still looked swollen to her, but not pregnant anymore. Amy was pale and her forehead dotted with sweat as she reached for the door latch. Jackson, who would admit later she was feeling spiteful toward Amy, threw a question at her before she got out.

"So how is your baby doing?" She knew it was a nosy question, especially a second time, but she thought Amy might open up to her since she herself was a single mother.

"I'm not pregnant, bitch." Amy jumped from the car, slammed the door, and walked away.

As much as it irked Jackson, she would keep the incident to herself, even as the case in the coming weeks and months attracted nationwide attention. No one, including prosecutors, ever knew about her. But she would find them.

As Amy settled into her seat in Recitation Hall, home of the Department of Art at the north end of the campus, she was hoping desperately for a routine day to let her forget about the Comfort Inn. But the sharp pains in her abdomen, along with her headaches and nausea, made that impossible. She didn't know it, but her toxemia, or preeclampsia, was now full-blown eclampsia, a postpartum illness that if left untreated can be fatal. In 20 percent of eclampsia cases the baby dies, and in 5 percent the mother dies.

Class ended early, and on her way back to her dormitory Amy stopped at CVS on Main Street to buy some pretzels, sanitary napkins, bubble gum, and sparkling water. Back in her room, Amy took a minute for the one comfort in her life she could always count on. She called Brian a few minutes after three P.M. It was a number she knew by heart, a call that she always charged either to his father's calling card or against one of the prepaid calling cards her mother had given her.

"How are you feeling?" Brian asked. He told her he had skipped his only class of the day after getting back on campus around two P.M.

"I'm fine. Just tired and my stomach's sore."

They talked for twenty minutes before she told him she was going to her last class. He said he would call her after dinner, around seven. Their usual time. They were a couple.

They would not talk again for a month. And then it would be in court.

Amy walked across campus to the university library and checked out three art books, all on the French painter Henri Matisse. After a quick stop at the campus bookstore for some art supplies, she went to class and then back to Thompson just as night settled over the campus, dropping the temperature toward twenty degrees. As her roommate lay on her bed in Thompson room 252, Amy returned a message to a friend on campus shortly before five-thirty. She was standing near her bed when Shooman noticed she had stopped talking and her head was swaying from side to side.

"Amy, what's wrong?"

No answer. Shooman went over to her just as Amy slumped to the floor, overcome by the first of several grand mal seizures she would suffer as a result of her eclampsia. Amy had put the Comfort Inn, the delivery, behind her and was trying to resume her life. It wasn't happening.

Everyone in Thompson Hall knew Amy had been pregnant. No one knew she had given birth just twelve hours ago.

"Amy passed out, Amy passed out!" Shooman screamed as she ran down the hallway for help. Others on the floor peered out of their rooms as Shooman ran by, hysterical.

Amy's convulsions were so strong that she bit her tongue, dripping blood onto her shirt collar and the rug.

Shooman returned with Nikki DeSanctis, the resident assistant on the floor, just as some floormates were rushing into the room, some going straight to Amy's side, others standing in the doorway, too shaken to help. After a few seconds the seizure stopped and Amy was awake and alert, but clearly shaken.

"We have to call an ambulance," Shooman insisted.

"No, I'm not going to the hospital."

"Amy, you have to go."

At 5:24 P.M. the dispatcher at the UD Public Safety Office answered the 911 call from DeSanctis at Thompson Hall. A girl had collapsed from what seemed like a seizure, DeSanctis said. The dispatcher told her to ask the patient if she had epilepsy, was pregnant, or had taken any pills. Amy answered no to all three.

Andrew Rubin jumped behind the wheel of the ambulance and Elmer Cherry took the passenger seat, and in six minutes the two ambulance volunteers, who were also students at UD, rushed into room 252 of Thompson, joined by campus police officer David Bartolf.

Cherry, a young black man with a slight frame and a whisper of a voice, walked into the room and went straight to the girl lying on the floor. Other students crowded the hall and the doorway but were cleared away by Bartolf. The first thing Cherry noticed was the blood on the collar of her white shirt. She was conscious but sluggish, her breathing clearly labored. He asked about the blood, and she pointed to her mouth and said she'd cut it when she fell. Before taking her vital signs and checking her reflexes, he asked if she was allergic to anything. Nuts, she told him.

He measured her pulse, which was racing at 136 beats per minute, and her blood pressure, dangerously high at 178/136. He also noticed that her abdomen was swollen. Running through a series of questions to check her response times and see if she was disoriented, he found she obeyed his commands and spoke clearly. But she was obviously in trouble, and her vitals were too high.

"Let's get you to the hospital," Cherry told her.

"No. I'm okay. I feel fine."

Shooman and DeSanctis begged her to go. Watching her crumple to the floor with convulsions had shaken Amy's roommate, and she pleaded with Amy to listen to Cherry.

But Amy was steadfast. For five minutes, then ten, for fifteen minutes she argued with everyone in the room as they reminded her that she had blacked out and suffered what seemed to be a severe seizure. Finally she agreed. She would go. But as she walked out with Cherry and Rubin, her legs weak, she made two final requests, requests that ambulance attendants hear frequently from college students on their way to the hospital.

"I'll go, but you can't call my parents. And I have to come back tonight."

What she forgot was that she was under her parents' health insurance plan.

Together, Rubin, Cherry, and Amy walked down the stairs to the ambulance waiting just outside the dormitory. The wind was picking up as they slowly passed a trash Dumpster and half a dozen bicycles locked up to a stand. Cherry climbed in the back with their patient, and Rubin drove away from the dormitory at 5:47 P.M. Ten minutes later he pulled into the driveway of Christiana Hospital, going straight past the small green "Maternity" sign that pointed to the right. All he knew was they had an eighteen-year-old girl with high blood pressure and a distended abdomen who was allergic to nuts and had suffered a seizure. They took her to the emergency room.

The ER was already a frantic scene as Amy was wheeled in. A junior at UD, a popular art conservation major, member of the Frisbee Club, and a freelance photographer, had been struck by a delivery truck earlier in the day while riding his bicycle on campus. It was a gruesome sight for students, David Toman thrown from his bike and dragged by the truck into a parking lot. He had been pronounced dead in the emergency room hours earlier, but doctors were meeting with his parents, who had just flown in from Illinois, when Amy arrived.

After Amy was asked for her home address and inadvertently gave her old Franklin Lakes house rather than the new town house her parents had bought, the medical questions were fired at her quickly.

"How do you feel?" "What do you remember?" "Do you feel any pain?" "Are you taking any medication?" "When was the last time you ate?"

"Yesterday," Amy said.

She sat up to talk. As soon as the nurses slipped off her clothes, she began to suffer another seizure. Her blood pressure shot up to 211/140. She trembled, her back arched off the table, and it was over in sixty seconds. Her tongue had swelled so much that she could barely talk, and her eyes were almost swollen shut.

Thanksgiving was two weeks away, and Alan and Sonye Grossberg could hardly wait. They hosted it for their relatives every year, a beautiful buffet spread for dinner, followed by watching football. Grandparents came. Aunts and uncles, nieces and nephews.

But like all parents, they most looked forward to the chance to sit with their children with no distractions, to talk to them about school, family, to see how they have matured and grown, to give them a hug. Quality time. It was hard to come by for most families in Wyckoff. Family dinners when everyone is present are special and rare occasions.

"Thanksgiving was their holiday," Amy's aunt, Andrea Grayson, would recall. "It was a time of family closeness, and the entire family shared its intimate issues before a roaring fire. Nothing was too intimate to discuss."

Thanksgiving in 1996 was to be particularly special. Alan and Sonye were alone for the first time in twenty years, and the holiday would reunite their family. Over the past few years their son, Jason, had been away at the University of Massachusetts, leaving only their teenage daughter, their baby, at home with them. But in August Amy, too, had left for college.

Without Amy around, life at home had become strangely quiet. No more girl talk on the phone with her friends, coming in late at night on weekends, studying in her room at all hours. They missed the commotion. But in two weeks Jason would come south from Boston, Amy would travel north from Delaware, and their parents would swell with pride at how they had raised their children.

Eager as they were to see both children, Alan and Sonye were also somewhat concerned about Amy and how she was handling her first taste of freedom. They were still thinking of their Parents Weekend visit in late October, strolling the beautiful campus and taking her food shopping. They never suspected that her suddenly baggy appearance was not a change in attitude or wardrobe taste, but a disguise.

Alan was driving home from work, and Sonye was alone, relaxing in their town house, when the telephone rang at 6:15 P.M. on the Tuesday evening of November 12, 1996.

"Is this Mrs. Grossberg?"

"Yes, it is. Who is this?"

"My name is Cheri Gray. I'm calling from Christiana Hospital in Delaware. Your daughter is very ill. You need to get here as soon as possible."

Sonye's heart raced after hearing every parent's worst nightmare.

"I'd like to speak to her," she said quickly, her body trembling and her eyes welling with tears.

"You can't now," Gray said.

"Why can't she speak?"

"She's having seizures."

"What kind of seizures?"

"Your daughter is very sick. She's having seizures, the doctor is with her, and she can't speak. Please try to get here as soon as you can."

Hysterical, Sonye wrote down the directions to Christiana Hospital and the telephone number and hung up. She wanted to call her husband on his car phone but was afraid to tell him about Amy while he was driving because she was worried he might lose concentration and have an accident. Instead she called her sister, Andrea, who told Sonye to call Alan and tell him to hurry straight home. Alan walked in the door at 6:45 P.M., and fifteen minutes later they rushed out the door together, carrying only the hospital phone number and directions and a small bag of Amy's clothes.

They had no idea how dramatically high Amy's blood pressure had risen or that her eyes were nearly swollen shut. They knew one word: seizures.

The New Jersey Turnpike is a 118-mile stretch that connects the most densely populated part of New Jersey at the north with the farmland of southern Jersey. Driving from the top, in Bergen County just west of New York City, to the Delaware Memorial Bridge takes about two hours. Two monotonous hours of concrete and steel that end with the handing in of a toll ticket and $4.60.

The speed limit on the turnpike was fifty-five mph, but seventy mph has always been the pace more likely to flow with traffic. When a driver's view is not blocked by one of the eighteen-wheel rigs rumbling beside them, he can soak up the sight of marshlands and the New Jersey Sports Complex near Exit 18, the Newark skyline at Exit 15, and the jets at Newark International Airport at Exit 14, followed by the mammoth blue-and-yellow Ikea furniture store in the industrial hub of Elizabeth. In that brief northern stretch, the superhighway cuts through field after field of smokestacks from the sprawling Exxon Bayway Refinery, where gasoline, heating oil, and jet fuel are all manufactured. The rancid smell of chemicals creeps through car windows, inevitably causing drivers to wince and speed up in search of cleaner air.

Farther south, the sights and smells improve, past the high rises of New Brunswick at Exit 8, past the state capital, Trenton, past the farms at Assunpink Creek, past the density of trees at the Pennsylvania Turnpike, past the greenland of the farms at Oldman's Creek in Salem County. Even after the journey ends by passing through the wide toll plaza at Exit 1 and into Delaware, two miles later, crossing the Delaware Memorial Bridge leads to another toll plaza and another anonymous hand stretching out from a cramped booth to demand money. This time, $2.

As they drove south to be with their daughter, the exits along the turnpike passed like a blur. They needed to talk to someone who might know more. First, Sonye called the hospital back on the car phone. Maybe Amy was better.

In the emergency room, doctors had just discovered why Amy had been so swollen and so reluctant to be hospitalized, as the ambulance attendants, Rubin and Cherry, had explained. Amy's seizures had subsided when the staff around her noticed her extremely distended belly.

Kelly Bailey, the resident emergency room nurse, helped start an ultrasound to listen for a fetal heartbeat. Nothing.

"Are you pregnant?" Bailey asked. Others joined in, asking the same question.

"Am I going to be okay?" Amy asked.

"Have you had a period lately? Have you missed a period?"

"No," Amy said.

"Have you been pregnant?"

"No."

"Where is the baby?"

"I don't know."

A doctor from OB/GYN was called in and immediately recognized the signs of eclampsia, the extreme swelling, the high blood pressure, the seizures. The emergency room team looked at her belly and then lower and saw what looked like the stub of an umbilical cord. When they examined closely, they saw a small amount of blood and the placenta at her cervix. And an enlarged uterus.

"Where is your baby?"

Amy said nothing.

"Where was your baby born?"

Nothing.

The doctors treated her with magnesium sulfate, which helps stem convulsions, and Valium to calm her nerves, and they kept questioning her. William Marshall, the emergency room's psychiatric nurse who had been called in to talk to Amy, stormed into her room. His face was red with anger as he leaned in close to Amy.

"Where is the baby? We know you gave birth. Where is your baby?"

Bartolf, the campus police officer who had responded to the 911 call from her dormitory, tried to interview Amy but was held off by Dr. Elisa Benzoni, a third-year OB/GYN resident.

"You're not going to go back to the university unless you tell us where the baby is," Bartolf said to Amy from the doorway.

Silence. And then a third seizure, more convulsions.

Dr. Lisa Phillips, a fourth-year resident in obstetrics and gynecology, gently reached inside Amy at eight P.M. and manually delivered an intact placenta. Tests done later on the placenta would show that it had been stretched and kicked by the fetus, signs that the baby had been alive inside Amy.

As Amy lay sick in the emergency room, her worsening condition had divided the staff. Some of the nurses were focused solely on her health, worried less about why she was there and more about making her well. Marie Essex, a labor and delivery nurse, would say later that Amy exhibited the most edema, or swelling, she had seen in sixteen years of nursing. But others in the emergency room were less sympathetic, angry and suspicious about this young girl's seemingly secretive behavior.

Sallylee Potts, a resident nurse in labor and delivery, saw Amy a few minutes later and noticed her eyes were swollen shut, her tongue so swollen she couldn't close her mouth, and her blood pressure very high. The preeclampsia Amy suffered during her pregnancy would play a critical role in her case. Her attorneys would use it to argue that not only did it keep a steady flow of oxygen from reaching her baby, contributing to the baby's ill health, but it left Amy so sick and weak that she was unaware she ever gave birth.

"What happened?" Potts asked Amy as she lay in her bed.

"I had a miscarriage," Amy answered.

"What time was that?"

"Late Monday or early Tuesday."

A few minutes later Amy's mother got through to the emergency room on her car phone, and Bill Marshall spoke with her.

"Did Amy just have a baby?" Marshall asked Sonye.

"A baby? What are you talking about? Of course not."

"Well, it appears Amy had a baby, and we're trying to locate it," he told her.

Sonye was speechless. She shrieked and cried as her husband continued to drive and asked what was the matter. She told Marshall they would be there by nine-thirty P.M. and hung up.

Amy had been at college for only a little more than two months, and Sonye, desperate to speak with someone else, didn't know her friends there. But she did know her closest friend for the last three years, her boyfriend throughout high school, who had just seen Amy over the weekend. Sonye picked up her cellular telephone to call Brian, but she didn't know his number. She knew only his home number in Wyckoff and dialed it. No answer.

Frantic, she called information and got the home number for Tara Lermond, Amy's best friend, who had also been visiting Amy that previous weekend along with Brian. Tara's sister gave Sonye Tara's number at college, and Tara gave Sonye Brian's number at Gettysburg. Once, twice, three times, Sonye called Brian and kept getting a busy signal. She dialed over and over, and then it rang.

When Brian had called Amy at seven P.M. as he had promised and no one had answered, he had no reason to worry something was wrong. Amy was in the hospital, and Shooman was with her, but he didn't know that. He figured his phone ringing now at seven-thirty was her calling back. Instead he heard another voice, screaming into the phone.

"Brian, this is Mrs. Grossberg. Amy's very sick. She's having seizures. She's in the hospital. They don't know what's wrong with her. We are on our way there now. Do you know anything that could help the doctors? Can you help her?"

There was silence. Brian had come to know Sonye as closely as he knew any adult aside from his parents and coaches. She wasn't a mother to him, but he liked her. She always treated him well. But she was Amy's mother, the one person Amy had been most terrified of telling she was pregnant. Brian had always told Amy he would do what she wanted. If she didn't want to tell, he wouldn't tell.

"Brian, you have to tell us," Sonye pleaded. "Please. Anything. She's so sick. She could die."

"I don't know," Brian shot back. "I don't know."

Loyal to the end. But he wasn't convincing. Sonye didn't believe him.

"Please, Brian, if you know something that would help her, we need to know so we can make her better. Please, tell us."

"I don't know. I don't know what's wrong."

"Brian, is Amy pregnant?"

The question knocked the wind out of him. Barely twelve hours ago Amy had been pregnant, and Brian, at her insistence and without hesitating, had taken their baby and thrown him in the trash. It solved their secret. The baby was gone, out of their lives. No one would find out, and their parents would never know she had been pregnant. But now they were asking. He was sweating and shaking all over again, just as he had in the motel room with Amy.

"Well, she was."

"What do you mean, she was?" Sonye fired back at him.

"She just had the baby today, but I took care of it. I got rid of it."

Before Sonye could respond, her husband shouted for Brian to drive immediately to the hospital and meet them there. But Sonye cut him off.

"No, no. Brian, stay there in your room. Don't leave. We're almost at the hospital. We'll call you from the hospital to let you know how she's doing."

She hung up and called the hospital back.

"Nine-one-one operator. Police, fire, or rescue?"

It was 7:52 P.M., and the hospital staff, frustrated with Amy's unwillingness to talk, had no choice.

"Police," the caller said.

"How can I help you?"

"This is Bill Marshall calling from Christiana Emergency Room. I think the best location is University of Delaware. What I have is a possible missing newborn infant."

"Okay, are they missing from the University of Delaware or are they missing from the hospital and you think they are at the university?"

"Well, essentially we have a woman here who is unable to tell us where the child is that she gave birth to, and the roommate, she is a student at University of Delaware, didn't even know she was pregnant. She has obviously given birth, but she, when she first came in, she denied she was even pregnant. We have already documented or established that she gave birth to some child."

"At somewhere besides the hospital?" the operator asked.

"Somewhere besides the hospital," Marshall answered quickly.

The 911 operator said she would transfer Marshall to

the Newark Police Department, since the university is in Newark. But that only frustrated Marshall. The Newark dispatcher Tacey Burton heard the word "university" and simply followed her protocol. The University of Delaware Police Department—"UDPUD," as it's sarcastically called by outside police agencies—handles campus problems. Newark police must know both the college town and the business district. They blend occasionally, when college students find themselves off campus, maybe drunk or speeding, or when a businessman on campus gets in an accident. But for the most part, the college, and its students, are isolated from town. That's why the school has its own police to handle its own problems.

Burton listened to Marshall's crisis. He repeated the situation about the girl and her missing baby.

"We don't know where the baby is," he said. "And her roommate doesn't know anything about a baby, and she is just pretty much post-seizure right now and can't tell us."

He gave Burton Amy's address at Thompson Hall and spelled out her name for the dispatcher. Burton told Marshall to keep pressing the girl for information and said she would send an officer to the hospital and also call university police.

"Can you express the concern I've been working that there might be a baby in a Dumpster somewhere nearby because there is clearly reason of that?" Marshall asked Burton before hanging up. No one had said anything about a Dumpster, but Marshall had heard the horror stories before of babies being pulled from trash bins, and he suspected this might be another one.

"Okay, so we are talking in the last twenty-four hours?" Burton said.

"That would probably be a fair estimation."

Burton called UDPD and told them of Marshall's plea, but a few minutes later Marshall called back with the same cry for help. This girl had a baby, and the baby was missing. Burton transferred the call to UDPD again. She figured that was the end of it, until a few minutes later the hospital called one more time. Burton was flustered and frustrated, and Detective Steve Fox could see it.

A stocky five feet eight, with a bald head, bushy mustache, and a cop's gleam in his blue eyes, Fox at thirty-five years old was in his tenth year with the Newark police, one of the more respected and outspoken veterans on the fifty-person force. Dressed in a suit, no matter how sharp and tailored, he still looked out of place, uncomfortable, rumpled. In a uniform, or in jeans and a T-shirt, he looked at home, his hairy, muscular forearms and paunch more visible.

He was standing near Burton's desk, just back from municipal court, winding down his two to ten P.M. shift as the on-call detective, when he overheard Burton's third conversation with the hospital.

"What's that all about?" Fox asked her after she had transferred the call.

"The hospital keeps calling. They have a girl from the university who had a baby. She's not saying where the baby is."

"Anything else?" Fox asked.

"I keep transferring them to campus police."

"Okay, I'll go over to UDPUD and see what's up."

This was a routine Fox never really enjoyed. Campus police and Newark police work together all the time, but both departments are sensitive about it. Each wants jurisdiction over investigations. It's a common gripe among law enforcement departments. The smaller forces resent the heavy hitters who swoop in to try to take over their case, and the heavy hitters, from the FBI on down, are invariably shocked when smaller departments don't simply hand over the work they have done and let someone else claim the glory and headlines.

Fox knew the game. He had played it from both sides over his career.

Born and raised in Pennsylvania Dutch country, he spent one year at Penn State University studying electrical engineering before leaving. He married young, at twenty, and moved with his wife, Sherryl, to Newark when she was hired by the Du Pont Chemical Corp. He was working for an electrical contractor when he saw that the university police had an opening. He applied and got it, going through the police training academy and starting work as a campus officer in the summer of 1983. For three years he stayed, before being hired by Newark police as a patrolman in May 1986. With Newark he bounced from the special operations unit investigating gangs and street crime, to being a street cop, to working as a detective in the criminal division. He was gruff and arrogant, too gruff for some. He didn't care.

Fox had just finished up months investigating child crimes, both those committed by children and those committed against children, when he walked into the small office of the college's Department of Public Safety around eight-thirty P.M. The dispatcher there was repeating the story to him that Burton had told when the telephone rang. It was Lieutenant Garrett Moore of the UDPD calling.

When the hospital calls were transferred to campus police, Moore had driven over to the waiting room at Christiana Hospital. He found Holly Shooman there, sitting quietly. Having her roommate collapse in her arms, shaking violently from a seizure, had traumatized her. She had known Amy for barely two months, and although she, like most of her floormates, was confident she was pregnant, they had not discussed it once. When Moore approached Shooman in the waiting room, he asked what she knew about Amy. Shooman told him Amy had left their dormitory room early that morning with her boyfriend, and they had returned a few hours later. She said Amy's boyfriend's name was Brian Peterson, and he was a student at Gettysburg College.

Moore immediately ordered his officers to begin searching trash bins around campus in search of a baby. Then he called his office and spoke with Fox.

"Garrett, whaddya got?" Fox asked.

Moore gave him the same report everyone else had about the girl and her missing baby. He said his officers were searching trash Dumpsters on campus, where students at UD were already reeling from the fatal bicycle crash. And all month they had been following the trial of David Stevenson, a 1993 UD graduate who was facing charges of shooting to death a Macy's security guard.

None of that was on Moore's mind as he talked with Fox. He didn't mention that Amy's roommate had told him Amy and her boyfriend, a student at Gettysburg College, had left the dormitory early that morning and returned a few hours later. But Moore did tell Fox something else about the girl in the hospital.

"She's lawyered up," he said firmly. She was done talking.

Fox offered his department's help.

"People don't lose kids," he told Moore. "I tried losing mine, and they always find their way home."

Moore chuckled but said he had the situation under control. He promised to call if he needed the manpower, and they hung up. Fox was about to leave when Andrew Rubin, one of the ambulance attendants who had driven Amy to the hospital, walked in.

"What happened?" Fox asked him.

"She's on the floor, she had a seizure before we got there," Rubin recalled. "Now they're telling us she had a baby."

Fox asked him if Amy had her pants on when they found her in her dormitory. Rubin said she did. He said there was no blood, no mess. Fox knew right away that if she did have a baby, she didn't have it in her dormitory room. But it wasn't his investigation. Nothing he could do but wait for Moore's call.

He left for his office at nine-thirty P.M., around the same time the Grossbergs pulled into the parking lot at Christiana Hospital. This was no dormitory they were going to now. As they ran inside, there was no loud music playing, no smell of dirty laundry, no parade of giggling teenagers bouncing in the hallways. The hospital was quiet. They were coming to her room when a nurse stopped them and explained that Amy was extremely sick and that the police were involved.

Inside the hospital room, Amy was awake but visibly weak and sick. Sonye rushed to her and hugged and kissed her, sobbing uncontrollably.

"I'm sorry, I'm sorry," Amy said as she cried in her mother's arms.

"It's okay, it's okay. That's what happens when little girls do grown-up things," Sonye said softly as she leaned in to her daughter. Amy was eighteen, a college freshman and talented artist who had dated one boy for three years and been sexually active for two. But in her mother's eyes she was still a "little girl."

Amy was so swollen all over, she looked nothing like the bubbly girl in all those photographs on their shelves back home. Nurses were everywhere. So were university police, standing outside her room.

The next day Amy would gain enough strength to tell her mother what her plan had been: to tell them at Thanksgiving, when everyone would have been home, including Jason. The whole family would have been able to support her, it would have been so much easier. Amy didn't mention that she had told Brian there was no way she could go home for Thanksgiving looking so pregnant.

"When did you know you were pregnant?" Sonye asked her.

"Right before I left for school. I felt different."

That would have been late August. She said nothing about the two abortion appointments, including one in early August, or of the phone call to Brian after the doctor's appointment when she'd told him how relieved she was that the doctor had missed her pregnancy.

Back at the Newark Police Department, Fox's shift was ending. He saw the commander for the four P.M. to two A.M. shift, Sergeant John Deghetto, and filled him in on what little he knew. Anticipating Moore's call during the night, Fox told Deghetto to call him as soon as the campus police called asking for help. A few minutes after ten P.M., Fox left for his home, which was twenty minutes away in Chester County, Pennsylvania. Before he climbed into bed, he pulled a dark gray suit from his closet and hung it on the door. He suspected his night was far from over.

# "I GOT RID OF IT"

Ninety miles farther west into Pennsylvania, Brian was lying in his second-floor room at Hanson Hall. His roommate saw that he seemed down and more distant than usual. He left him alone. But another friend asked Brian what was wrong, and he said his grandmother had emphysema and he had missed his class that day to visit her in the hospital.

Normally on a Tuesday night, he would have been out with friends, or studying, or hanging out on the first floor, where most of his teammates from soccer lived, or talking on the telephone to Amy. Now Amy was in the hospital, her parents knew about the baby, and he was paralyzed.

A knock at his door at nine-thirty P.M. startled him. Scott Simonds, the area coordinator for residence life at Gettysburg College, stood with Sergeant Charles Witt, a college security officer. Brian invited them in and quickly began crying and shaking.

"Brian, the reason we're here is we have a report that your girlfriend gave birth to a baby and the baby is missing. Do you know where the baby is?" Witt asked.

"I'm not sure," Brian said.

They asked him to take a walk with them.

As his dorm mates stared, puzzled to see their clean-cut friend who always said hi to them leave with security, Brian walked slowly, with his head down, out of Hanson onto North Washington Street. His soccer teammates had met Amy twice, and there were rumors that she might be pregnant. But no one knew.

Outside, the red neon sign inside Pizza House was still glowing as the three of them turned left and walked past the chapel to the small white house of the security office. Brian sat across from Simonds and began talking.

"Things didn't go as we had planned," Brian said.

He took Simonds through the pregnancy, their decision to keep it a secret, their failed attempts at having an abortion, and his visits to her in Delaware. He recounted the midnight phone call from Amy and the delivery in the motel room.

"We took the baby and wrapped it in something and got rid of it," he said.

"Do you remember where?" Simonds asked.

"No."

Simonds stood up and left the room to call Dennis Murphy, the dean on call for the College Life Division. Murphy immediately called the college counselor on duty that night.

Frances Parker, a slight woman with short brown hair, a soft voice, and a motherly look to her, was at home when the call came a few minutes after ten P.M. A psychologist and the associate coordinator for the college's Office of Counseling Services, she specialized in building students' self-esteem, helping victims of sexual assaults, working with students who were learning disabled, and helping those fighting eating disorders. She was available at all hours for emergencies and was the counselor on call when Simonds needed someone to talk to Brian.

Parker would say later it was "just pot luck" that she got the call that night instead of one of the other counselors. She walked the two blocks from her home to the college security office. When she got there just after ten-thirty P.M., she was escorted back to a small room, where she found Simonds sitting with Brian, who was wearing jeans and a sweater over a white T-shirt.

"Thanks for coming," Simonds said to Parker.

For any counselor, walking into a first meeting with a student requires a delicate touch, particularly when the student is a freshman. The students are away from their homes, their friends, their parents, their security blankets, and even though they want to act and feel like adults, and be treated like adults, they are really just big kids. Parker was experienced, but even for her, every student, every session, brought new challenges.

In a few sentences Simonds summarized for Parker what police in Delaware had told him. He also told Parker that Brian was worried about his girlfriend and seemed distressed to the point of panic. After a few seconds of introductions, Brian began talking, taking his audience of two back a few hours in time, back to Delaware, back to his pregnant girlfriend, back to a call she'd made to him almost twenty-four hours ago. He had just started sharing when Parker stopped him.

In the pamphlet Gettysburg students receive outlining the role of the counseling center, the word "confidentiality" is typed in boldface. "Information about those sessions or their content will be released only upon the student's written request, in circumstances which would result in clear danger to the individual or others, or as may be required by law," the pamphlet reads.

Parker recognized that her role as Brian's crisis counselor would be compromised if he talked to her while Simonds was in the room with them.

"Scott, you should leave," Parker said. "I don't think if you stay that it would be confidential."

Parker had no idea what Brian was about to tell her, if it would take five minutes or five hours. She sensed he was in trouble and wanted to be sure to protect his right to privacy. Simonds left reluctantly and agreed to go find the phone number for Brian's mother or father. With Simonds gone, Brian asked Parker a few questions before continuing with his story.

"Is whatever I tell you confidential?"

"Yes."

"I don't want my parents to know what happened," he said. He was oblivious of the trouble he was facing.

"You have to tell me what you want me to share with people and what you don't," Parker assured him. "That's your right. I can't divulge any information without your permission."

For almost an hour they talked. It would become one of the critical missions for police investigators to find out what Brian told Parker. It was before the police reached him, before he had an attorney, before he had a chance to rehearse his lines or collect his thoughts. He spoke from his heart and let everything out. To Parker, Brian seemed depressed, despondent, isolated. He had been awake for thirty-six straight hours. Brian cried as he recalled what he had just been through.

"I tried to take care of things as best I could," he told Parker.

"Brian, is there a chance that the fetus is viable, and that we should have authorities look for it?" Parker asked him.

Brian looked at her, puzzled. *Viable?*

"Is there a chance the fetus is viable?" she repeated.

"You mean, is the baby alive?" he said.

"Yes. That's what I mean."

"No."

Throughout their conversation his thoughts were on Amy, how she had mentioned suicide to him and how he'd taken her threats seriously.

"What could I have done? I felt so bad for her," he said.

He said he wished he could have done more for her, but that it was her body, she was the woman, and he could only stand by her decisions. He talked without being prompted. He said Amy was worried about her mother finding out and that he thought Amy's mother was never very fond of him.

He seemed almost numb to Parker, worried only about disappointing his own parents and, especially, his grandmother. When Parker warned Brian that he might be facing arrest, he looked at her, startled.

"He shook his head from side to side at this information," Parker would say later. He was crying as he said he was afraid he might have hurt Amy during the delivery and that maybe she had died in the hospital and that she wasn't okay as Simonds had told him. Parker assured him Amy was alive.

"Nothing will ever be the same," Brian said.

When they were done, Gettysburg police detective Kevin Wilson walked in and asked Parker to leave. Parker called Brian's father in Long Island and told him what was happening. His father told her he knew Amy but had no idea she had been pregnant. He said he would be in Gettysburg by the morning.

Wilson's investigation had begun the way most of them did: with a phone call to his department. Shortly before midnight on November 12, he was dispatched to the college. Timon Linn, the chief of security at Gettysburg, told Wilson that a lieutenant with the campus police at the University of Delaware had called him. All that was known was that a girl at the Delaware school was in the hospital, that she had given birth, that her baby was missing, and that her boyfriend was a student at Gettysburg. Linn told Wilson that the student, Brian Peterson, was with a counselor, and Wilson drove quickly over to the campus security office.

Sitting down with Brian, Wilson saw a handsome, clean-cut teenager with bloodshot eyes. Brian was slight, five feet six, barely 160 pounds, and he was shaking as Wilson, a stocky thirteen-year veteran, sat down and pulled out his small pad with pages that flipped over from bottom to top. Brian was not in custody, but he was a suspect in an apparent crime, and if he was willing to talk, Wilson was more than happy to listen.

His interview was just getting started when police officers in Delaware rummaging through the Dumpster outside Thompson Hall on the UD campus discovered a brown paper bag. Inside was a pair of gray ladies' underwear and a white washcloth.

Wilson started writing in clear, printed words, first the time, 23:59, and then the date, 11-12-96. He wrote, "Brian Carl Peterson, w/m 18 6-10-78," followed by Brian's home address and telephone number, as well as his Social Security number.

As Brian started talking, Wilson stopped printing and started scribbling to keep up with him, flipping to a new page every thirty seconds. He advised Brian of his rights at 12:02 A.M. on November 13. To make sure he understood his rights and was aware of his surroundings, Wilson asked him to define the word "attorney." His experience had taught him that an interview with a suspect is no good if it can't be used in court. Brian said an attorney was a person who represented people in a court of law.

Satisfied that Brian knew what was happening and was willing to speak without a lawyer, Wilson first told him what he had learned in the last hour. He told him his girlfriend was being treated at a hospital and appeared to be out of danger. Wilson asked if the baby was okay.

"No," Brian said.

"How do you know the baby is not okay? Is he dead? And if so, how do you know?"

"I did it," Brian said.

"You did what?"

"Got rid of it."

"How did you get rid of it?"

"Just threw it out."

"Where at?" Wilson asked. He was looking for as many specifics as he could get with each question, but he got little help. Brian said he did not remember where. Then he said he threw it in a Dumpster. Hopeful, Wilson persisted, trying to pin down where the Dumpster was.

"I have no clue," Brian said.

He knew exactly where the baby was, but he didn't

want them to find it. He would admit later that he lied because the baby had caused so much stress and tension on everyone that he just did not want it to come back into his life or Amy's. He told Wilson the baby was in Delaware, but that he couldn't remember the town.

"When was the baby born?" Wilson asked.

"About four-thirty A.M."

Again, Wilson probed for details and got nothing. Brian said the baby was born at a hotel, but he didn't know what hotel or where it was or the room number. He did remember paying cash and that it wasn't expensive.

"Was it near the college?" Wilson said, referring to Grossberg's Delaware campus.

"I don't remember how long we were driving for," Brian said.

Wilson turned his attention to what Brian knew about the infant.

"Was the baby born alive?"

"I'm not sure."

Wilson kept hoping Brian would just start talking, telling him everything, instead of one-, two-, and three-word answers.

"What happened when the baby was born?"

"It was lying there. I put it in a bag of some sort."

Brian said it was a plastic bag, but he couldn't remember what color. He said he didn't know how long his girlfriend had been pregnant. He said she had called him at about 12:45 A.M. on Tuesday and that he had picked her up at the University of Delaware about two hours later. All Wilson knew was there was an abandoned baby somewhere in Delaware. That was it. Maybe it was freezing and crying, maybe it was dead. Maybe it never took a breath. He had no idea.

"Brian, babies have lived in Dumpsters for days and lived," Wilson said. "Can you tell me where the Dumpster is just in case the baby is alive?"

"I don't know where it is," Brian said.

"Any idea?"

"No."

Barely thirty minutes after he began, Wilson decided to take a rest. Just to make sure the baby was not in Brian's car, Wilson asked Brian to take him to his Celica. They drove Brian to his car and, after a quick search, arranged to have it towed to the police department, a block off the main square in the center of town inside the cream-colored, cinder-block Gettysburg Municipal Building. Back at the police department, Wilson walked Brian to his office. A tiny and cramped room with a cluttered desk, a rolling chair, a folding metal chair, and a bulletproof vest on the floor, this was where Wilson felt most comfortable talking.

Wilson obtained a warrant for Brian's arrest shortly after two A.M. and then returned to his office to continue his interview. He asked Brian the route he drove from Delaware back to Gettysburg, then asked if he had washed his Celica. Brian said he had not and agreed to let police search the car.

Holding on to a flicker of hope, Wilson asked one last time if Brian knew where the baby was.

"No."

"Do you know if the baby was a boy or girl?"

"No."

Wilson could see Brian was tired and went to make some calls. He put Brian in the holding room, a small square room of cinder-block walls with nothing but a brown folding chair, a metal bar on the wall for suspects to be handcuffed to, and a one-way mirror.

After all the questions and all the answers, Wilson still was a long way from the most important answer. He called the Delaware campus police shortly after one A.M. to see if they had learned more and to check on the condition of the girl. Lieutenant Moore in Delaware felt as helpless as Wilson did. Moore had a mother, Wilson had a father, and no one had their baby.

Knowing only what Wilson had told him, that Brian

admitted to throwing the baby in a Dumpster near a motel, Moore called the Newark police, who launched a search to cover a ten-to-twelve-block radius in town. They knew that if the teenagers had left campus, and had probably not gone far, the selection of motels on South College Avenue would have been too convenient to pass by.

Wilson, meanwhile, was growing desperate. He was ready to charge Brian, at least with child endangerment, but that seemed almost senseless as long as the baby was missing. Along with Corporal Thomas Grissman, Wilson sat back down across from Brian and had him sign a waiver showing he had been read his rights. Wilson knew Brian was exhausted, but he also knew that with the temperature outside in the twenties, every minute was critical if police were going to find the baby. Wilson started from the beginning, with the phone call Brian received from his girlfriend, which Brian said was around 12:45 A.M. on Tuesday.

"What did she tell you?"

"Um . . . that her stomach was bothering her and that she might be going into labor."

He said he did not know how long she had been pregnant and that he had driven to her college dormitory, picked her up, and driven with her to a hotel.

"Then what happened?" Wilson asked.

"She gave birth to the baby."

"What happened at the birth?"

"Um, I don't know. The head of the baby came out . . . I don't know."

Brian was speaking so softly, he was difficult to understand.

"Do you remember the baby crying?"

"No."

"Was the baby breathing?"

"I don't know."

Wilson knew this was crucial. A breathing, crying baby thrown in a Dumpster was an obvious crime, and if it died, it was probably murder. But if the baby was stillborn, or if there was no full-term baby and it was a miscarriage, charging Brian would be difficult.

"Okay, who cut the umbilical cord?"

"Um, I did."

"How did you do that?"

"Well, when I picked the baby up it tore."

"It tore and ripped. Did you ever tie it off?" It was a medical term, but Wilson presumed a college student would understand what he meant.

"No," Brian said.

Brian said he'd put the baby in a plastic bag and left his girlfriend in the room to put the bag in the Dumpster.

"Do you know where the Dumpster is?" Wilson asked, knowing he had already asked twice before.

"No."

"Do you know if the baby was alive when you put it in the Dumpster?"

"I don't know."

Wilson reminded Brian of the earlier interview, when he had given police permission to search his car. Brian had denied that he had taken his car to be washed, but the search had turned up a receipt from the White Glove Car Wash in Delaware stamped 11:28 Tuesday morning.

"Why did you wash the car for?" Wilson asked.

Brian stammered.

"Just . . . I . . . just killing time on my way home. I just had the car washed. It needed to be washed anyway."

Wilson had assumed that when Brian had left the baby in the Dumpster, he had simply walked outside through the parking lot and put the bag with the body in the trash. But the car wash receipt gave him a new theory.

"When you had the baby, did you take the car to get rid of it, just drop the baby off in the Dumpster?"

"Yes." Brian was flustered and beat. The baby had never been in the car with him, but his mind was wandering.

There comes a turning point in almost every interview police do with suspects, and Wilson thought this might be it. Brian had lied about having the car washed, and now Wilson believed he had the explanation. The baby must have been in the car with him at some point, even if just for a few seconds.

"Where did you have the baby at?"

"Um, it was either like in front of me or—"

Wilson cut him off. "In front of you like on the floorboard or on your lap?"

"Yeah, on my lap or on the floor and then, ah, or on the passenger side."

Brian said he got out to put the bag in the Dumpster, went back to pick up his girlfriend, and drove to her dormitory room. They slept for a few hours, and he said he left for his college that morning, stopping at the car wash before getting onto Route 95. Again, he said he did not know where the Dumpster was, even when Wilson almost pleaded with him, telling him the baby deserved a proper burial.

The interview had given Wilson conflicting pictures of Brian. One was of a scared kid, a confused freshman who seemed to recognize he had done something wrong but, for whatever reason, could not bring himself to admit it. Then there was the second image. Brian had lied in the interview and had apparently had his car washed for a reason. Did he really not remember the name of the hotel? Or the location of the Dumpster? Or did he just not want police to find the baby?

Those questions still unanswered, Wilson felt he had enough to hold Brian, at least to allow time for police in Delaware to search for the baby. Brian was charged with concealing the death of a child and endangering the welfare of a child. His bail was set at $20,000, and Wilson drove him three miles north of town to the Adams County Prison, the home for some 150 pretrial prisoners and those convicted and awaiting sentencing.

Then Wilson joined other officers searching Dumpsters around his town. Just in case. By that time, University of Delaware police had scoured their campus and come up empty. Lieutenant Moore finally dialed the number of the homicide pager for the Delaware Attorney General's Office in Wilmington, the number police departments know to use for late night emergencies.

The homes in Wyckoff, New Jersey, vary from million-dollar mansions to quaint contemporaries; but every neighborhood is tree-lined and beautiful.

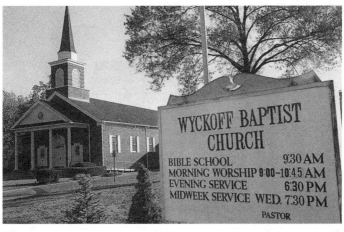

WYCKOFF BAPTIST
CHURCH

| | |
|---|---|
| BIBLE SCHOOL | 9:30 AM |
| MORNING WORSHIP 9:00–10:45 AM | |
| EVENING SERVICE | 6:30 PM |
| MIDWEEK SERVICE WED. 7:30 PM | |

PASTOR

At the Wyckoff Baptist Church, a landmark in town, Reverend Jeff Boucher asked members of his youth group to write letters about their problems and concerns. One teenage girl wrote that she "want[s] to go to heaven because I'm going crazy with this pressure."

ALL PHOTOGRAPHS BY MEL EVANS FROM *THE RECORD* ARCHIVES.

Amy Grossberg exited the courthouse in Wilmington, Delaware, July 1997, surrounded by reporters and photographers moments after her lawyer Robert Gottlieb (in glasses) was thrown off the case for violating the gag order.

After pleading guilty to manslaughter on March 9, 1998, Brian Peterson left the courthouse sandwiched between two of his lawyers, Joseph Hurley (right) and Russell Gioiella.

Amy Grossberg spent her high school years in this elegant home in Franklin Lakes, New Jersey, one of the country's most exclusive suburbs.

After growing up in a modest Long Island suburb, Brian Peterson moved into this spectacular house in Wyckoff with his mother and stepfather.

Teachers at Ramapo High School joke about how to tell the student parking lot, shown here, from the teachers' lot. The students' cars are nicer.

Ramapo High School in Franklin Lakes is one of the state's top high schools.

Behind the Comfort Inn in Newark, Delaware, on a freezing night in November 1996, Brian Peterson ran to this corner in the rear parking lot and threw his newborn son into a Dumpster.

Newark police detective Steve Fox (center) investigated the baby's death for twenty months, during which time his marriage and health deteriorated. Here he stands behind Brian Peterson's lawyers, Jack T. Litman (left) and Russell Gioiella, after the July 9, 1998, sentencing.

After Amy Grossberg pleaded guilty on April 22, 1998, her parents left the Wilmington courthouse hand-in-hand with their son, Jason.

After Gettysburg College officials and local police questioned Brian Peterson about the whereabouts of his baby and then released him, Brian's father, Brian Peterson Sr., drove him back to his childhood house on Long Island. His second wife, Ann Marie, frequently attended court with him.

Days before Brian's arrest, Barbara Zuchowski, his mother, briefly considered sending her son out of the country to avoid prosecution in what was then a death penalty case. Brian was rarely seen without her by his side.

Never without one of his polka dot ties, Joseph Hurley, Brian's Delaware lawyer, is regarded as one of the finest and most flamboyant criminal attorneys in the state. He orchestrated Brian's very public surrender a day after the FBI labeled Brian a federal fugitive.

After the gag order was lifted, Delaware Deputy Attorney General Peter Letang, the lead prosecutor and the father of two young children, told reporters what he thought of what happened to Amy and Brian's baby: "Horrible. Horrible."

Minutes before the sentencing, Amy Grossberg's third defense team gathered outside the courthouse. Robert Tanenbaum (left), Jack Gruenstein (center), and John Malik (right) were hired after Amy's first lawyers quit and her second lawyer was thrown off the case.

The sidewalk in front of the Wilmington courthouse was frequently a mob scene and became a second home for reporters covering the case.

Prosecutor Peter Letang answered a critic who thought the sentences were too light: He said that proving murder was difficult and he was satisfied with the guilty pleas to manslaughter, but would have liked more jail time for Amy and Brian.

# "WE GOT THE VICTIM HERE"

It was two A.M. and forty-eight-year-old Pete Letang, wearing only his boxer shorts, was sound asleep, sandwiched between his two favorite ladies. And loving it.

On his left lay his wife, Debbie, a woman almost twenty years younger who had enough energy to light up their house all by herself, attractive and petite with short black hair, an irresistible smile, and an infectious laugh. They had met on Valentine's Day in 1990 when she was a recent graduate from University of Delaware who started interning with him at the Delaware Attorney General's Office in Wilmington. They were introduced by the attorney general, Charlie Oberly, one of Letang's closest friends, and three years later they took their vows on the shore of the Sassafras River at the northern tip of Maryland's Chesapeake Bay, before sailing off on their honeymoon.

On his right, in a bassinet, lay Samantha—"Manth," as he called her—all of nine days old and nine pounds and a miserable sleeper. Debbie had given birth on November 3, and Letang had taken the previous week off to be with his wife, his newborn daughter, and his two-year-old son, Nicholas. Monday had been Veteran's Day, and Tuesday, his first day back at work, had been routine. In by eight-thirty A.M., out by six P.M. He had taken home a briefcase full of work to catch up on and never even opened it.

His first two marriages had ended without children, and now with two of them at home, he was suddenly finding himself wanting to do nothing but play dad all night. Before he put his head down at eleven-thirty P.M., he made sure that the homicide pager, which was rotated among the prosecutors every week, was on his bedside table.

"When you have it, you fully expect it to go off," he would say later. "Sometimes it's just a question about a search warrant. Sometimes it's a homicide."

Sure enough, the piercing beeps jolted him awake a few minutes after two A.M. Beeper in hand, he crept downstairs in his boxers, careful not to wake Debbie or Samantha. As he glanced at the beeper and dialed back the unfamiliar number, he noticed that, outside, a winter freeze had settled on the impressive wooden swing set and slide behind his house and even on the tiny birdhouse hanging off his front porch.

"This is Pete Letang, I was paged."

Garrett Moore explained to him about the girl they had in the hospital, her boyfriend in Pennsylvania, and something about their missing baby. Letang instructed Moore to immediately call a police agency, either Newark police or the Delaware state police, and to keep him posted throughout the night.

Hanging up, Letang thought briefly about going back upstairs to sleep, to be with his wife and baby, whose umbilical cord he had cut a little more than a week ago. Then he looked at the beeper. It was quiet for the moment, but he knew that wouldn't last. He grabbed a comforter from the closet, walked into his living room, and lay down on his couch, the beeper resting on his chest.

As if one baby weren't enough to worry about, now he had two.

As he lay there, Letang had no way of knowing that these two teenagers from well-off families in northern New Jersey, who had graduated high school just five months earlier, were about to become his most famous defendants, replacing a mammoth 350-pound serial killer whose execution he had watched.

Boyishly handsome and built like a six-foot-tall bear with graying sandy brown hair and blue eyes, Letang was imposing. His voice boomed. He spoke the way he walked, with a purpose. He had broad shoulders and a slight paunch, but in a suit he looked more athletic than heavy. And he was. Sailing, skiing, even scuba diving, were all passions. He looked like someone who was in his element telling stories and jokes on a sailboat in the middle of the ocean, with a beer in his left hand, a fishing rod in his right. He was hard to dislike.

"What you expect from him is charm and wit," one attorney and friend of Letang's once said. "He does it naturally. You can try to out-nice him. But it's impossible."

Letang was born and raised in Wilmington. His father worked his way up from being a chemist to a vice president with the Du Pont Chemical Corp. Letang attended public schools and then the prep school Wilmington Friends, where he played linebacker on the football team. He enrolled at Bucknell University in Pennsylvania, and after graduating in 1970, he joined the campaign of Pierre S. "Pete" du Pont III, a Republican state representative running for Congress.

The du Pont family is to Delaware what the Kennedys are to Massachusetts, and Letang recognized that any contact with the du Ponts could only help him down the road. He did what he had to, fetching coffee, playing chauffeur, copying. When du Pont was easily elected in 1971, Letang took a job with him in Washington for a year.

"He was a very optimistic, very positive person," du Pont, now a Delaware lawyer and the editor of an on-line magazine, recalled of the young Letang. "He was a good companion on the trail."

Eager to go to law school and get it over with as quickly as possible, Letang left Delaware for Texas and Baylor University. Two and a half years later he had his degree, finishing in the top third of his class. He passed the bar exams in Texas and Washington but failed Delaware's. Nevertheless, he landed a job with the Delaware Attorney General's Office in 1975, low man on the team, prosecuting drunken drivers. He passed the state bar on his second try.

As most prosecutors do, he started slowly, working long hours, handling small cases. But he developed his own style that would lead to later successes. No wild hand gestures when he talked in court, no shouting or flamboyance, just a confidence, an air about him. Judges liked him. Jurors liked him. With his slightly tousled hair yet professional look, he managed to come across as friendly and unpretentious yet tough and sincere. A combination every lawyer strives for but few achieve.

"He's very laid-back, he's not at all self-conscious, and he's disarming to people who don't know him with his friendliness," said Joseph Gabay, a criminal defense attorney in Wilmington who has known Letang for almost twenty years. "He talks to a jury as if they're sitting in the backyard talking about how many hamburgers to put on the grill. Juries like that."

By 1980 Letang was handling murder cases and establishing a solid reputation when du Pont called again. He wanted Letang to help lead his campaign for governor.

"By then he knew the state so well, he knew the people," du Pont said. "He had good insight into people, and that was what I needed from him."

The partnership worked, and du Pont won easily. But Letang missed lawyering. In 1982 he opened a practice in Wilmington, handling mostly wills, property transfers, divorces, and some criminal work for the public defender's office. It was hardly thrilling work or lucrative. He earned maybe $45,000 a year, and it had just about worn him out when another old friend came calling.

Letang had known Charlie Oberly for years, and during the late 1970s they had worked together in the Delaware Attorney General's Office. When Oberly was elected to lead the office as attorney general in 1986, he asked Letang to come back. On one brutally hot August afternoon Letang walked out of Gander Hill Prison in Wilmington after suffering through inmates fighting over a fan and decided he needed a change. He accepted Oberly's offer for a senior prosecuting position.

Less than a year later, in 1987, Steven Brian Pennell became Letang's first big catch, a repeat killer of young women. Letang and fellow deputy attorney general Kathleen Jennings convicted Pennell of killing two women. The murderer was sentenced to death. Letang was just back from a skiing vacation in Europe with Debbie in 1992 when he watched Pennell, a mountain of a man wearing size fourteen orange sneakers, get strapped in for a lethal injection.

"It's macabre," he would say years later. It was not a solution he enjoyed seeking as a prosecutor, but he conceded reluctantly that in some cases death is the only answer for a crime. "I'm in favor of the death penalty, but don't think it should be universally applied," he said. Pennell, both Letang and Oberly were sure, deserved death. He was Delaware's first serial killer, first execution in forty-six years, and first case in which state prosecutors relied heavily on DNA evidence to get their conviction.

But as Letang and Oberly would learn later, seeking the death penalty can bring either the public's support to a prosecutor or the public's wrath. Seek it for a Pennell, and no one argues. Good riddance. Seek it for a wealthy and white teenager, and be prepared for scorn and scathing attacks.

Pennell's trial and execution attracted national media coverage. For prosecutors, the result was nothing short of a home run. Prosecutors are driven by such cases. They are statement cases, the ones that allow prosecutors with limited state budgets to show they can stack up against any high-powered law firm, no matter how much the defense spends, and prove that money doesn't always buy freedom.

With Pennell as his launching pad, Letang continued to climb, and no one was prouder than his former boss.

"When you hire a kid as your gofer, to drive you to barbecues, and he ends up as a chief prosecutor in the state, you have to feel good about that," du Pont said.

After running the rape unit for five years, Letang took over the drug unit, consistently being assigned some of the office's biggest cases. He prosecuted David Dutton, getting him a life sentence for the murder of a college coed whose body was found on a golf course fourteen months after she vanished. He won the conviction and execution of James Clark, who murdered his parents just months after he had finished serving twenty years in prison for another killing.

Until Pennell, Letang had been viewed as an ordinary, maybe above average, prosecutor, but hardly a leader in his office. He was always laid-back, sometimes too laid-back for certain attorneys who wondered if he was simply going through the motions on their cases. But by the time Oberly left the office for private practice following a failed run for the United States Senate in 1994, Letang had risen about as high in the office as he could. In the office he was always ready with a story or a nibble of gossip. A running joke became that they have the telephone, the telefax, and the tele-Peter. With his popularity and seniority came more responsibility, and that meant more time tied to the office homicide beeper.

The Grim Reaper. That became his nickname among the senior prosecutors, because whenever he was the prosecutor on call for their office, trouble seemed to find him. The homicide pager system was started after some Delaware prosecutors had started to complain that the biggest and best cases, the high-profile murders, kept being assigned to the same people. The pager, rotated among prosecutors every week, was supposed to give each of them a fair shake at the big trouble.

Just minutes after Letang hung up with Moore, the officers who had fanned out across Newark to search Dumpsters got their first break. At 2:14 A.M. Sergeant John Potts and Patrolman Frank Gillespie found a plastic bag filled with bloody sheets in a Dumpster in the left rear corner behind the Comfort Inn. Potts immediately called Steve Fox at home, waking his wife and, briefly, their children, Kyle, ten, and Kaitlin, six.

"Don't touch a thing, I'm on my way," Fox told him. He grabbed his suit from the closet door.

The back roads of Pennsylvania were as quiet for Fox at two-thirty A.M. as they had been for Brian twenty-four hours earlier. Fox raced to his office and dialed the homicide pager number of the Delaware Attorney General's Office. He assumed that the prosecutor tied to the pager had already been briefed, and he was right. Letang was still awake when his beeper went off again at two-fifty A.M. This time, he recognized the number. Newark police.

"This is Pete Letang, I was paged."

"Hey, it's Steve Fox over in Newark."

Fox and Letang would form a friendship and a mutual respect for each other over the next eighteen months that neither could have anticipated as they talked on this morning.

"I wanted to let you know what's going on," Fox said. "We got some bloody sheets we found in a Dumpster at the Comfort Inn. But we don't have a victim yet."

"Keep me informed," Letang said. "If I don't talk to you soon, we'll talk first thing in the morning."

Fox went to work. It was almost four A.M. when Newark detectives began piecing together where Brian and Amy had been the previous morning. Potts had checked the guest records at the Comfort Inn and asked where the bloody sheets had come from that were found in the Dumpster. He was handed the guest slip to room 220 with Brian Peterson's signature.

In the two hours since university police had called Newark police, Newark officers had found bloody sheets thrown out from a motel room paid for by Amy Grossberg's boyfriend. Fox was excited about the detective work they had done, but he knew the search would not be a success until the baby had been found. Searching Amy's room was critical. For that, Fox needed help.

Bob Agnor was asleep when Fox called him at four-thirty A.M. He told him only that they were looking for a baby.

"Meet me at the HoJo's," Fox said. "I need a ticket, Bobby."

Agnor knew a ticket meant a search warrant. And he knew HoJo's was the Howard Johnson on South College Avenue across from the Comfort Inn. He was scheduled to work the eight A.M. to four P.M. shift, but Fox didn't care. A huge man, six feet one, portly, with dark brown hair and a bushy mustache, Agnor was out the door in five minutes, with Fox in ten, underneath the unmistakable blue-and-orange sign of the Howard Johnson. Fox walked straight to the trunk of his car and pulled out the bag of bloody sheets Potts and Gillespie had recovered.

"This was found in one of the Dumpsters near here," Fox said to Agnor.

Fox started to explain why they were there. He told Agnor that university police were investigating a girl at Christiana Hospital who doctors said had recently given birth. Her boyfriend had told police in Pennsylvania that he had helped her deliver their baby in a motel and then got rid of it in a Dumpster. What Dumpster, or what motel, the boyfriend had not said.

Police had been drawn to South College Avenue by simple reasoning. They knew the girl was a UD student and that if she and her boyfriend had gone looking for a motel to deliver their baby, they would have had to pass the three along the strip before reaching Route 95: the Sleep Inn, Howard Johnson, and Comfort Inn.

Sunlight was two hours away, and the freezing wind had dipped the temperature toward twenty degrees. All the officers were wearing their long winter coats. Fox knew if there was a baby out there, and it had been lying in a trash bin for a full day, there was little chance it was still alive. He was talking with Agnor and Gillespie a few minutes before five A.M. when he spotted trouble.

"Son of a bitch!" he yelled as he ran toward his unmarked white Ford LTD.

The sight of a garbage truck rumbling along the strip in the early hours of a weekday morning, from one building to the next, emptying Dumpsters along the way, would normally not alarm a Newark officer. But when Fox saw a brown Harvey & Harvey Waste Handlers truck backing up to a Dumpster behind the Mobil station, he knew he had to stop it. Its next Dumpster would have been behind the Comfort Inn and the adjacent Mother's Kitchen. The diner, open round the clock, was marked by a bright pink neon triangle sign. Its late night customers were mostly the truckers and the occasional pack of UD students with a sudden craving for a stack of blueberry pancakes.

Fox and Agnor ignored the traffic light, and the foot-high concrete median on South College Avenue, and raced in their cars across the street, screeching to a halt next to the trash truck. Fox jumped out of his car.

"You're done!" he shouted at the driver, Steve Garabaldi. "Stop what you're doing."

He told Garabaldi they were looking for a child and he would not be allowed to empty any more trash bins until police had searched them first. They prayed that he hadn't already dumped a baby into his truck without even knowing it. Garabaldi, panicked that he had, climbed into the back of his truck and began throwing aside everything in sight.

As he was checking his truck, Lisa Nyland, out of sight a few hundred feet away, walked her two-and-a-half-year-old yellow Labrador, Jesse, toward the Dumpster along the side of the Comfort Inn, behind the diner. A handler with Maryland Natural Resources Police, Nyland had been called that morning to bring in her dogs to help with the search for the baby.

Together, Nyland and Jesse had recently taken a basic

cadaver search class in Quantico, Virginia, and they had
been on eight searches. None had turned up bodies. The
dogs she worked with, Labradors and German shepherds,
were known for their strong retrieving instincts and
trained to track any human scents, from bones and hair to
clothing, blood, and sweat.

As soon as Jesse neared the Dumpster at 5:10 A.M., he
started barking, jumping toward it with his paws, and tug-
ging Nyland to go behind it. Jesse smelled something
other than trash. Nyland climbed into the Dumpster, rak-
ing through cardboard boxes, empty cans of corn and
peas, and several trash bags weighing more than twenty
pounds but filled with more food and empty cans. She
reached into the right rear corner and pulled out a shiny
gray plastic trash bag, its yellow drawstring handles tied
tightly.

Back on the ground, not wanting to disturb the handles,
she tore a hole in the top of the bag and peered inside. She
immediately called to the officers, including Corporal
Brad Geesman, who were with her. Fox and Agnor were
just around the corner when they heard their radios
crackle.

"C-fifty to forty-three," Fox heard. He grabbed his
radio.

"Fifty, go."

"We got the victim here behind the Comfort Inn."

Fox and Agnor sped around a fence into the motel
parking lot, shining their car lights on the Dumpster. They
saw Geesman and other Newark officers along with
Nyland and Jesse, sitting calmly. Walking toward the
group, they saw the plastic bag on the ground. Fox was
steamed. The bag should have been left where it was
found, in the Dumpster.

He gently opened the hole that had been ripped there
and saw a clump of white towels stained with blood—and
an obviously dead baby with a full head of dark, matted
hair. The body was lying with its right side down, its right
hand up by its mouth, almost in a thumb-sucking position.

He was surprised to see how clean the body was, almost no blood. He saw no sign of any injury.

Suffocation, he thought. The baby must have died from lack of air.

As police sealed off the parking lot, Fox determined that the crime scene was the motel room and the plastic bag. Not the Dumpster. After photographing the inside of the Dumpster and sifting through the flattened boxes and empty cans, he left the trash alone. No officers protected the Dumpster or the trash in which the baby had been found. It would be one of the few mistakes police would make, but a critical one that would come back to hurt them.

With one search finished, Fox turned his attention to the next search: Amy's dormitory room. He told Agnor to write up a search warrant application and try to recover any hairs, fibers, or blood, whatever could link her to the baby. He also gave Agnor and the officers who would be combing the room with him an odd instruction.

"Pay more attention to what's not there than what is," Fox told them. He said they should look for prenatal vitamins, books on childbirth, abortion pamphlets, anything related to babies, but that they should not expect to find anything like that. He suspected this baby was a secret to everyone but the mother and father.

When Rick Pretzler, an investigator for the Delaware Medical Examiner's Office, arrived, he wrapped the body in a white plastic sheet, placed it on the stretcher, and drove it to the office for an autopsy. Fox made a final search of the Dumpster, hoping to find more evidence. He found nothing.

While campus police officers were banging on the doors of students, asking what they knew about Amy's collapse and her pregnancy, Agnor was piecing together what he needed for the search warrant. It had been a frantic last two hours for him, starting with the four A.M. call from Fox and the discovery of the body. He hurriedly typed out how the case began, with UD police being contacted by the hospital, and how Gettysburg police became involved. He hadn't been present for Wilson's interview with Brian, but he had talked with Wilson, and he had Lieutenant Moore's UD crime report.

That report read: "Suspect Grossberg delivered a baby *alive*. The baby died by unknown reasons and was disposed of. Suspect Peterson assisted in delivery and disposal."

With that information, Agnor typed his search warrant application.

"Police officials in Pennsylvania located Peterson and obtained a post–Miranda statement," Agnor typed. "Peterson admitted taking Grossberg from dorm room 252 Thompson Hall University of Delaware to the Comfort Inn, where the delivery of the baby occurred. Peterson indicated that the baby was alive when placed into the plastic bag."

Brian had indicated no such thing. Wilson had asked him over and over if the baby was alive, and Brian had said he did not know. Agnor was working off of other officers' reports, and Moore's report said the baby was alive.

Agnor was just winding up his application when his phone rang. Letang wanted an update. Agnor told him he was typing up a search warrant at that very moment for the girl's dormitory room.

"We found a baby in a trash bin behind the Comfort Inn," Agnor said. "It was in a plastic bag."

"Does anybody know how the baby died?" Letang asked.

"Not yet."

"Who's doing the autopsy?"

"Perlman," Agnor said.

"I'll stop in to see her before I go to work and talk to you after I get in."

Letang showered, dressed, and told Debbie about the dead baby, then kissed Samantha and Nicholas good-bye. Agnor, meanwhile, was having Magistrate Wayne R. Hamby approve the search warrant for Amy's room at seven A.M.

Agnor arrived at Thompson Hall half an hour later. It was bustling more than most mornings because of all the commotion overnight, from Amy being rushed to the hospital to Dumpsters being overturned outside. University police knocked on the door to Amy's room, and no one answered. They entered the room, announcing themselves as they walked in, and found a typical college dorm setting.

A refrigerator with a microwave on top of it. Two beds and two sets of dresser drawers, two desks, two closets. A pile of clothes and a beanbag chair lay on the floor between Grossberg's bed and desk. A backpack was on top of the pile. Agnor looked inside the backpack and found a three-ring binder. He opened it and fumbled with a letter along with art notes and materials. The two-page letter began: "Dear God."

Agnor and Detective J. B. Walker both noticed that the trash can was filled with clumps of wet paper towels and that the bag lining the can, gray with yellow drawstrings, looked identical to the one the baby had been found in. From Amy's desk, police took a prescription bottle of Donnatal, a muscle relaxant, and three pictures of Amy and a young man they presumed to be Brian Peterson.

The search took two hours. When it was over, officers had collected two boxes of maxipads and one box of tampons, a bag of cotton balls, all of Amy's bed linens, Amy's letter to God, the Donnatal pills, a white cotton shirt with bloodstains, gray sweatpants, white pajama bottoms, a pair of red panties, the gray trash bag filled with paper towels, a letter written by Amy to Brian and another from Brian to Amy, and the pictures of the couple.

The Donnatal pills would become an immediate concern of prosecutors. As they learned of the secret pregnancy, they wondered if the Donnatal might have been swallowed to try to abort or induce the fetus. Not sure what illness the pills were for, prosecutors would later have them analyzed to see if the side effects could have harmed the fetus. Only after doctors told them the pills would not have harmed a fetus did prosecutors forget about the Donnatal.

Fox's prediction, meanwhile, was accurate.

In his report from the search, Agnor wrote: "Conspicuously absent was the lack of any items for the care of a newborn infant. No diapers, blankets, clothing, bottles, etc."

Amy's attorneys would use that notation as proof that she was completely unaware of her dire situation, of just how advanced her pregnancy was. The police had a different theory. She had nothing for her baby because she'd never planned to keep him.

Driving the ten minutes into Wilmington in his 1980 gold-colored diesel Mercedes, a classic car that he cherished, Letang thought about the body he was going to see. He had seen dozens of corpses but had never grown comfortable with it. Logic told him this baby, found in a plastic bag on a freezing night, had died from asphyxiation and maybe hypothermia. In the elevator going down to the basement of 300 South Adams Street, he thought he was ready for this. He just wanted to ask Adrienne Sekula-Perlman, the deputy medical examiner who had been on call that morning, a tall, stylish, and sometimes headstrong woman, for a cause of death.

But just before he saw Sekula-Perlman, an old case popped into his head. Two years earlier Letang had found himself looking at another dead baby, a newborn girl whose body was recovered from a toilet in a home. Katherine Jones, a forty-two-year-old woman, told police she thought she had suffered a miscarriage and not actually given birth. Letang charged her with murder, and eventually she pleaded guilty to manslaughter and served two and a half years in prison.

He tried to put the image of Jones's baby, and his own Samantha, out of his head. But the instant he walked into the chilly, wide-open, windowless room, with yellow tiled walls and rows of fluorescent lights shining down on two stainless-steel tables, he turned pale. Fox was there. So was Sekula-Perlman.

Autopsies on adult bodies are ably performed by medical examiners everywhere. A medical examiner's job is to decide whether a death occurred under circumstances that require an autopsy. But medical experts agree that completing an autopsy on a tiny infant, with organs so small they must be measured with special scales, are more complicated. There are signs that tell whether the baby ever breathed beyond the simple air-in-the-lungs test. It's a specialty, autopsies on newborns. The tests on the body and the organs are more delicate and complicated and, as a result, take longer.

From fifteen feet away Letang saw the tiny body lying on its back on one of the tables, its head elevated, its eyes closed, its body small enough for him to cup in his two hands, almost ten inches of the umbilical cord still attached. Ten fingers, ten toes, mouth slightly open, matted black hair. His stomach gurgled.

"Oh, man, I can't go in there," he told Sekula-Perlman. He backed up into the main room, where bodies are first wheeled in and weighed, and stared at the brown tile floor. He motioned Fox and Sekula-Perlman to come over to him.

Autopsies are never very pretty. And when the deceased is a cute and tiny newborn, it's only that much more depressing. Like most labs, the city morgue had a blackboard for the medical examiner to jot down any findings, anything from surface injuries, to height and weight, to the appearance of the organs. Sekula-Perlman had already started the autopsy on the cold and tiny body when Letang arrived, but she had made only a few notes on the blackboard, instead writing mostly in the small notepad she carried.

The standard autopsy incision is the Y-cut, running diagonally down from the left and right shoulders to a meeting point at the base of the ribs and then continuing down in a single line to the pubic bone. On an adult, the incision from top to bottom covers roughly eighteen to twenty-four inches, but on this baby it was barely six inches. The incision completed, Sekula-Perlman peeled away the skin and muscle and cut open the ribs to expose the lungs, heart, liver, kidneys, and other organs.

It was not the first newborn she had examined. In her nearly three years with the office, she had seen deaths by gunshot, poison, illness, suicide, drowning, just about any imaginable manner. And for the most part she had become numb to the sight of a dead body. Including a baby. It was her job.

But just as Letang was struggling to collect himself, both Sekula-Perlman and Fox also found themselves linking the baby to their personal lives. On Sekula-Perlman's desk upstairs were photos of her teenage son, a year younger than Brian and equally preppy and good-looking. She knew few details of this case, only that the baby had apparently been born to two teenagers in a motel room. What would her son have done? she wondered. Fox was reminded of a miscarriage his wife had suffered a decade ago. They'd had two children since then, but the miscarriage, the lost baby, had always stayed with them emotionally.

The newborn on the steel table, at six pounds, two ounces, and twenty inches long, with dark eyelashes and blue eyes, was no miscarriage. It was a cute, full-term baby. No doubt about it. From the doorway of the autopsy room, Letang could see that the chest and skull had been opened. The body was clean, almost no blood.

The head was another story. On the outside, there were no abrasions. But when Sekula-Perlman cut open the scalp and removed the skullcap, what it revealed shocked both her and Letang when he caught a glimpse.

Standing outside the room, Letang saw the depression fracture first, a deep indentation slightly larger than the size of a postage stamp on the top of the skull, as if someone had put their thumb into the top of a hard-boiled egg. To a layman it looked brutal and vicious. Then Letang noticed the linear fracture, the crack in the skull that looked like a piece of a puzzle that hadn't quite been pushed in all the way. This skull was not just bruised, it was broken.

Out in the hallway, Letang took a deep breath and listened to Sekula-Perlman. She told him the infant had been born alive, that there was clearly air in the bowel and lungs and hemorrhages in the brain, all indications that the child was almost certainly breathing and his heart pumping when he was thrown in the Dumpster.

"I came down here to see if it was asphyxiated," Letang told her. "That baby's head looks caved in."

"Yes, it has major skull fractures," she answered him.

They both knew that the head of a baby is softer than an adult's skull, more pliable so that it can slide through the birth canal, which also made it more vulnerable to injury and easier to crack. Letang talked briefly with Fox and then left Sekula-Perlman to complete her autopsy.

What the hell happened to that baby? he thought as he walked back to his car.

The autopsy took almost three hours. With half a dozen people walking in and out of the room, from technicians in lab coats, to Fox in his business suit, to Pretzler, the office's investigator who had picked up the body from the motel, to the state medical examiner, Richard Callery, the body was X-rayed, photographed, and its organs removed one by one. Unlike the organs from an adult body, which are weighed in the hanging tin scale above the table, the baby's organs were so small that they had to be measured in a tiny white plastic scale with a bowl the size of a coffee mug. The liver, smooth and shiny brown, weighed 112 grams, one-tenth the size of a normal adult liver. The right kidney weighed 12 grams. The brain weighed 400 grams.

The body had no sign of decomposition to indicate how long it had been in the trash. But it was the head that had Sekula-Perlman's attention. She had cut the skull from ear to ear and peeled back the scalp. The skull fractures were impossible to miss, and she had no doubt that they were the single most significant factor in the baby's death.

In her preliminary report she wrote that the cause of death was "multiple skull fractures (linear and depressed) caused by blunt force trauma, with epidural, subdural, and subarachnoid hemorrhages, hypothermia, and asphyxia." The baby, Sekula-Perlman believed, died from having its head bashed, causing bleeding in the skull, as well as being out in the freezing cold for twenty-four hours in a plastic bag that deprived it of oxygen.

What she could not tell, and what would become another mystery for Letang, was the nature of the "blunt force trauma" that had caused those fractures. Was it an intentional whack by Amy or Brian to keep the baby from crying and "get rid of it"? The toss into the Dumpster? Or something heavy landing on top of the body as it lay in the trash bin?

Steve Fox, after learning of the skull fractures, returned with officers to the motel room the next morning and seized virtually every blunt object. They took the blood-stained mattress, a silver pipe and faucet, the bathroom sink, the bed, the telephone, and the desk chair. Everything had already been wiped clean by the maid, but Fox held out hope that if there was a tiny hair, a speck of blood, any sign that the baby had come in contact with something hard in that room, they would find it. And that might explain the skull fractures. Fox sent officers behind the motel to drag a net through the creek there, hoping to pull up something that Amy or Brian might have tossed there in their rushed exit.

They found nothing in the creek, and every object they seized from the room was clean. Officers even took an ultraviolet light through the room to look for blood splatters away from the bed. Again, nothing.

Sekula-Perlman would eventually tell prosecutors, and later the media, that she believed the chair may have been used to hit the baby.

"Babies fall all the time and never suffer these kinds of injuries," she said.

But she would never be able to prove her theory.

Fox would have his own suspicions. He believed that a foot, a heel, Amy's heel, might have caused the fractures when Brian left her alone with the baby for ninety seconds. He, too, would never be able to prove anything.

But both Fox and Sekula-Perlman would never believe the eventual defense argument that the fractures were caused by the toss into the Dumpster or by something sharp and heavy landing on top of the body after it was dead.

Only two people would ever know for certain what happened inside that motel room. Everyone else—the lawyers, the police, the press, the public—would be guessing, theorizing, and speculating.

# BARBIE GETS BUSTED

*A* *my did nothing wrong.*
  They were the four words that any lawyer, police officer, reporter—anyone who spoke with Amy's parents—would hear, over and over. It was her parents' position, and nothing would change it. Nothing else was acceptable. It would prove to be, in the eyes of many, her parents' gravest mistake.

Amy and Brian were a good fit, a cute couple. White, young, clean-cut, smart, no blemishes in their past, strong family support. They had it all. Together. As the case against the teenagers unfolded, and defense lawyers were brought in, a conflict arose almost immediately. Amy's parents kept repeating their position: *Amy did nothing wrong.*

There was a sentiment that if Amy and Brian went hand in hand into court and threw themselves on the judge's mercy by showing remorse and tears, apologizing for an act they committed out of fear, throwing them in jail would have been difficult. The public would have seen their faces, and their families, and accepted their apology. A judge would have, too. Prosecutors, especially an attorney general sensitive to the voters, might have been willing to be lenient if that's what the public wanted.

But every time Alan and Sonye Grossberg said their daughter did nothing wrong, they drove a wedge between

Amy and Brian, each time a little deeper. A dead baby was found in a trash Dumpster behind the motel where it was delivered. Amy's baby. If Amy did nothing wrong, that pointed a finger directly at the only other person in the motel room with her. Alan and Sonye never said Brian did it, only that Amy didn't do it. No different.

Amy's version of the early morning hours of November 12, 1996, would remain largely consistent throughout her defense. But it would raise so many more questions than it would answer that the authorities believed only pieces of it, because of evidence they would uncover showing how desperate she was to keep the secret.

*I called Brian because I was having some pains, but I don't remember asking him to come. Then I saw his car pulling up to my dorm. I didn't understand why he came.*

Still, Brian had driven two hours and arrived at Amy's dormitory at three A.M.: police found it difficult to accept Amy's vague bewilderment. Brian would not have rushed to be with her at that hour unless she had given him a reason.

*Brian drove us to a motel, and I was too weak to object.*

It might be believable given her advanced state of preeclampsia, but Amy walked herself into the motel room and walked herself out. No one carried or forced her. She could have asked Brian to drive her to a hospital, just as Brian could have driven her without asking.

*I remember lying on the bed with my knees up and felt a sharp pain in my pelvic area, and I started to shake. I don't know how, but my pants were pulled down. Then I felt this squish, but I didn't see or hear anything. I heard Brian go out of the room twice, and when I asked him what happened, he told me not to worry, everything was okay. He helped me back to my room at college, and later he left for his college. When I asked him later on the telephone what had happened, he again told me not to worry about anything.*

Prosecutors recognized that only two people would ever know for certain what happened inside that motel room. But accepting that Amy never heard or saw anything, that Brian acted entirely on his own, and that she was a sick and innocent bystander through her own delivery called for a leap of faith verging on the impossible.

"Having just watched my wife go through her pregnancy and delivery, I found her story just so hard to accept," Letang would say months later. "It defied logic that she was so unaware of what happened."

But that was what Amy was saying. One day she was pregnant, so pregnant that she had felt the baby kick inside her. The next day she was not, and she never saw fit to find out what happened to her baby. That was the condensed story, right up to her seizures in her dormitory room, that her defense attorneys would have to work with. *Amy did nothing wrong.*

His business card says Charles Slanina, but to everyone he is Chip. With his glasses, young face, and thick brown hair, he resembles a forty-something computer scientist more than a lawyer. An associate for one of the top firms in Wilmington, Biggs & Battaglia, he was known among fellow lawyers mostly for his stint as the disciplinary counsel for the Delaware Bar Association and as a former Deputy Attorney General. He was the watchdog for their missteps, and that was a key reason Andrea Grayson called him on Wednesday morning. Andrea Grayson was Sonye Grossberg's sister and a New Jersey divorce lawyer. Grayson needed a Delaware criminal lawyer for Amy, someone the family could trust, whom they could afford.

Slanina agreed to visit Amy in the hospital that night. It would be the beginning of a strained relationship between Amy and her family and their Delaware legal team. "Amy did nothing wrong" would not sit right with Slanina or the lawyers he would ask to join him.

Amy did a lot wrong, Slanina would tell her parents. She hid her pregnancy. She sought no prenatal care. She gave birth in a motel room. She told no one about it after returning to college. But what the lawyers wanted to argue was that while Amy may have been morally wrong, socially wrong, wrong in just about every way, she was not criminally wrong, and she did not deserve to go to jail. That was the argument Amy's lawyers would advise her to make.

For Alan and Sonye, it was not good enough.

"What they wanted in this case was not to have the charges reduced or mitigated, or to have her disciplined, but they wanted her totally exonerated," said Harlan Giles, a renowned obstetrician and perinatologist from Pittsburgh who was hired by Amy's lawyers and interviewed her.

Not long after Slanina got his call, Jeffrey Cook received a similar one at his office in downtown Gettysburg. Forty-three years old, the Philadelphia native had a small private practice while also helping with some public defender cases. When his secretary told him John Rogers Carroll was on the phone for him, he couldn't help being a tad excited. To Philadelphians, particularly lawyers, Carroll was admired, almost revered. He had launched his career in 1953 by helping to defend nine Communists charged with advocating a government coup. He never spoke with the press, and he never had to. Those who knew him, respected him.

Carroll told Cook that there was a Gettysburg freshman in the Adams County Prison who needed a lawyer. He was facing charges of at least child endangerment. Cook, a Gettysburg graduate from the 1970s, agreed to help and drove to the prison a mile away, where he met Brian's father and uncle, Ted Will. The three men went inside to a private room and met with Brian, who was wearing the standard orange prison uniform.

Brian was stone-faced as he told Cook what he had told Detective Wilson. The baby didn't look right, palish blue. They talked for forty-five minutes, after which Cook called District Attorney Mike George.

George was prepared to hold Brian. He had no proof that a crime had been committed in his state, but he also had a dead baby and the father, who'd admitted to throw-

ing the baby away, in his grasp. He didn't want to let Brian
go. But when officials in Delaware told him they planned
to file more serious charges and ordered George to release
Brian, he did. Reluctantly. By five P.M. Brian, his father,
and his uncle were gone, driving to Long Island, while
Brian's mother boarded an emergency flight back from
her vacation in the South Pacific.

"Delaware has expressed no interest in us holding him
any longer," George said. "There came a point when there
was nothing else we could do to keep him."

The story, meanwhile, was about to reach Wyckoff.
Patrick Crosetto, a Ramapo sophomore at the time, and a
few friends were working in the Franklin Lakes Public
Library after school when they saw a man in a trench coat
looking through the Ramapo High School yearbook. The
reporter for the *Wilmington News-Journal* in Delaware
asked the group of teenagers if they knew Amy Grossberg
and Brian Peterson. He told them police had found a dead
baby in the trash and that Amy was in the hospital.
Crosetto was two years behind Amy and Brian, but he
knew them. Everyone did.

"Are you sure you've got the right people?" Crosetto
asked. For three days the *News-Journal* was the only media
outlet covering the story. It would have company soon.

The reporter wasn't the only one in Wyckoff from
Delaware. Fox, the lead investigator on the case, had sent
two of his detectives, Susan Farrell and Ralph Johnson, to
the New Jersey town first thing Thursday morning. Fox had
a theory that Amy had been the controlling one in the relationship and in keeping the secret. He told his detectives to
visit the high school and anywhere else people could
describe how Amy and Brian were together. Later, Fox
himself would travel to Wyckoff to do his own snooping.

That night, as Letang walked up the stairs into his
house with the names "Grossberg" and "Peterson" dancing in his head, he knew this case would be more difficult
for him than for the other prosecutors in his office. So did
his wife. She was so sure that she asked him if he should

take it. She had seen the developments on the news and been shaken at hearing about a baby being thrown in the trash and the horrible head injuries. She asked her husband if he could handle it, almost hoping he'd say no and pass it off to someone else.

"I'll be okay," he reassured her. It wouldn't be easy.

As the Letangs sat down for dinner, Slanina was arriving at the hospital to meet for the first time a terrified young woman and her equally frightened parents.

"I thought I had a blob," Amy told him from her bed in the intensive care unit of the OB/GYN wing.

She was extremely puffy. Her feet, hands, and face were swollen. The hospital had given her a private room and allowed her parents to stay with her at all hours. After he heard about the baby and the secret pregnancy, Slanina left to call Letang. Letang pressed Slanina to let Amy make a formal statement about what happened to her baby. But Slanina would not allow it unless he had assurance that she would not be charged with a crime. Letang wouldn't make that promise.

For three days the two men went back and forth. Letang kept asking, Slanina kept refusing.

While Amy remained hospitalized, and Brian lay in seclusion with his family, the tiny body of their son lay in a refrigerated compartment of the downtown Wilmington morgue. Unclaimed.

"It could be released for burial," Dr. Richard T. Callery, the state medical examiner, told the *Wilmington News-Journal* on Friday. "It's just a matter of somebody asking. But at this point, we have not had any request for the release of the child."

The next day, three days after the baby's body had been pulled from the trash, Amy and Brian were officially charged. Sekula-Perlman told Callery her conclusion. The baby had been born alive and died from multiple skull fractures, with injury to the brain caused by blunt-force head trauma and shaking. The death, she said, was a homicide, which was all Letang needed to hear.

"The Newark Police Department has obtained arrest warrants charging Amy S. Grossberg and Brian Peterson with murder in the first degree of their newborn baby boy on Tuesday November 12, 1996," read a press release that went out at six P.M. on Saturday. "The arrests of Grossberg and Peterson are proceeding at this time."

Grossberg was accounted for, and the police knew she was not going anywhere from her hospital bed. But Peterson was missing. Newark police searched his parents' home in Wyckoff, and his father's house in Long Island, and came up empty. Immediately for Letang, Alex Kelly came to mind. The high school wrestling star in Darien, Connecticut, a similarly affluent town to Wyckoff, was charged in 1986 with raping a classmate in his car. Instead of surrendering, he fled to Europe, where he lived for eight years, before finally being arrested and returned home for trial. He was found guilty and sentenced to sixteen years in prison. Letang hoped Brian hadn't done the same.

It was that night when Jane Brady, the elected attorney general for Delaware, made a decision that would haunt her and her staff for the duration of the entire case and bring criticism down on her from lawyers, parents, and teenagers across the country.

Because the baby was under the age of fourteen, Delaware law allowed prosecutors to seek the execution of the suspected killer or killers. Perhaps worried about coming down too softly on a pair of wealthy white New Jersey teenagers, Brady told Letang they would pursue the death penalty, even though the case clearly did not fit the capital punishment profile. Letang argued with her. He was livid. He knew it was wrong; he was sure this wasn't a death penalty case. Pennell, the serial killer he had prosecuted and executed a decade earlier, was a capital case. Amy Grossberg and Brian Peterson were not. Infanticide is never a capital crime. But it wasn't his call, it was Brady's. That night at home, frustrated and upset, Letang called his father to vent. The biggest case of his career was barely three days old, and already a part of him was wishing it on someone else.

On Sunday he followed his orders and said the state would seek the death penalty for Amy and Brian because their act of leaving a baby outside in cold weather, in addition to the head trauma found in the autopsy, showed an intent to commit murder. Brady's decision left Letang taking the criticism. He was the one speaking with the press, not her. He had a listed home telephone number and was easily accessible at work. Brady was unlisted and was referring calls on the case to him. Though the decision was Brady's, Letang's name was attached to it. He knew it. His friends knew it and told him how bad they felt that Brady had hung him out to dry.

Amy and Brian were suddenly targeted to be Delaware's youngest death row inmates.

"It's like Barbie getting busted," said one mother in Wyckoff.

### Monday, November 18, 1996

In a giant twenty-screen movie cinema in Commack, New York, off Exit 53 of the Long Island Expressway, an hour east of New York City, a cleaning lady was working her way through the seventeen stalls in the women's bathroom. It was close to one A.M. on Monday, the movies were all done, the crowds gone, the maroon velvet ropes holding back no one. The cleaning woman pushed open one of the stall doors to clean the toilet.

Soaking in the water was a baby, a dead white baby boy.

He had been delivered in the bathroom, police said later, and suffocated, either by the water, the mother, or the failure to have his throat cleared. It was a murder, and Suffolk County police appealed to the public for help in finding the mother. The case was virtually ignored by the media, warranting a few days of stories in the New York newspapers and then forgotten.

As Suffolk County investigators went looking for their

suspect, without any bother from reporters, a throng of television and newspaper reporters had converged on the courthouse in Wilmington, Delaware, from New York, New Jersey, Philadelphia, and national magazines. Who were these teenagers from this affluent town, and why had they thrown their baby in the trash? Two hours north, Wyckoff was besieged. The town had not seen a media frenzy since 1992, when convicted rapist Donald Chapman, who served twelve years in prison, was released to live with his parents in town. But this mob dwarfed that one.

The headline Monday morning in the local newspaper, *The Record*—DEATH SOUGHT FOR BERGEN TEENS—was stripped across the top of the front page, and suddenly reporters were hiding in the woods outside Ramapo High School, photographers were climbing on the roof, and the circular driveway was jammed with news crews. The tranquillity the residents were so accustomed to was gone. Principal John Mucciolo, who arrived at his school by six A.M. anticipating a media mob, urged arriving students to not talk with reporters, and in his morning announcement over the loudspeaker he said if they did talk, they should be careful about what they said about their former classmates.

As so often happens when a small town is invaded by a media crush, the people in town lashed out at the intruders. *The Record* had nine reporters on the story. The *New York Daily News, New York Post,* and *New York Times,* along with *Time* and *Newsweek* magazines, all joined the fray, as did every New Jersey and New York television and radio station. The reporters were looking for a reaction anywhere they could find it, from shopping center parking lots, to the popular Harned's General Store, to the grounds of every school in town where they knew parents would have to arrive to pick up their children. The residents hated it, particularly the references to their town as "bucolic" and "affluent."

But the readers couldn't get enough of the coverage.

*The Record* sold almost three thousand more newspapers on Monday than it did the previous Monday before the case broke. Bergen County, like the rest of the country, wanted to know why.

The police in Delaware did, too. On Monday morning Newark police lieutenant Roy Clough said the focus of the investigation was on the head injuries to the baby.

"These were not just bumps," he said. "We're trying to determine how the baby was struck in the head. We're very interested in that, but we don't know."

He said what was most disturbing to police was that if Amy had not collapsed in her dormitory, "it's very possible and scary no one would have ever known what happened."

Around noon one of Amy's doctors at Christiana Hospital called Letang and said they were ready to release her but had been told there was an agreement that she would not be arrested upon her release. Letang immediately called Slanina and Oberly and said he had agreed to no such deal.

"We are arresting her," Letang said.

"This wasn't supposed to happen," Slanina insisted angrily. "The deal was she would be released and available for comment. You told me she wouldn't be arrested in her hospital bed."

"We have to arrest her," Letang repeated. "I'm acting under orders." Attorney General Jane Brady's orders.

He promised Amy's attorneys the arrest would be discreet and calm, that she would be escorted by officers out a back door. None of that was comforting to Amy's parents.

Amy hugged and kissed them inside her hospital room. Right up until she was taken from her parents' arms, Amy had a team of people fighting to keep her in bed. Doctors discharged her after talking with corrections officials to ensure she would be watched closely and explaining she should refrain from strenuous activity, eat lightly, and take her medication religiously.

Her lawyer and her parents all pleaded with Letang to hold off arresting her until she was stronger. But she was handcuffed and led from the hospital and driven to the Newark Police Department station, where she was photographed and fingerprinted. Emerging from the station, she looked like a tired monk. She wore a borrowed long blue coat, its hood covering her head to keep her warm. She walked slowly, her eyes fixed on the ground, her wrists cuffed, clutching a can of Coke in her hands. She trudged alongside Grayson, her aunt, who nuzzled close to her and held her left arm. From there it was a quick drive to Magistrate Court 18 at Gander Hill Prison for her arraignment.

The small room was packed with reporters, and when Amy was escorted in just after five P.M., hushed gasps escaped from reporters' mouths. She looked thirteen, maybe fourteen, but nothing like eighteen. She had bags under her teary eyes, her long dark hair was mussed. Wearing a long-sleeved white shirt, black-and-white pants, and a sweater tied around her waist, she let the lawyers do all the talking.

"The state intends to seek the death penalty," Deputy Attorney General Donald Roberts told Justice of the Peace Rosalie O. Rutkowski. He asked that Amy be held without bail.

Slanina told Rutkowski that Amy pleaded not guilty and did not challenge the request for no bail. He knew asking for bail would be fruitless. Rutkowski ordered that Amy be held and undergo a psychiatric evaluation, a standard move. As Slanina left the prison, he was swarmed by the reporters just outside the front door, the bright camera lights making him squint. He admitted he was stunned the state was taking such a hard line in seeking the death penalty.

"She's not a danger to anyone, and she is not a risk of flight," he said. "Both Amy and her family are upset there has been a rush to judgment. Without commenting on the facts of the case, we remain confident Amy will be vindicated."

The "we" Slanina referred to was his new co-counsel. The Grossbergs had told him earlier that day to hire whatever help he needed. His first call was to Eugene Maurer, a bit of a free spirit who is regarded as one of Delaware's finest criminal lawyers. He was not in. Slanina then called another free spirit and equally sharp lawyer, Joseph Hurley. But he, too, was unavailable.

Slanina's third call was to Charlie Oberly, the former state attorney general turned defense lawyer, a straight arrow and bulldog of an attorney. Oberly, and his partner, Kathleen Jennings, who a decade earlier had prosecuted the serial killer case with Letang, signed on immediately to help. The three lawyers then divvied up the duties, with Slanina taking the investigation side and Oberly and Jennings handling the brunt of the media barrage and interviewing and hiring defense experts. Medical experts were needed to study whether the baby had been healthy at birth, as well as the physical and mental states of Amy and Brian.

Just as Oberly and Jennings were joining the case, Brady, already feeling the criticism for her decision to seek the death penalty, tried to take a softer stance toward the teenagers and justify her reasoning.

"We realized how traumatized these young people must be, but I said the fact remains there were intentional injuries to this newborn child, and I have to do my job and take whatever steps I and my staff believes are necessary," she said in her office for a small group of reporters. "I realize their hearts are broken, but I have a tough job."

Outside observers agreed at the time with her assessment, if not her decision.

"The attorney general is in a very difficult position here, because she is darned if she does ask for the death penalty and darned if she doesn't," said Lawrence J. Connell, an associate law professor at the Delaware campus of Widener University School of Law. "Prosecutors tend, the argument goes, to seek death in disproportionate numbers against minorities and the poor. Here we have two middle-class white college kids who appear to have committed a capital murder. If the attorney general did not charge them with capital murder, she would be criticized for giving them preferential treatment."

From her arraignment, Amy was taken to what would be her home for the next two months.

Traffic on Baylor Boulevard is light, all the time. It's a dead end with only one building, about five miles outside Wilmington. As the trees along the road end, the bright green roof of the two-story Delores J. Baylor Women's Correctional Institute, which opened in 1992, comes into view. There is no mistaking that it's a prison, set out in the open, a security chain-link fence twenty feet high with barbed wire on top surrounding the brick building. Inside, the jail is surprisingly clean and quiet. The brick walls are painted peach and lime green, giving it a soft look. A long hallway lined with windows runs next to the recreation area, where green park benches sit beside a volleyball net.

The police car carrying Amy pulled up around six P.M. to the door behind the prison, where inmates get their first glimpse of their new accommodations. Two pay telephones hang in a room off to the side, with flyers posted on the wall showing the names and numbers of bail bondsmen. In the booking and receiving room, Amy gave her name, date of birth, and Social Security number. She was ushered into a corner concrete shower stall, where she had to strip, squat, cough, and shower. It's the routine every female inmate is put through to make sure she is not trying to smuggle in a weapon or drugs by hiding anything in her mouth or vagina. Cleaned, she was given her new wardrobe, a baggy white cotton shirt and white pants. Her picture was taken as she held a slab beneath her chin with her name, the date of November 18, 1996, and her birthdate.

No longer were her floormates Holly Shooman, Seth Chorba, and Nicole DeSanctis, young and carefree students just like her. Amy was in the same building with forty-three-year-old Vicky Chao of Queens, New York, also known as Susan Chao, Virginia Chao, and Judy Chao, sentenced in 1989 to three life terms for three premeditated murders, arson, and burglary.

After a brief stop in the infirmary, where she gave her medical history, Amy was taken to her cell. In the last week Amy had been in the small room 252 at Thompson Hall, a smaller room 220 at the Comfort Inn, and a cramped room at Christiana Hospital. All were bigger and brighter than cell 207 at the Delores J. Baylor Women's Correctional Institute. The entire prison holds three hundred women, and in an effort to help rehabilitate, rather than just incarcerate, it was designed with an open, airy look so the inmates could spend hours at a time in a vast room instead of cooped in their cells. Breakfast was served at five-thirty A.M., lockdown was at ten P.M. From one to two P.M. was recreation time, after which, every day, the women had to be in their cells for a head count.

On the second floor, in a corner, cell 207 had a stainless-steel toilet and sink just inside to the right of the door, a bunk bed in the right corner, a fluorescent light on the ceiling, and a tiny window at eye level along the back wall. The view of the woods was obstructed by the coiled barbed wire that lined the top of the fence surrounding the prison. As Amy settled into her strange bed, she heard for the first time a taunt that would follow her wherever she went in the jail.

"Baby killer!"

The jail was dark and quiet as Amy dozed off. She had no idea that the woman who had wanted her there so quickly was going on national television to explain why killing a baby was not simply murder in Delaware, but first-degree, capital murder.

Since starting his program, *Rivera Live*, on CNBC, Geraldo Rivera had built something of a cult following among lawyers. His guests could always be counted on for spirited debate about the latest hot legal battle brewing somewhere in the country. His viewers ranged from the lawyers who fantasized about trading barbs with him on the air to the simply curious newshounds.

In late November the fiery host with the wire-rimmed glasses and bushy brown mustache was consumed by two cases: the Oklahoma City bombing case against Timothy McVeigh and the Unabomber. Then along came two baby-faced New Jersey teenagers and a state seemingly intent on demanding their execution, and Rivera was salivating. His guests on November 18 were Christopher Darden, one of the losing prosecutors against O. J. Simpson; Alan Dershowitz, the nerdy and eccentric defender of Klaus von Bulow and a Harvard University law professor; and, by telephone, Delaware attorney general Jane Brady.

"The murder of a newborn infant is obviously a horrendous crime under any circumstances, but when the alleged killers are the young, fresh-faced parents of that child, the event soars, really, beyond our comprehension," Rivera said in his show's opening.

In a brief story by NBC reporter Pat Dawson previewing the discussion among Rivera's guests, a woman from Wyckoff was interviewed on a pretty side street.

"I think we live in our little cocoon here, and we think that all of these problems are elsewhere, and they're not," she said.

Rivera jumped right in on Brady.

"Why murder one for both of them at this stage?"

"Based on the information we have and the autopsy results, we believe the injuries were intentionally inflicted, and in our state, that crime is—those acts constitute murder in the first degree," Brady said.

Rivera turned to Dershowitz.

"We have a lot of discretion in this country," Dershowitz said. "There are thirty-five hundred people on death row for more than one hundred thousand murders. You don't just charge a mother with first-degree murder and capital punishment for the post-traumatic birth syndrome of killing a child."

Rivera cut him off and asked Brady to respond.

"Well, first of all, the way our statute works in Delaware, when we made the determination based upon the information we have in the autopsy reports that murder in the first degree was the appropriate charge—because the age of the victim is less than fourteen, the case is a capital case," she said.

Dershowitz scoffed at her explanation. "I guarantee you, I'll bet you that in the end they do not ask for the death penalty. They're just using it as a tactic and a political gimmick."

"The bottom line is that we don't make decisions based on politics," Brady shot back. "And with the exception of trying to clarify the law in Delaware and respond to some of the media's questions, we don't intend to comment on the case in the media. We don't try our cases in the media. We try our cases in the courtroom."

"What are you doing on this television show?" Dershowitz asked with a chuckle.

The banter continued for another few minutes, ending with Rivera asking Brady if Delaware actually uses the death penalty, actually gives people on its death row the lethal injection.

"Yes, we do, and we've had several executions during my tenure as attorney general."

Rivera thanked his viewers for watching just as it was approaching lights-out time at the Delores J. Baylor Women's Correctional Institute. The spotlight was about to shift onto Amy's boyfriend and squarely onto Joseph Hurley, exactly where he likes it.

## Tuesday, November 19

He says his polka-dot ties are his trademark, that he has the largest collection of them in every possible color combination, from purple and orange to red and blue, and he never steps into court without one.

But really his trademark, as his friends like to say, is "just being Joe." Just being Joe means just being loud, just being witty, just being crude, just being friendly, just being the center of attention, and most of all, just being one of Delaware's, and the country's, finest criminal defense lawyers.

His summer of 1996 had been consumed by one of his most gratifying and emotional victories. A restaurateur had been charged with causing the death of his eighteen-month-old son by leaving him in a closed vehicle for three hours on a scorching summer day. Mike Chase said he did not know his wife had placed their child in the car, but police said he simply forgot his son was there. The jury acquitted him of criminally negligent homicide, reducing the defendant and Hurley to tears in the courtroom. That was also just being Joe, and that was why Brian's family hired him when the Grossbergs did not.

On Tuesday Hurley told prosecutors and the press he did not know, nor did he want to know, where Brian was. He admitted he had seen him Sunday and had told him and his mother to call him only from pay phones. As his lawyer, if he knew where Brian was and did not tell police, he could be charged with obstructing justice. And Brian's family could be charged with harboring a fugitive.

"This is about a mother not wanting to turn her only-born child over to the state of Delaware so they can murder him," announced Hurley on Tuesday, addressing what had become the daily horde of reporters who shadowed his every move. "This is an incredibly painful situation for all of them."

The newspapers, meanwhile, especially the tabloids, could not have scripted a story more tailor-made for their headline writers. On Tuesday the *New York Daily News* ran the yearbook picture huge on its front, sandwiched between these words: "They are 18 and sweethearts. They had it all. Now they're charged with killing their infant and they are Facing Death."

The police had already searched the two homes where Peterson should have been. Hurley promised a surrender, but the police were unconvinced of his sincerity. Three days had passed since the warrant was issued. Police began pressuring Hurley, and by midafternoon he acknowledged Brian had to turn himself in.

"We can't drag this on," he said outside the courthouse. "He'll turn himself in as long as there isn't a SWAT team waiting for him at the state border and it can be a peaceful arrest."

William Hogan, the police chief in Newark, a tall, burly, balding man, assured Hurley the arrest would be simple, as long as it happened quickly.

"He will be arrested peacefully and treated with absolute respect," Hogan said. "We just want to turn this over to the courts, where it belongs."

But Brian's mother was petrified of that idea. Barbara Zuchowski met with Hurley on Tuesday and asked him what countries the United States does not have extradition treaties with, what countries Brian could flee to without fear of being returned. Hurley discouraged her from shipping her son out of the country.

"At least he'd have a life," she responded.

Hurley couldn't argue with her. He was as baffled as anyone as to why the state seemed so intent on seeking the death penalty for Brian and Amy. At Amy's college, students were split. Most could not forgive and were livid at one of their classmates for not turning to the services they all knew were available on campus. Others saw themselves in Amy and couldn't help wondering if they would have had the courage to tell their parents. Karen Stoltzfus saw a lot of Amy in herself. Stoltzfus, a freshman at UD from the tiny town of Gap, Pennsylvania, was four months pregnant when Amy was arrested. She wrote a letter to the student newspaper, the *Review,* that appeared Tuesday.

"I am also a freshman, so it was difficult for me to make a decision whether to keep the baby or give him up for adoption," she wrote. "Today, I have shed a million tears for that innocent little baby whose life was taken so horribly."

In an interview that afternoon she recalled the conversation she'd had with her mother after telling her boyfriend she was pregnant.

"I'm in trouble," she'd told her mother on the couch in their house.

"What kind of trouble?"

"I'm pregnant."

"Omigosh."

That was it. Stoltzfus, a pretty brunette mature beyond her years, said she started to cry and her mother hugged her. "It was very comforting," she remembered. "I didn't want to let her down. That was my fear. She knew how much I wanted a career. I felt like I let a lot of people down."

Asked what advice she might have offered Amy had she known she was pregnant, she said she would have told her to talk to other women. Women, she said confidently, are compassionate and less judgmental.

"Your parents don't want to see you struggle or in pain," she said.

Tuesday night, with Brian still missing, police became fed up with Hurley's promises and the FBI was called in. The Bureau issued a federal arrest warrant for Brian, charging him with unlawful flight to avoid prosecution. He was a fugitive, and the entire country was wondering where he was.

"We want him now," Newark chief Hogan said late Tuesday. "We wanted him before now."

## Wednesday, November 20

As each day passed, Hurley was drawn like a bee to honey toward the microphones, cameras, and notepads that waited outside his small, red-brick brownstone office two blocks from the courthouse. He never avoided them. He would come out, his silver hair perfectly combed, his glasses snug, his silk polka-dot tie knotted neatly, and speak as calmly as a news anchorman.

For two days the calls had been tying up the switchboards at the offices of the lawyers for Amy and Brian. And the lawyers whose home numbers were listed found their answering machine tapes full when they returned home and simply flipped the tapes without even listening.

Newspaper reporters, television producers, and some of the biggest media stars all begged to tell "the true story" of Amy and Brian, or at least the story most likely to get them the coveted interview. NBC's *Dateline* called, and Katie Couric wrote. CNN, *Hard Copy,* German Television, Maury Povich, Larry King, Montel Williams, Geraldo Rivera, Oprah Winfrey, Sally Jesse Raphaël, and *Redbook* magazine all wanted the story. So did *The New York Times* and *The Washington Post, People, Time,* and *Newsweek* magazines. A movie producer from Beverly Hills called to promise millions for the rights to the story.

On the streets of Wyckoff, the same question was being asked about Amy and Brian that was asked after a group of star high school players in Glen Ridge, New Jersey, was arrested in 1989 and charged with the gang rape of a mentally retarded teenage girl.

Why would these children who had everything commit such a frightening act?

Hurley knew that each interview he gave, each quote, each sound bite, was an opportunity to present an image of Brian as a terrified teenager and of his mother as a woman unwilling to give up her only child to a state seemingly hell-bent on executing him. The longer the delay in arresting Brian, the more spin Hurley could put on the case and the more potential jurors he could make feel sorry for his client. Spin was just being Joe.

To this former prosecutor, eighty-hour work weeks were typical, and the only thing he loved as much as his work were his horses. At fifty-three he was at his peak professionally. His two marriages had failed, and after losing touch with his grown daughter for years, she was back in his life. But just when it seemed as if Hurley might soften, and maybe even hide from the spotlight, an interview appeared in which he said his dream life would be "with a twenty-seven-year-old babe who loves oral sex," or photographs showed up of him in the shower, and everyone in Wilmington chuckled and shook their heads. There he goes again, just being Joe.

Sitting in his office on Wednesday, his feet on his conference table, his secretary fielding calls from *The Montel Williams Show* to *The New York Times,* Hurley looked remarkably relaxed.

"I can't tell you what happened, but I can tell you what didn't happen," he said. "These two kids did not go to the hotel to have their baby with the idea of killing it. They went to the hotel with the idea of giving birth." He said if they had really been plotting to kill their baby, they certainly would not have registered in the motel under Brian's name.

Then he made a promise: The surrender will come Thursday morning in downtown Wilmington.

"There will be a tearful hug. He's scared. He's scared. He's scared. He's going into an environment with a bunch of predators."

He might as well have come right out and said: Don't put him in jail. He'll get hurt. That was not the FBI's concern on Wednesday. Their agents were growing angrier by the hour, knowing that Hurley could turn his client in whenever he wanted. Tim Munson, a supervisory special agent for the Bureau in Wilmington, made what amounted to a guarantee on Wednesday night.

"The FBI has been very successful at bringing in fugitives, and I am confident we will do that in this case," he said.

Back in Wyckoff, the neighbors of the families and other residents in town were shell-shocked. They were criticizing the press for overblowing the story, but at the same time some were sitting down with their own children.

"We have this lonely sorrow that this could happen," a lawyer in town, Anthony Benevento, told *The Record* that afternoon. "We pretty much have to accept some of the responsibility—communally. Because this can't be a one-family or two-family alone grief. We're grieving over this."

They were also grieving in Gettysburg. Students there received a campus-wide e-mail from Dean of College Julie Ramsey. It gave no details at all, frustrating the students who were being besieged by reporters.

"We are working closely with everyone involved," was all it said.

Brian's soccer teammates and coaches were distraught. Brian had played his freshman year with enthusiasm and hard work, getting little playing time but not once griping about it.

"He was a real even-keeled kid," said the soccer coach, Dave Wright. "He never let on that there was anything going on in his life that was a problem."

That night, the surrender imminent, Hurley made one more act of just being Joe. Jim Graham, a longtime local photographer and freelancer for the Associated Press, had asked Hurley for permission to shoot a portrait of Brian before he surrendered. Hurley knew the right picture would be splattered on front pages across the country and maybe make prosecutors look like the bad guys for being so hard on such an innocent-looking kid. Hurley told Graham to be at the Holiday Inn, three blocks from the courthouse, on Thursday morning. He made no promises.

**Thursday, November 21**

Graham arrived in the Holiday Inn lobby on King Street and Eighth Street around seven A.M. and sat in one of the lounge chairs in the corner by the window. An hour later Hurley arrived with Brian and his parents, and after brief introductions, the group went up to the roof. Two blocks away, at King and Tenth, was the FBI office that since Saturday had been coordinating the manhunt for Brian.

It was an overcast day, and with a backdrop of drab office buildings, Graham shot several portraits of Brian alone, while his parents stood off to the side. When he fin-

ished, Graham thanked Brian and went to put his gear
away. That's when he looked up and saw the spontaneous,
touching scene that every photographer dreams of captur-
ing. He snapped away the photograph that would appear
around the country. Brian's mother, in a worn-out brown
leather jacket, her graying hair bushy in the back, touched
her hand to her son's left cheek as she fought back tears.
Her red fingernail polish was the brightest color Graham
saw. Brian wrapped his arms around her back and gazed
down into her eyes. Looking like the athletic teenager he
was, he wore blue jeans and sneakers and a blue fleece
zippered jacket over a white T-shirt. A blue Villanova
baseball cap, Hurley's suggestion to make him look more
youthful on television and in print, was pulled tightly over
his short brown hair.

The good-byes done, it was time to surrender.

Outside the courthouse, more than a hundred reporters
and photographers were overflowing the sidewalk. People
arriving for work, or for court appearances, fought their
way through, cursing and shoving. Suddenly, just after
nine-thirty A.M., one reporter spotted Hurley walking up
King Street with Brian and his parents and sprinted
toward them. The mass of reporters, photographers, and
cameramen followed, ignoring pedestrians, and "Don't
Walk" signs, pushing each other out of the way to get as
close as possible. As Brian's mother clutched his arm
from behind him, Brian looked dazed, his blue eyes staring straight ahead. He ignored the questions shouted from
reporters, but his mother could not ignore one yell from a
woman standing on the sidewalk.

"Baby killer, baby killer!"

His mother started to cry.

Another voice shouted: "Brian, you are in my prayers."

Reporters drowned out each other with their questions:
"Brian, why did you do it?"

"Brian, where have you been hiding?"

"Brian, did you kill your baby?"

Tears welled in Brian's eyes. Knocking over newspaper boxes in their path, the reporters clung to every step Brian took. As they neared the One Rodney Square building with the FBI office on the fourth floor, Special Agent Tim Munson broke through the pack.

"FBI! Everybody back!" he shouted. He was clad in a suit, his gun holstered on his belt for everyone to see. When nobody listened, he simply threw bodies out of the way to reach Brian in the middle of the scrum. He grabbed Brian's left shoulder and pulled him along. To the press, Brian was a story. To the FBI, he was a fugitive wanted for murder.

"I want to go with him, I want to go with him," his mother cried out.

The family and Hurley disappeared inside the building. Brian hugged his mother tight, both of them crying.

"Mom, it's okay," Brian told her. "I'm not afraid. I'll be all right. I want you to be all right."

Downstairs, the reporters took a collective deep breath, gathering in small groups to share details from what they had just witnessed. Upstairs on the fourth floor, Brian cried as the FBI fitted him with a bulletproof vest at the request of Hurley, who said he had received threats on Brian's life. When Hurley came back down, the reporters were waiting.

One asked about Brian's clothes, opening the door for Hurley to begin eliciting as much sympathy as he could for his client.

"He's an eighteen-year-old kid who wears a baseball cap, plays soccer, loves God, and loves America."

The spin was on. For the first time Hurley hinted at what would become the critical issue in the defenses of both Amy and Brian.

"There's always an issue in a case like this of when the life started, and when it ended," he said. "Was it a stillborn baby or was it a live-born baby?"

As Hurley was talking, Brian, just as his girlfriend had been three days earlier, was whisked to the Newark Police Department station for fingerprints and mug shots. From there, just like Amy, he was driven to Gander Hill Prison for his bail hearing, in the same packed room she had been in on Monday. When he walked in wearing white prison scrubs marked "DOC" on the back for Department of Correction, and "PT" on the front for pretrial, he, like Amy, looked much younger than his age. Judge Vernon Taylor ordered him held without bail.

An intimidating-looking gray slab of a building surrounded by a chain-link fence, Gander Hill is Delaware's only prison set on a city street. The recreation courtyards are next to the housing units. Worried that a skinny, fresh-faced teenager charged with killing a baby would be in danger in a prison built for 1,200 inmates and holding 1,800, correction officials put Brian in the infirmary, in isolation. Hurley was relieved.

"I told him to be obedient, soft-spoken, and to carry a small stick," he said when asked what advice he had given Brian.

Brian had barely been booked into Gander Hill Prison when Dr. Michael Baden arrived in Wilmington Thursday afternoon from his home in Albany, New York. Formerly the chief medical examiner of New York City, he was recognized as one of the leading medical examiners in the country, participating as an expert for O. J. Simpson in his successful murder defense. Oberly, who had worked with Baden on a case a few months earlier, had called him to perform his own autopsy on the baby, to try to determine a cause of death that contradicted the state's.

He did. The fractures, Baden said, were postmortem. The baby was already dead when they occurred. That directly countered what Sekula-Perlman had ruled in her autopsy: that the baby was born alive, and the fractures were a cause of his death. It was the first of what would be many disagreements over the baby's health between the two opposing teams of doctors in the case.

Brian's first night in prison passed quietly. He ate chicken hot pockets, green beans, salad, peaches, and bread and slept in the infirmary in a private room. It was a privilege prison officials, worried for his safety in the overcrowded jail, felt he needed. Despite being packed, Gander Hill is kept surprisingly clean, its floors waxed regularly by inmates, its walls freshly painted green and white.

The next morning, responding to Hurley's intimation that the baby might have been stillborn, the Delaware Medical Examiner's Office reiterated what it had already said.

"The autopsy showed it was a full-term, healthy baby boy," said Alexis Andrianopoulos, the spokeswoman for the Delaware Department of Health and Human Services. If the baby had been stillborn, she said plainly, the state could obviously not have charged murder. You can't murder what is already dead.

On Thursday night, the town of Newark, and the campus of UD, let out a collective deep breath. For five days news crews had taken over, patrolling the campus in search of the student who knew something, the professor willing to talk, the cop with all the details. Then, suddenly, peace was back. Amy and Brian were in jail, and the satellite news trucks, hovering helicopters, and droves of reporters cleared out. The only sign of the chaos that had been was on the front page of the student newspaper, the *Review*: PETERSON TAKEN INTO CUSTODY.

"There's not much news happening today," said Leo Shane III, the reporter covering the story for the *Review*. "But it's still the topic of discussion in every dorm and at every dinner table."

It was also the topic among talk shows around the country. But the talking had to be done by anyone but those connected to the case. Henry duPont Ridgely, the president judge of the Wilmington Superior Court who had assigned himself the case, had heard enough talk from the lawyers, from Brady and Letang, from Hurley, and from Oberly and Slanina. He imposed a gag order on all of them, hoping to protect any potential jurors who hadn't yet been affected by the coverage.

While Brian sat in isolation, in a twelve-foot-by-twelve-foot cell with only a stainless steel toilet and sink alongside his bed, his former classmates at Gettysburg were still reeling from the news of what had put him there. Help was provided for students, with counselors even visiting some of Brian's classes to let his friends and classmates share their emotions. More than three hundred students and staff attended a vigil at the college chapel, directly next to Brian's dormitory, to help the students cope with his arrest and to pray for his future.

So much had changed in his life, and Amy's, but one thing had not. Just as in high school, they were five miles apart. And they were a couple.

# IN JAIL, IN LOVE

With their children behind bars, Alan and Sonye Grossberg and Brian Peterson Sr. and his ex-wife, Barbara Zuchowski, joined forces for a mutual goal: to get their children out of jail as quickly as possible and back home.

Their lawyers signed what's called a joint defense agreement and set out on their investigation with an agreement to share any information they discovered. Brian and Amy were a couple, and so were their lawyers.

As with any defense investigation, the first priority in this case was to find out what the prosecutors knew. The only way to do that was to follow the state's footprints with the help of their own bloodhound, Michael Leyden, a former FBI agent turned private investigator.

One of the first things Slanina had Leyden do was to watch the trash be thrown out from the Mother's Kitchen Diner. Slanina wanted to know what time it got tossed, how big the bags were, what was in the bags, how they landed in the Dumpster, everything that prosecutors were studying. Slanina knew, just as Letang knew, that not saving the trash from the Dumpster had been a big mistake. It would allow the defense lawyers to raise the question that the baby's skull fractures were caused by something landing on his head in the Dumpster.

Leyden and Slanina went together to Amy's dormitory

room, a spot police detectives had already scoured. Not only did Slanina want to know what Letang had, he wanted to know what Letang believed was important. On campus, and by telephone, Slanina called dozens of students, hoping to catch them before they left for winter break. He asked about Amy, about how often they saw Brian, and about her pregnancy.

Amy and Brian were still a couple, and their lawyers were hoping they stayed that way. It was a critical point of their defense strategy. The vision of the lawyers was for Amy and Brian to stay tight, walk into trial arm in arm, throw themselves on the court's mercy with their innocent faces, claim that the baby appeared to be dead, and almost dare a jury to throw them in jail. They had taken every step of the pregnancy together, and in their lawyers' eyes there was not one convincing reason to split them up now from one case into two.

It was without question more risky for Amy to stay with Brian than for Brian to stay with Amy. Brian had admitted taking a baby and throwing him in the trash. Amy had said nothing damaging, and the seizures she had suffered after giving birth clearly made her the more sympathetic of the two. Amy's irregular periods would allow her lawyers to argue that she was never quite sure she was pregnant until it was too late to do anything about it and that instead she believed she had suffered a miscarriage in the room. Brian's statement to police would hurt him, and as long as Amy was his co-defendant it would hurt her as well. Still, her lawyers were confident that the benefits of presenting jurors with a scared young couple outweighed the good that might come from splitting with Brian and blaming him for the baby's death.

At Ramapo High School, at high schools around the country, Thanksgiving is a reunion, the first time the last graduating class is back home together after three months at college. The football game at Ramapo is an annual frenzy of students hugging and screaming as they catch up on girlfriends, boyfriends, fraternities, sororities, classes, and campuses.

But when the Ramapo Class of 1996 returned home in late November from college, they were a subdued bunch. Two of their friends were in jail, facing the death penalty for allegedly killing their baby, a baby Amy had been carrying right in front of them in the spring and summer. Now they were thinking back. Had there been a clue that she was pregnant? Their parents had told them about the arrests while they were still at college, but really all they had to do was watch their evening news or read *Time* or *Newsweek,* or almost any newspaper, and there was that smiling yearbook picture of Brian and Amy from the Senior Holiday Ball.

Thanksgiving weekend was to have been the end for Amy and Brian. She would go home, her family would take one look at her puffy cheeks, her obviously swollen belly, wrists, and ankles, and she would break down. Brian could have then told his parents, and all the pressure that had been tearing them up inside since the spring, all the lies and pretending, would have been released like a rush of air from a balloon.

The problem was they miscalculated. Amy was pregnant by early March and full term by November. They had pegged April as the month she began missing her period and were confident she would make it to Thanksgiving. She didn't, and they ate their turkey, stuffing, and cranberry sauce alone, in their cells, five miles apart from each other, 150 miles from their families. College was a world away. They went to bed with the nightmare of being strapped down and put to sleep forever by lethal injection.

In the first few weeks after the arrests, Wyckoff residents were reeling. Opinions on what to do with Amy and Brian ran the gamut, from those who wanted their heads to those who wanted them released for making an error in judgment. Good kids who did a bad thing.

The gossip started flowing quickly in Wyckoff, and

Amy's mother was the frequent target. Brian was more of an outsider to many, except his friends. He hadn't grown up in town, his family had no roots there, his mother was hardly known. But people who knew Amy's family began murmuring that while she was a sweet girl, Amy was always a little snobbish, never shy about mentioning her maid. And her mother was selfish and extremely image conscious, the rumors went. That would explain a lot, the people said, believing they had found the simple answer to the most complex of crimes.

They were more eager to look for a way to explain Amy and Brian as an anomaly, a fluke, anxious to ignore the possibility that other teenagers in Wyckoff might be feeling the same pressures they had. Accepting the smaller picture would be much easier than confronting the bigger one.

Everyone was hoping for a trial, to learn what really happened. They would have to wait. And wait. And listen as tempers flared, stories changed, and lawyers quit. The end was not an hour away, as it is on those television legal dramas.

The occasional television news truck or newspaper reporter continued to pass through town every so often in the weeks after the arrests, looking for a reaction to each development. That only angered parents more. Their children, particularly the high schoolers, were upset, and many of the parents were unsure how to handle them. Ramapo was quiet as Christmas break approached for students. Parents were debating whether they should confront their children, remind them that there was no reason ever to keep such a huge secret from them. Many did, sitting down with their children for heart-to-heart talks. Plenty didn't. Maybe it wasn't necessary. *My children know better.*

"I know in my family there has been a lot more communication since this began," said Katrin Ramsey, a parent in Wyckoff who came to know Brian through the soccer league in town. "Other parents have said the same thing."

Mucciolo, the Ramapo principal, was struggling with

the story just as parents were, and he wanted to help them. He spoke with Brian's mother and Amy's parents and asked their permission to hold a sort of rap session for their classmates, to let them vent their emotions and cry with friends if that's what they wanted. The families agreed.

Through the clergy and parents in town, he spread the word that before the football game at ten A.M. on Friday, November 29, the classmates of Amy and Brian were welcome at the school to just talk. They jumped at the chance. More than one hundred students showed up starting at eight-thirty A.M.

"I know you're all aware of what's happened," he told them. "We know the media is having a field day with this."

He told them what he could, the facts as he knew them, and that professional counselors were there to help them cope, along with clergy from most of the churches and temples in the area. But the students were most interested in talking among themselves, and they did for almost two hours. They prayed for their classmates, a few of them crying, and huddled in small groups.

Nobody, meanwhile, had given a passing thought to the tiny body still lying unclaimed in the downtown Wilmington morgue, identified only as Baby Boy Grossberg-Peterson. Most murders have a victim and a family crying out for justice. But the only people crying out for this victim were complete strangers from around the country, bombarding newspapers with letters to the editor, calling the talk radio programs, demanding to know how two teenagers could have been so plain stupid. Why not leave the baby on a church doorstep? Near a hospital? Anywhere he could have been found and cared for by someone who wanted him?

Prosecutors were less interested in what Amy and Brian did not do and more concerned with what they did.

On December 9, 1996, one year to the day after Brian and Amy had danced and laughed the night away at their Senior Holiday Ball, their futures so bright, Letang walked the two blocks from his office in downtown Wilmington to the courthouse on King Street.

Occupying the entire block on King Street between 10th and 11th Streets, the Daniel J. Herrmann Courthouse is an eighty-year-old block of stone gray granite, three floors aboveground, two floors below. Its nine pillars in front tower over the steps leading up to the front door at the right corner. Across the street, a bus stop always attracts a crowd, as does the small park on a beautiful spring day.

The courthouse is the anchor of the city, the magnet to which everyone seems drawn for one reason or another, to file lawsuits, accompany loved ones to court, meet an attorney for lunch. Come five P.M. the courthouse closes, and so, it seems, does the rest of downtown Wilmington, except for a few restaurants. From bustling business district to virtual ghost town with the simple locking of two glass doors. During the day lawyers come and go from the courthouse, most within walking distance of their offices. The pedestrians who stroll in and out, through the metal detector, are usually there to support a friend or relative in court or pay a fine. But some people walk in free and walk out in handcuffs.

Letang entered the courthouse on this Monday, as he often did, through the private doorway for employees in the rear. He knew a swarm of reporters, photographers, and television cameramen was waiting in front to catch a glimpse of him and thrust a microphone in his face, and he wasn't in the mood.

After a brief stop at the office he kept in the courthouse basement, he took the elevator up to the third floor, the grand jury room. What he wanted, an indictment, didn't take long. Steve Fox had walked unnoticed in the front door of the courthouse, past the slew of reporters there, who had no idea he was the lead detective. Upstairs, behind a sealed door, Fox addressed the grand jurors like a college professor lecturing his students and outlined the facts of the case, from the secret pregnancy, to the discovery of the baby in the trash, to the arrests. It took four hours, and at day's end the grand jury handed up the indictment.

"Murder in the first degree: Amy S. Grossberg and Brian C. Peterson Jr., on or about the 12th day of November 1996 in the County of New Castle, State of Delaware, did intentionally cause the death of the newborn baby boy of the defendant Grossberg and of the defendant Peterson." The punishment is life in prison or, if the prosecution so chooses, death.

"Murder by abuse or neglect in the first degree: Amy S. Grossberg and Brian C. Peterson Jr., on or about the 12th day of November 1996 in the County of New Castle, State of Delaware, did recklessly cause the death of the newborn baby boy and had engaged in an act of abuse or neglect of the baby." The punishment is fifteen years to life.

Everyone had anticipated the first charge, intentional murder, but the second one, the abuse claim, caught the defense attorneys by surprise. The statute had been introduced in 1994, when Oberly was the attorney general, to address cases of babies killed by extreme shaking—in which the intent is not to murder, but death is caused by a person's reckless act.

"It gives them two arrows in the quiver, one theory which is harder to pursue and one which is easier," Hurley explained. "It relaxes the burden on the prosecution because even if they can't prove intention, they can still establish a reckless state of mind."

As inseparable as they were in high school, Amy and Brian were reunited on the indictment. It listed them by their new identities. Brian was 9611007811. Amy was 9611007818. Hours after learning of the indictment, Amy was released from the infirmary of her prison into the maximum-security wing, joining sixteen other inmates charged with varying degrees of violent crimes. Wyckoff was a world away.

Their first three weeks in jail passed quickly. Their attorneys had talked with Letang about possible plea bargains with both of them. But as soon as they said they were looking for no jail time, Letang stopped listening. Out of the question. See you at trial.

"They are going to jail," he told the lawyers.

It had been almost four weeks since Amy and Brian had last seen each other, since Brian had left Amy at college. They missed each other desperately. They had never gone that long in their relationship without contact. Their parents visited every weekend, often staying longer than the allotted one-hour time limit for most visitors.

Harlan Giles, a Pittsburgh doctor, met with Amy and Brian at their respective prisons on December 12. Giles had been hired by Oberly even though he had never worked a criminal case. At first he'd declined. He had heard about the case. It was murder, not his game. But Oberly pressed him, insisting the story was not as it seemed. Giles flew to Philadelphia and met with Oberly, who took him to meet Amy first and then Brian.

From his interviews, Giles would form a picture of Amy and Brian that could probably have applied to almost any upper-middle-class family in affluent America.

"This case illustrates two kids who are on a high career program who would never want to disappoint very animated parents who are extremely ambitious," he said. "The parents are high achievers, very bright, and they wanted the moon for their children."

Amy was quiet and subdued when Giles met with her in the small, well-lit visitors' room, with blue carpeting and a dozen tables. Giles noticed immediately that she was still swollen all over, a common condition of women who have eclamptic births. She told him she could not have been far enough along to have a full-term baby because she had been bleeding when she saw her doctor in July and the doctor had told her she wasn't pregnant.

Because she'd told her doctor she was having her period on that day, and worn a feminine pad as proof, the doctor had taken her word and never questioned her.

"That's all it takes for a teenager who doesn't want to

be pregnant to convince herself that she isn't at that point," Giles recalled some months later.

He left Amy, feeling confident that Oberly was right: this was not premeditated murder. There was no plan, no intent. His meeting with Brian did nothing to change his mind. He found Brian to be immature emotionally for his age, and while extremely bright, he was medically naive.

"He didn't understand the symptoms of pregnancy," Giles recalled. "Their stories jibed. They both told me the same thing. It was totally believable. He said he would wait until Amy told her parents, and they would do it at the same time over Thanksgiving break."

Giles said Amy and Brian were extremely afraid of the "ramifications and repercussions, and of hearing their parents say, 'This won't do. You can't do this. We're paying for college, and your whole life is ahead of you.'"

Instead of paying for college, their parents were now financing their children's defense. Sparing no expense, Brian's family hired a second attorney to join Hurley, and he would quickly take over their case. He was recommended to them by Brian's uncle, Ted Will.

Certain attorneys have a presence when they stand and talk. They are not the tallest, the loudest, the most clever, or the most sharply dressed. They have an intangible appeal, and the fifty-three-year-old Jack Litman has it, managing to tightrope-walk that line between confidence and arrogance. His posture is perfectly erect, his broad shoulders forming a straight line across his neck. His baritone voice is easily understood in any courtroom, and when he talks he rests his hands firmly on the podium and eyes the judge squarely through his glasses.

None of that is what earned him his reputation as a fierce defense lawyer in New York City's criminal courts and an expert in forensic evidence. What led Brian's family to hire his firm, Litman, Asche, & Gioiella, was his success, his brilliant defense tactics, and his devotion to each case and each client he takes. His clients, and his peers, praise him. Victims' rights groups, particularly feminists, are less fond. A glance at his client list—many of his cases become front-page fodder for the New York tabloids—explains why.

Robert Chambers, the so-called Preppie Killer, was charged with the 1986 slaying in Central Park of eighteen-year-old Jennifer Levin. A hung jury led to a plea bargain and a reduced charge of manslaughter. Richard Herrin, a twentysomething Yale graduate, crushed the head of his girlfriend with a hammer while she slept in her parents' home in posh Scarsdale, New York, in 1977. Facing life in prison if convicted of murder, he was instead convicted only of manslaughter when Litman convinced the jury that Herrin had been jilted and his act had been the result of extreme emotional disturbance. Herrin served eight years in prison.

In both cases involving handsome, privileged young men, Litman, the former deputy chief of the homicide bureau in the Manhattan District Attorney's Office, focused as much on his clients' alleged victims as on his clients. It became his modus operandi, somehow finding ways for jurors to look at the victim as more than an inno-cent bystander without actually blaming the victim out-right.

That was impossible with Brian Peterson.

Brian's victim was a defenseless, vulnerable, six-pound-two-ounce baby boy born in secrecy in a motel room. The public was already expressing outrage with Brian and Amy and sorrow for their infant, so their lawyers knew they had to deflect attention from the teenagers. They also knew the only two people who could say for certain what condition the baby was in when he was born were Amy and Brian. And they were a couple.

Everyone else would be guessing and speculating, based on their examination of the body. As long as Brian and Amy stuck with the story that the baby appeared to be blue and maybe even dead when it came out, prosecutors would have to prove otherwise beyond a reasonable doubt if they wanted to convict them of murder.

What caused the baby's head injuries was the one question Steve Fox knew he would probably never answer. He was determined to make it the only question he could not answer. When he wasn't at work, he was investigating the case on his own time, tracking down any shred of evidence he could find. Piece by piece he put together a timeline of what happened when. He was like a sponge, soaking up as much information as he could. He spent hours flipping through books at the University of Delaware library, reading about neonaticide and what would drive a young woman to commit such an unthinkable crime. This case angered him. He'd had nothing handed to him as a child, and his annual salary as a cop was the equivalent of the cost of some of the cars that parents in Wyckoff simply gave their children. This case made no sense to him. But the evidence, some one hundred pieces, was coming together.

With receipts that police had found in Brian's car and Amy's dormitory room, he knew that Brian got gas at 1:00 A.M. before he picked up Amy, that he had his car washed at 11:28 A.M. on the morning after the birth, and that Amy went to CVS that afternoon. Thanks to a subpoena that enabled him to access Amy's records at the university, he learned that she had been to the library thirty minutes after stopping at the drugstore. He was curious to see if she had checked out any books recently on babies or giving birth, but she had not. After talking to students, he knew she had attended her twelve-thirty P.M. and four P.M. classes the day she'd given birth.

At home he spent hours on the Internet, searching for every article written on the case. When he saw a story that mentioned a student who had been interviewed, he found and questioned the student himself. But by far his most interesting reading was the stack of cards and letters, mailed by Amy, that police had taken from Brian's dormitory room. None were found in Amy's room from Brian. Each note to Brian was almost a mirror image of the previous one, apologizing, venting, crying, praying. What amazed Fox was that the reading he had done at the library told him that girls who commit neonaticide typically deny their pregnancy to themselves. Amy, as her letters showed him, clearly hadn't done that.

"She was dumping everything onto Brian," Fox said months after the case. "She's not denying that she's pregnant. She's acknowledging she's pregnant and saying that it's the worst thing that could happen to her."

A small army of a dozen suits crowded into the basement morgue of the Children's Hospital of Philadelphia on the morning of December 13, 1996. They came from around the country to watch a brain almost the size of a softball be removed from a plastic container filled with a clear solution of formaldehyde and methanol, placed gently onto a ten-foot-long stainless-steel table, and sectioned with what looked like a household bread knife.

It was, in the scope of the case, pivotal, with the two sides aligning like opponents on a football field, staking out their positions and digging in for battle.

Prosecutors, based on Sekula-Perlman's findings, had said this baby was born alive and full-term and died from any of four factors: head trauma, shaking, asphyxia, or hypothermia. The defense, buoyed by Brian's claim that the baby "looked blue," was intent on showing that the baby was in fact stillborn, or at least appeared to be stillborn, which, they would then argue, would explain why Brian did what he did.

Letang and his co-prosecutor, Paul Wallace, were at the sectioning, and so were Litman and Oberly, as well as two of the medical experts they had hired, Baden from New York and Dr. Jan Leestma, a renowned Chicago neuropathologist, whose late arrival delayed the sectioning by about half an hour. Sekula-Perlman was there, along with her boss, Richard Callery, and the medical examiner investigator, Rick Pretzler. Steve Fox was there, too, in his capacity as the lead police detective on the case. There was not much room in the tiny, windowless morgue.

"We wanted to see what the brain looked like," Leestma said of the defense experts. "The allegation is it had been traumatized or beaten to death, and we wanted to look for reflections of that. Is there blood or injury?"

Holding the cutting knife on this Friday was Dr. Lucy Rorke, acting chief of pathology at the Children's Hospital of Philadelphia and one of the experts hired by prosecutors to support their claim that the baby was born alive and healthy and was murdered. A short and silver-haired spark plug of a woman, she had taught Sekula-Perlman much of what she knew and was respected by both the defense and prosecution. Sekula-Perlman, Rorke had told prosecutors, was one of her best students.

As Rorke started cutting, Litman began sketching the shape and direction of the skull fractures on a small notepad he pulled from his pocket. Some gentle pushing and shoving began among the doctors watching so they could get a clear view of the brain. After Rorke's third slice, she paused and pointed toward a spot in the brain.

"Look at that," she said to her audience. "There is a malformation."

She pointed with her knife to an empty space in the brain at a spot where there was not supposed to be a space. As Rorke leaned in close, so did the cluster of doctors and lawyers around her, everyone trying to get an up-close look at what was obviously not a perfectly normal, healthy brain. Everyone agreed that what they were looking at was a cleft on the right side of the brain. A smaller cleft on the left side would be found later. To a layman, the clefts look like an extra fold. But to doctors it's an obvious, rare, and serious congenital brain defect called schizencephaly.

It strikes fewer than one in every ten thousand newborns and usually begins forming in the first twelve weeks of a pregnancy. As a person born with it develops, schizencephaly can cause developmental delays, seizures, delayed speech and language skills, and vision and eating disorders. Many people born with the defect have normal intelligence, while others suffer mental retardation, partial or complete paralysis, and reduced muscle tone. Exactly what causes schizencephaly has remained a mystery, though some doctors suspect that an in utero stroke may be responsible.

Leestma leaned in close next to Rorke and nodded his head to her, acknowledging the clefts and letting her continue. Rorke would tell the prosecution that the brain defect was absolutely not life threatening, had nothing to do with the infant's death, and may not have even been noticeable until the child started to walk. But the defense would counter that while the schizencephaly may not have caused the baby's death, it was a significant factor in why the baby appeared to be blue.

It would be the first of half a dozen debates over the infant's health that the two sides would engage in over the coming months, as the defense lawyers sought to punch holes in the autopsy findings and show that all Brian did was dispose of what he believed was a dead baby.

On the skull fractures, Sekula-Perlman refused to waver in her belief that the head injuries were intentionally inflicted by repeated blows to the top of the head. Dr. Mary Case, the chief medical examiner in St. Louis and one of the country's leading authorities on head injuries, was hired by prosecutors soon after the autopsy and given every photograph, every shred of documentation on the baby's health and injuries. She supported Sekula-Perlman's claim that the fractures occurred before the baby was thrown into the Dumpster and were not caused by that toss.

"I've seen lots of injuries from babies that were thrown into Dumpsters," Case would say later. "None of them had injuries like this baby."

But Leestma and Baden, the defense doctors, argued that because they saw no blood in the fracture lines of the skull, the fractures had to be postmortem. And because they were on top of the head instead of the back, front, or side, the more typical sites for inflicted head injuries, it was more likely they had occurred either during the toss into the Dumpster or while lying in the Dumpster upside down for twenty-four hours, head down and feet up.

"There is a skull fracture, but no mass of blood in it," Leestma would say. "If this had occurred in life, the massive nature of this would have caused clotting in the brain. It's impossible that the baby cried. Not with the brain problems this baby had."

As for the baby's lungs, in her autopsy Sekula-Perlman found the lungs and bowels to have healthy amounts of air, both signs that the baby breathed.

Again, Leestma and Baden disagreed. They said the presence of air in the lungs did not prove that the baby breathed and disputed Sekula-Perlman's claim that they were well aerated. They said the air in the organs came from simple elastic expansion of the chest during the precipitous delivery of the baby and did not require life to be present.

The battle lines were drawn. It no longer was simply a war over the guilt or innocence of Amy and Brian. It was now just as much about the health of their baby, exactly what the defense lawyers wanted.

With their new medical evidence in hand, the defense attorneys set out on their next mission: to collect as much background on Sekula-Perlman in an attempt to discredit her and, ultimately, her autopsy. They started looking at her past cases, including a completely different case in which a mother was shot while nine months pregnant. They explored why Sekula-Perlman had never become board certified by the American Board of Pathology. They found critics of her and they found supporters, but Sekula-Perlman, married to a Philadelphia lawyer, shrugged it off. She was confident in herself, her findings, and most important, her pictures of the fractures. She was itching to show those pictures to a jury.

In an e-mail to Paul Wallace, the co-prosecutor working with Letang because of his expertise in child abuse cases, she wrote: "It is my opinion that: Baby boy Gross-

berg was a full-term, live-born infant. Baby boy Grossberg lived a separate existence from his mother. Baby boy
Grossberg died as a result of a combination of blunt force
cranio-cerebral trauma, shaking, asphyxia, and hypothermia. Baby boy Grossberg's birth anomaly did not con-
tribute in any way to his death."

The first chance for prosecutors and defense attorneys
to air their differences publicly was coming next.

Seeing the judge in Courtroom 301 is easy from every
angle, every corner, every one of the ninety-six seats in
the six rows of dark oak benches. Hearing the judge is not
so simple. The acoustics are horrible. Voices bounce
around the room like pinballs, echoing off the high ceiling. Sunlight beams in from small arched windows up by
the ceiling. The heavy doors at the back of the courtroom
squeak just loudly enough for everyone to hear someone
walk in during a hearing. Judges hate that. Every head
turns toward the door.

When all the lawyers and parties are ready, a bell
sounds and the judge walks briskly through a door in the
rear left corner and straight to the leather chair behind the
bench. From there the judge looks down on everyone, and
everyone looks up at the judge, leaving no room for doubt
as to who's in charge.

Henry duPont Ridgely makes sure of it. A Delaware
native, the president judge of the superior court in Dover
and Wilmington since 1990 and the father of two teenage
boys, Ridgely runs his courtroom with a firm hand. He
gives lawyers enough slack to let them flash their flamboyance but is known to rein them in when they start talking just to hear themselves speak. When opposing lawyers
get snippy with each other, in court or in briefs they file
with him, he's quick to cut them off and remind them to
focus on the case. Boyish looking at forty-seven years old,
with neatly parted graying hair and glasses, Ridgely looks
the part, a former attorney for the state senate, turned
judge. He has no connection to the du Pont family of the

chemical fortunes. But relation or not, the name alone carries a certain weight in Delaware.

Arraignments are usually the most boring of all proceedings in court. Defendants almost always plead not guilty, and bail is either set or not set. Five minutes, in and out. But on December 17 reporters from the smallest newspapers and radio stations in Delaware to *The New York Times* and every national television and cable network swarmed the steps of the courthouse in Wilmington. No one expected to learn much. They were there not to see how Amy and Brian pleaded, but simply to see them. Together. For the first time since their arrests.

It was the titillating side of the case. The love-struck teenagers from the affluent New Jersey suburb. So much attention focused on them and their relationship that the reason for their court appearance became secondary. The question of the case had shifted from "Did they kill their baby?" to "Were they still dating?"

They arrived separately, half an hour apart, through a back entrance for prison inmates. Amy wore a bulletproof vest. The courtroom was packed with reporters, except for the front row, which was reserved for the families. Amy's parents sat with Sonye's sister, Andrea Grayson, and next to Brian's parents and his stepfather. They were in it together, or so it seemed.

All eyes focused on the door from the judge's chambers through which Amy and Brian would walk into the room. Brian entered first, in gray corduroys, a white dress shirt, and a blue tie. He sat quietly at the long table to the far right and joined everyone in watching the door for Amy. She came in seconds later, wearing a black business suit, her protective vest gone. She sat at the same table, on the left side of Kathleen Jennings, while Brian sat to Jennings's right.

"How are you?" Brian said softly to Amy.

"Fine," she mouthed back to him.

Whispers filled the courtroom until the ringing bell startled everyone.

"All rise," the bailiff belted out, and in walked Ridgely in his black robe. He sat behind his long table, on which sat a small lamp with a green glass shade that softly lit the judge's face. Over his right shoulder hung a massive portrait of Albert J. Stiftel, the prior superior court president judge.

Hurley stood first and made a motion to enter the two newest attorneys for Brian's defense into the Delaware courts. Ridgely welcomed Litman and his partner in his New York City firm, Russell Gioiella. Lanky, with long hair and a nasally voice, Gioiella was less rigid and more friendly than Litman.

Litman's entry to Brian's defense had immediately worried Amy's parents. He was a high-powered New York City lawyer, and they worried that their lawyers, even though they were among Delaware's finest and Oberly was a former state attorney general, would stand in awe of Litman. Oberly knew Delaware's judges better than anyone, he had been the boss to the prosecution team for years, and he was known as a tireless worker. Even Hurley, Delaware's top criminal defense attorney who had been with Brian throughout his surrender, saw Litman's presence as a sign that Brian's family lacked total confidence in him.

"The mentality of the folks in the New York area is that if it's any good, it's in New York," he said. "They think of Delaware as a backwoods province."

At the arraignment, after Litman and Oberly said their clients pleaded not guilty to the murder charges and requested bail, which Ridgely denied, Litman dropped the first of many bombs on the courtroom, outlining what would become the meat of the case.

"Neither Amy nor Brian intended to cause, or in fact did cause, any harm to the deceased infant, let alone did they kill the deceased, as the prosecution alleges," Litman told Ridgely and the packed courtroom. "You will hear, Your Honor, that the viability of the infant, which the prosecution must prove at trial was a viable child, independent of the mother, is a critical issue, as is both Amy's and Brian's state of mind with respect to that viability. Your Honor, there has already been developed incontrovertible proof that the infant had congenital brain damage, damage to the brain that occurred months before the baby came into the world, that seriously compromised the viability of that infant. And you will also hear that there will be incontrovertible proof as well that the mother, at the time of the birthing, had serious medical problems which imperiled the viability of the child as well, the viability outside and independent of the mother's support."

The entire courtroom seemed to take a collective gasp. It was the first public statement about the health of the baby. The defense strategy was under way: Humanize the defendants, dehumanize the victim so that it doesn't appear to be murder anymore, only the disposal of what looked like a dead baby. The baby was brain damaged. Not viable. Incapable of living outside Amy's womb. And Amy's health had hurt her baby.

Litman also began his calculated attack on how prosecutors and the medical examiner's office had handled the autopsy and, in his mind, rushed to release a judgment on how the baby died. Litman made a motion asking the state to release the exact time and cause of the baby's death, not simply that the baby was born alive and killed by blunt force trauma. He waved in the air the press release the medical examiner had given out the day after the autopsy.

"When they issue a press release the day after they did their autopsy and the prosecution doesn't want to tell us they stand by this opinion, something is not right," Oberly said. "We think we are entitled—we are not asking for the evidence or the manner in which, for example, they stand by this opinion, the fractures occurred, whether it was done with a baseball bat, a sledgehammer, or grasping and throwing. We're not asking for the manner. We're not asking for their evidence with respect to the issue, but we are asking, what is the cause of death?"

"Mr. Letang," said Ridgely, turning to the prosecution

table. Letang quickly saw where the defense lawyers were going with their argument. He had seen the baby and the skull fractures. But he also knew about the brain damage and the further tests being done on the brain.

Prosecutors would eventually stand by their story. So would Sekula-Perlman. The cause of death, as Perlman had said from the first day, was multiple skull fractures, linear and depressed, with epidural, subdural, and sub-arachnoid hemorrhages, as well as hypothermia and asphyxia. Schizencephaly was present but was not a factor in the baby's death. But before Letang said that, he wanted to wait.

"My first thought in dealing with this is that it is pre-mature," he said. "Because we do not have the investiga-tive work through the medical examiner completed yet. So if they want the medical examiner's office to opine now, where the work is not yet completed, I think that is unfair. My first request would be, let's postpone this and revisit this, if needed, after all the discovery is completed."

Litman had no desire to be patient. He continued to wave the press release from the medical examiner and demanded to be told if the prosecution was standing behind that release, which said the baby died from multi-ple skull fractures caused by blunt force trauma and shak-ing.

"Why do you need it again, Mr. Litman, if it's already in writing?" the judge asked.

"Because they don't want to tell us, in fact, if this is what they're doing or if they want to change it," Litman answered. "That's the entire point of this. We want to know if Dr. Perlman is in the process of changing her opinion, or whether or not they wish to stand by it. We're not asking for how the skull fractures occurred. We're ask-ing for the cause of death."

Oberly and Litman were beginning their attack. Their investigation into the background of Sekula-Perlman, who performed the autopsy, had shown her to be a vulnerable witness. A graduate of the Medical College of Pennsylvania, she had performed dozens of autopsies but was not certified by the widely recognized American Board of Pathology, to which more than 90 percent of pathologists go for certification. Litman and Oberly were confident they could match their experts, some of the leading forensics authorities in the country, against Sekula-Perlman, and jurors would have no struggle deciding who was more credible.

Before sitting down, Oberly made one more request. He asked for something he knew prosecutors could not give him: an inventory of the items in the trash Dumpster. His friend Letang could say nothing. There was no inventory. The trash was long gone. If the state was going to argue that the injuries to the baby's head occurred before Brian tossed him in the Dumpster, or during the toss, and were not caused by a heavy box or can or battery landing on top of the body, it would be difficult. They would have to rely on the testimony of the officers who had sifted through the trash, and Letang knew the defense attorneys would question why they had failed to preserve the trash.

The arraignment took ninety minutes, ending with Ridgely setting January 21, 1997, as the date to hear arguments regarding whether prosecutors had enough evidence to continue holding Amy and Brian without bail. He also set September 9 as the trial date. When the judge slammed his gavel, Amy and Brian turned and waved to their crying families in the front row. Then they turned to each other, and Amy, her nose red, mouthed, "I love you," to Brian as they touched hands briefly.

Outside the courthouse, Litman stepped up to a bank of microphones and repeated for the television cameras what he had said inside. He questioned the state's autopsy finding that the baby was healthy and died from shaking and multiple skull fractures caused by blunt trauma.

"There is incontrovertible proof that the baby suffered congenital brain damage months before it came into the world," he said.

The gag order had limited the attorneys from elaborating, which forced the reporters to seek outside analysis from attorneys who had been following the case but were not connected to it. Jerome Capone, a Wilmington attorney who became a media favorite for legal comments because of his experience in capital murder cases, immediately said the defense lawyers were walking a fine line with their argument that the baby was brain damaged.

"They better be very careful," he said that afternoon. "You don't have the right to kill a baby just because it's brain damaged."

What no one knew was how the two teenagers could have been sure the baby had brain damage in the few seconds before the body was left in the trash. Does a brain-damaged baby look any different from a normal, healthy baby at first glance? People were skeptical.

One question had been answered, though. Amy and Brian were still in love. Their lawyers were working together, and the teenagers were still close. They could not talk with each other from their respective prisons, but from their appearances in court, it was obvious their feelings still ran deep.

As the media and the public tried to make sense of the day's events, no one, including Amy and Brian as they were returned to their cells, had any hint of the arrangements being made for a small ceremony that would take place the next day.

Route 22 in Union, New Jersey, is no different from South College Avenue in Newark, Delaware, except that it's miles longer and the cars zip twice as fast. More fast food, more neon lights, more traffic, more ugliness. Off Exit 140 of the Garden State Parkway half an hour south of Wyckoff, it's a town, and a road, Amy and Brian probably never had a reason to see. Union and Wyckoff could not be more different.

The sign for Temple B'Nai Abraham Memorial Park is nestled among a growth of bushes along the eastbound side of Route 22. The cemetery almost seems out of place, hidden between strip malls along one of the busiest roads in Union County. Drivers taking the turn to enter the park are suddenly thrust into peace and beauty, where a dense forest of trees provides a soft blanket of shadows over the plush green grass and endless rows of gravestones.

On the afternoon of December 18, with his parents in jail and his grandparents at home in Wyckoff, Baby Boy Grossberg-Peterson was laid to rest there, thirty-six days after he was born in a motel room, thirty-five days after his body was found in a Dumpster. There was a death certificate, but no birth certificate since the baby had never seen a hospital.

No one had claimed the body for two weeks, and when Amy's parents finally did, it could not be released until all tests were completed. It sat in the thirty-eight-degree refrigerator in the downtown Wilmington morgue for another two weeks. The arrangements were finally made by their lawyers. The lawyers chose the funeral home. The lawyers chose the burial site, a Jewish cemetery.

Under Jewish tradition, a child is not named until its circumcision a week after birth and is not considered viable until it is thirty days old, which is why some families of stillborns choose not to name their babies.

The only people at the funeral of Baby Boy Grossberg-Peterson were from Krienen-Griffith Funeral Home in Elsmere, Delaware. It was the home the lawyers chose to handle the arrangements, and because no one had contacted him about a casket, Bill Krienen, the owner of the funeral home, had to arrange for one to be donated.

He and a small team from his home drove the tiny casket to New Jersey and buried it among dozens of other stones, all with names. Krienen performed a brief ceremony, reciting a generic prayer appropriate for any faith. When they left, the burial site was marked by a metal stick a foot high with a white piece of paper at the top and the name "Baby Boy Grossberg-Peterson" written in black ink. Jewish families typically unveil a gravestone a year after a death.

"It was long overdue," Slanina, Amy's attorney, said of the burial.

The holidays passed quietly for Amy and Brian. So did the twenty-sixth wedding anniversary of Amy's parents on Christmas Eve. At the women's prison, a local choir was let in to sing and Christmas trees were decorated. With only one Jewish prisoner, nothing was done for Hanukkah. A group called Prison Fellowship visited the inmates with cookies, punch, and candy and provided gifts to the children of the inmates. At Gander Hill Prison, no decorations were hung out of concern for fire and safety. A local band played a concert on Christmas.

Amy's parents, and Brian's, were struggling to cope. Their lawyers were working overtime to get their children out of jail at the January 21 hearing, but with the holidays approaching, the Petersons, and particularly the Grossbergs, were distraught. They were allowed one visit a week for one hour. But Sonye also found herself driving to Delaware just to stand outside Amy's prison, where her daughter could see her through her small window. Even though she couldn't see Amy, it gave her comfort to know her daughter was seeing a familiar face.

Amy hated the prison food but managed to make a few allies. Not friends, but at least women who would talk to her without calling her names. She helped some of the prisoners make rope bracelets for themselves and their family members. Amy made one for each of her parents and put on as strong a face as she could around the inmates. She was allowed only two calls a day, and her lawyers visited her at least once every day, sometimes twice, at her parents' orders.

On New Year's Day the defense lawyers got a belated, but much welcomed, holiday gift from prosecutors. They were handed all of the state's evidence, from police reports to warrant applications to room search results, and nowhere could they find exactly where and when Brian said the baby was alive when it was born, as Moore had put in his report and Agnor in his. It was not in the transcript of Brian's interview with Wilson.

"We don't think he said it," acknowledged one Delaware police official.

Brian's lawyers had suspected as much. And they were right. If Brian had said the baby was alive, their entire defense strategy crashed.

They were now clear to argue that the baby either was stillborn, or appeared to be stillborn, and that Brian simply panicked with what he thought was a dead baby. At worst, the lawyers believed, it was criminally negligent homicide. At best, it was desecration of a corpse, a gruesome charge, but a misdemeanor, and Brian and Amy could walk away unscathed. Their lawyers could not wait for January 21, when they hoped to get a glimpse of the state's case against Amy and Brian and, more important to the families, get the children home.

# FREE

After his frantic first night on the case, which ended with the discovery of the baby, followed by a week of building enough of a case to arrest Amy and Brian, Steve Fox had come to accept that this case would consume his days and nights.

On January 15 he and Bob Agnor, the detective who had searched Amy's dormitory room, loaded up a police cruiser with the bed and faucet from the Comfort Inn motel room, two pairs of Amy's underwear, the three towels that were in the bag with the baby, and the plastic bag itself. They drove two hours south on Route 95 to the FBI crime lab in Washington to have everything tested for DNA.

They did not expect to find Brian's DNA anywhere, and they didn't. But scientists did find something curious on one of the towels, the towel Brian had used to wipe up the spurting blood from the torn umbilical cord after he'd tried to move the baby. Along with finding Amy's blood on it, as expected, scientists found traces of the baby's DNA. Fox could not think of one reason why the baby's DNA would be on a towel unless the baby had bled or the fluid from the cord was the baby's. Either way, he knew the presence of the baby's DNA would hurt the defense argument that the baby was stillborn. Stillborns don't usually bleed.

The mystery surrounding the head injuries deepened. Since there was no abrasion on the head, and the baby's DNA was on the towel, Fox began to wonder whether a blow to the baby's head, while the towel covered it, was how the skull fractures were inflicted. He would never prove it.

As baffled as people were about what Amy and Brian were accused of doing, Bacilia Lucero's act on a frigid Saturday night in January made people shudder in disbelief. For a day. Maybe a week. And then they forgot about her and went back to wondering about the once promising futures of the Wyckoff teenagers. So did the media.

Bacilia Lucero was a twenty-two-year-old illegal immigrant from Mexico working at a textile factory and living in an apartment in impoverished Paterson, New Jersey, with a dozen family members. What she did was predictable, almost understandable to some.

What Amy and Brian did was none of those.

Minutes after she gave birth to a girl in the bathroom of her cramped third-floor apartment in a small house with light green aluminum siding, Lucero walked to the bathroom window overlooking an alley filled with garbage cans. Her twenty-year-old cousin, Juan Diego Lucero, who had helped her deliver, held open the window and watched as she flung her newborn, the umbilical cord still attached, to her death. Out of sight, out of mind. The young cousins had been in the United States for a year, on a mission to earn money that they could send back to their families in the poor rural town of Tecolutla. A baby would have compromised that. The newborn girl was later named Jaqueline Lucero Garcia and buried in an emotional ceremony in Mexico.

The story made the front page of *The Record* the next day and attracted television news crews to the alley where a neighborhood boy found the tiny blue body. But there was no outcry, no national media frenzy. The stories were straightforward, reporting the facts as police knew them. But no one saw a need to talk to psychologists about what makes young women kill their infants. No one sought out the details of Lucero's secret pregnancy. No one asked the questions they asked in their stories of Amy and Brian because the answers were assumed.

Poor, uneducated, no options. What more did we need to know?

"We expect the poor to behave this way, to act crazy," Charley Flint, an associate professor of sociology at nearby William Paterson College in Wayne, New Jersey, said a few days after Lucero's arrest. "We don't expect the rich to. The feeling is that the Grossberg-Peterson baby mattered. The public does not think that the Lucero baby mattered, however, and that's why there is not the same public fascination with this case."

How Lucero's case was handled compared with how Amy and Brian were treated would provide a stark contrast in how society views murdered babies and their parents. Neither young woman had wanted a baby, and neither was a danger to society, a threat to kill again, though Lucero was an illegal immigrant and possible flight risk. Yet after Lucero's arrest, her bail was set at $500,000, and when her family could not afford to pay it and her public defender lawyer could not get it reduced or raise any questions about the health of the baby, she was placed in a New Jersey mental institution. Her freedom was gone, and she would eventually plead guilty to aggravated manslaughter and be sentenced to twelve years in prison.

Amy and Brian were about to demonstrate how money talks.

The mere possibility that two defendants charged with first-degree capital murder could be walking the streets while awaiting trial seemed ludicrous at first appearance. No one could remember it happening in any state, at any time. Murder is murder. Or is it?

This was not just any death. And these were not ordinary murder suspects. Had there been a family of their victim angrily demanding justice, bail and freedom would have been much more unlikely. But the victim's families were the suspects' families. And what if Amy and Brian had been black and from Brooklyn? Make bail? Unlikely.

"These young people seek not to flee from the world, but to be vindicated by it," Kathleen Jennings, Oberly's partner and one of Amy's lawyers, told Judge Ridgely at the bail hearing.

It took just forty-five minutes, and when it ended, Sonye Grossberg sobbed and lightly banged on a courtroom banister, and Barbara Zuchowski wiped her eyes. Their children were coming home on $300,000 bail apiece. No more prison for the time being. No mental institution. All it took was an accepting prosecutor, aggressive defense lawyers, and six checks of $100,000 each. Three to get Brian out, three for Amy. Brian's parents had come up with the cash on their own, while Amy's parents had turned to their brothers and sisters and friends for help. Both families would later get their cash back by posting property as collateral to ensure that their children went nowhere while awaiting trial.

Throughout the hearing, Amy, wearing black boots, a black skirt, and a black sweater, and Brian, in his preppy khakis and blue shirt, displayed emotions they had not showed earlier, smiling, giggling, whispering to each other, appearing relaxed. Their parents sat behind them, holding hands and fighting back tears.

For a short while Letang had been reluctant to let Amy and Brian go home to await trial. Alex Kelly, the Connecticut fugitive, kept popping into his head, reminding him it would be a mistake. Letang had read the stories about Brian's mother asking Hurley which countries the United States did not have extradition treaties with, and Letang knew if he let them go home, and they did flee, his reputation would be tarnished.

"They're not going anywhere," Jennings assured Letang.

That was Letang's only concern.

"Our opinion is, they are not a risk to the community,"

Letang said. "If they were, we wouldn't be in this position."

Still, he wasn't about to let them lead the life of ordinary teenagers while awaiting trial for murder. The judge denied his request to take their drivers' licenses. But Letang won a few other requirements in addition to the bail money. Observe a curfew of eight P.M. to six A.M. Surrender their passports. Sign waivers of extradition so that if they did flee and were caught, they would have to be returned to the United States. Submit a daily log sheet of activities once a week. Report weekly by telephone to a pretrial officer in Delaware. Meet twice a month with the pretrial services department. Remain in New Jersey unless permission is granted by Delaware.

And wear some new jewelry.

Around one ankle, they were required to wear monitoring devices. The small black box about the size of a cigarette pack is attached to a tamper-proof black anklet. It is equipped with a transmitter so that when the person wearing it travels beyond the range of the monitoring device hooked into his telephone jack, a signal is sent to a monitoring center, quickly notifying authorities. In order to leave the home, the person must call and notify the center ahead of time.

It would be a restrictive lifestyle, but it would be a far cry from prison. Bacilia Lucero was still in her dark and private room at the Forensic Psychiatric Hospital in Trenton when Amy and Brian were told they were free to go back to their parents' homes in Wyckoff as long as they met their bail conditions. They had to stay in Delaware, at the homes of their attorneys, Brian with Hurley and Amy with Lisa Borin, an associate in Oberly's firm, before the monitoring systems were set up in their homes in New Jersey.

Until the bail hearing, Amy's and Brian's parents had not given one interview. The gag order had restricted them, and their lawyers, from discussing the case in detail. But an hour after their daughter was released on bail, Alan and Sonye Grossberg met with me in Oberly's ninth-floor office overlooking downtown Wilmington and into Pennsylvania.

They sat on a couch in his office, holding hands. Around each of their left wrists were the rope bracelets Amy had made for them in prison. Sonye wore a silver necklace that had been mailed to her by someone expressing support.

"Words cannot express how we feel," she said. She was shaking as she cried. "We're going to snuggle with her all night and not let go and tell her we love and support her."

Brian hoped to do the same. He had loved and supported Amy throughout their ordeal, and his feelings hadn't changed. Nothing in the bail conditions prohibited Amy and Brian from seeing each other, and they could not wait.

"They are young people who obviously have a close, loving relationship," Litman told the media throng outside the courthouse after the hearing. "There's no reason they can't get together."

They were still dating, and both their defense teams were hoping the relationship would last at least until trial.

Ten days later, on January 31, Amy and Brian returned home to be monitored with their ankle bracelets. Fifty newspaper and television reporters waited outside their homes. At Brian's house, two signs adorned the front door: "Brian, We Love You" and "Welcome Home, Brian."

To satisfy the reporters, Brian and his mother stepped out their front door with their attorney, Litman's partner, Russell Gioiella.

"They love him. They missed him so much," Gioiella said of Brian's parents. "It's been a very emotionally trying time. They want to thank their friends and family who supported them, as well as the officials in Delaware who worked to make it possible for him to come home."

Those officials who made it happen were not too happy about it. Delaware correction officials were annoyed at this sudden responsibility thrown at them to somehow keep tabs on two teenagers from another state, 150 miles away. Even with the eight P.M. to six A.M. curfew, the supervisor of Delaware's Home Confinement Program worried that if Amy or Brian made a break for freedom, New Jersey had no authority to detain them until Delaware arrived.

"This time lag could possibly result in a fugitive situation," the supervisor wrote in a letter to Judge Ridgely.

Brian and Amy were going nowhere. They were just thrilled to be together again. They were a couple.

With their clients back home, Litman, Oberly, Slanina, Hurley, Jennings—all of the attorneys for Amy and Brian hoped for two things to happen. First, that they would stay close and continue dating, so that when they walked into court together they could show genuine affection and love for each other. Second, they hoped, as all attorneys do, that their clients would avoid even the slightest trouble until their trial. No speeding tickets, no curfew violations, no sign that they were not treating their predicament as gravely serious.

A general rule among defense attorneys is to never ask your client: Did you do it? It's not what matters. What matters is providing them the best possible defense to get them acquitted of any charges.

One of the first things the attorneys for Amy and Brian did after they were released from prison was give them separate lie detector tests. They knew the results would not be admissible in court because the science was unreliable. But the lawyers wanted to verify the stories they were getting, and in the event that Amy and Brian passed, they could mention the results to prosecutors to try to gain a little leverage. It's a common practice. On separate dates, both Amy and Brian were hooked up to polygraph machines and asked a series of questions about what had happened. The results would stay quiet.

After having spent two months in tiny cells, Amy surrounded by women and Brian by men, they almost jumped into each other's arms once back home in Wyck-off. Their curfew had them paranoid. They had to be home every evening by 8:00 P.M., but from their first day home, they never walked in at 7:55 P.M. They left themselves lee-way, always, to guard against a traffic jam or any unfore-seen snag. On weekends Amy often went to Brian's house, and they would cuddle in front of the television in the basement. Brian was almost always toting a gift when he saw Amy, usually a Beanie Baby, the hot-selling line of small beanbag animals that come with their own name and birthdate.

Just going out to a movie presented a dilemma. They wanted to enjoy some semblance of a normal life, but they knew if they were seen in public smiling, they could alien-ate people, who would say they were treating their situa-tion lightly.

Amy went back to work at the Market Basket, putting together gourmet food baskets out of sight of the cus-tomers. She also found religion. Her family's synagogue, Temple Beth Rishon, invited her to volunteer there, to put her art skills to use by decorating the bulletin boards.

One of the first people on the telephone to Brian at home was Evan Baumgarten. During Brian's four years at Ramapo High School, they had formed a bond, a friend-ship, that started on the soccer field and extended off it. Evan had coached Brian on the high school team and watched him mature from a pipsqueak freshman with lightning quick feet to a vocal leader, a captain the other players looked to for leadership.

Baumgarten, pleasant, soft-spoken, and a short and stocky thirtysomething, saw Brian as a boy any parent would be happy to meet as his or her daughter's boyfriend. When Brian's lawyers said in late January that they needed letters from his friends to convince the judge of his good character for his release on bail, Baumgarten was first in line with pen in hand.

That's why he called Brian so quickly to welcome him home, to make him an offer to keep busy while awaiting trial. Knowing how much Brian loved playing soccer, Baumgarten asked him to help coach the team of ten-year-old boys in the Torpedoes league that Brian had played in, a league with long roots in the town and some four hundred boys and girls playing on thirty teams. Brian was thrilled at the opportunity to be outside, playing his favorite sport, spending time with Baumgarten.

"Everybody is very supportive of this," Baumgarten said.

Not everybody. Some parents were offended that a young man charged with murdering his baby was not only free on bail, but was coaching children, acting as a role model. When the president of the Torpedoes Soccer Club, Dan Caldwell, learned of the invitation, and *The Record* reported it in a front-page story, the league was under pressure. Parents in town left messages on Caldwell's answering machine, some irate, some supportive, but enough of a split to get his attention.

"I believe Coach Baumgarten acted with the best of intentions out of his concern for Brian, and did not consider the implications for the club," Caldwell said. A week later, February 7, he rescinded Brian's invitation.

"The club considers Evan a wonderful asset to the club, the community, and the youth of this county, and in no way questions his motives. But right now, we feel this would be inappropriate until Brian's legal status has been resolved."

That was a long way off.

His defendants, the parents of this victim, were home in Wyckoff as Letang's full attention turned to the baby's skull fractures and what caused them. Unlike most of his previous murder cases, the whodunits where the accused denies involvement, this was a case of why something was done. There was little sleuth work for detectives; it was a case for the doctors and scientists, like the ones Letang flew out to visit in El Segundo, California, on February 12. At Biomechanics Research and Consulting, Inc.,

Letang met with Terry Smith, a bespectacled man with curly black hair and a round face. His background was in head injuries and the protective effects of helmets and headgear. At Biomechanics, which specializes in injury analysis in automotive, sports, and occupational accidents, Smith focused on sports-related head injuries and car crash injuries.

It was a technical company for which Letang had a technical question: What degree of force would it have taken to cause this baby's skull fractures? He gave them pictures and autopsy reports, he told them everything he knew. The problem Smith had was that he had no data on newborn head injuries like this baby's. All Smith could tell Letang was that the head injuries were not consistent with hitting a flat surface, like the side of the Dumpster, as the defense attorneys had been suggesting, and were more consistent with hitting a corner or sharp side of a heavy blunt object.

"It was clear to us this baby had suffered a force capable of causing a significant fracture, not something that occurs from a flat surface," Smith said months later.

Letang left Biomechanics with a stronger belief that the injuries had been inflicted intentionally, but not with a stronger case.

Just as Ramapo High School students compete against each other with cutthroat attitudes, the television networks were banging down the doors of the lawyers, pleading for that critical first on-camera interview. The Grossbergs, believing that Amy was being portrayed as a spoiled rich girl, were eager to tell their story, and Oberly was assigned to handle the media crush. He was well aware of the gag order and determined not to discuss any evidence in the case. But that didn't rule out a soft interview to show a loving and terrified family to the world and, more important, to potential jurors.

It was a strategy that Brian's lawyers shied away from. Litman rarely sought out the media's help in a case, and although Hurley never saw a camera he didn't like, it was not his call alone to make.

This was not the kind of case that a no-name producer went after. To land this interview, the names and faces everyone knew would have to beg personally. And beg they did, even offering invitations to posh dinner parties in Washington. On a Monday evening in early February, with Amy home with her parents in Wyckoff, Oberly drove to New Jersey to meet with Barbara Walters and Katie Thomson, an editorial producer for ABC's 20/20. No one takes more criticism for her interviews than Walters. She's not a journalist, her critics say, she's an entertainer, and it's true that softball questions leading to teary-eyed answers is her signature. But no one lands more of the most wanted interviews than she does, for exactly that reason.

If Amy and her parents were going to do a television interview, Oberly was determined not to let her go anywhere near the camera without weeks of practice questions and mock interviews. They all realized that how sincere and heartfelt she and her family came across to a nationwide audience, and to potential jurors in Delaware, would be the single biggest step toward getting either the public's sympathy or their scorn. They also knew they had just one shot at television, because Judge Ridgely would undoubtedly threaten to sanction them if they did it again.

While meeting with Walters, Oberly outlined the defense position that Amy and Brian may have committed some moral mistakes, but neither of them did anything criminal or homicidal. He told her that the Grossbergs would like to know how the piece would be handled and wanted to watch other examples of similar interviews Walters had done. He said evidence questions were off limits, but he suggested that the unfairness of the gag order, the faults with medical examiners, and the life of Amy were all areas he hoped to see explored.

Ever the experienced competitor, Walters wrote a brief

but gushing letter to Oberly the day after they met.

"It was a great pleasure to meet you Monday evening. What a very special man you are. I do hope we will be able to bring the true story of the Grossberg family to the public. Your dedication to the family is enormously moving. I was affected by them as well and would like to offer any support I can give."

Steve Fox had seized a minicassette tape from the answering machine in Brian's dormitory room. On first listen the tape revealed nothing unusual. But Fox knew that answering machines continuously tape over old messages and that there might be a revealing old message underneath the immaterial new ones. That called for an expert, the best, and Letang turned to Paul Ginsberg.

When FBI agents retrieved tapes from inside the fire-ravaged Branch Davidian compound in Waco, Texas, in 1993, they found that a transmitter they had slipped inside recorded indecipherable sounds, mostly explosions, gunfire, and muffled voices. In his home office in Spring Valley, New York, Ginsberg enhanced the tapes enough so that jurors in the criminal case against the surviving cult members could hear them as they planned to set the compound on fire.

On a Thursday morning in early March, Fox, Letang, and Paul Wallace drove four hours north to Ginsberg's home and asked him to tell them what was on that tape that they couldn't hear. For $5,000 he did it in one week. It was hard to hear, but Amy's voice was on the tape.

"Hi, it's me. It's seven o'clock. I guess you're not calling me. I hope my worst nightmare isn't coming true."

It was an ominous message and potentially damaging to Amy's defense. But it would prove to be useless because there was no way to tell when she had left it. Or what the nightmare was that she mentioned. Was it her fear of Brian leaving her? Or that the baby was coming? Or that her parents had found out?

\* \* \*

On March 11, 1997, a Tuesday afternoon, Amy and Brian looked like any pair of eighteen-year-olds in love, giggling, his arms draped over her shoulders, her arms wrapped around his waist where his tan sweater vest met his khaki pants. Standing in the hallway of Oberly's office, Amy looked straight into Brian's eyes, her head tilted slightly up, her eyes peering out from behind her oval-shaped, wire-rimmed glasses. The hallway where they stood was dark, but not dark enough to hide them. It was an unusual display of affection for one simple reason. Their parents stood just feet away, gobbling M&M's around a small round table.

So did their lawyers. The families had come to Delaware on this day to ask permission to take the monitoring bands off Amy and Brian. They promised to stay in Wyckoff, and they asked the judge to look at them, look at their supportive communities, their loving families, and accept that they were not going anywhere. They hated having to be home from eight P.M. to six A.M., being restricted by a curfew at the age of eighteen.

Ridgely listened and looked. And said no. The ankle bracelets would stay. They used to be like any other teenager, like any other couple, and their town used to be like any other town. But no more. Ridgely denied their request to lose their ankle bracelets, but he did allow them to start spending more time outside their homes, to work or study.

Now they were back in Oberly's office, relaxing as much as they could. As Brian whispered to Amy, and she smiled, her mother turned over the nearly empty bag of M&M's and studied the calories. She shook her head. Her daughter came up behind her and read with her.

"Are M and M's kosher?" Sonye Grossberg asked, knowing that Passover was less than a month away.

"I doubt it, Mom," her daughter said, laughing while reaching into the bag for a few more.

They hardly resembled murder defendants. It was the kind of chitchat you might hear at any house in Wyckoff, maybe the gray condominium in the complex where the Grossbergs lived or the red-brick Tudor where Brian lived with his mother and stepfather.

That afternoon, in her first interview since her arrest, Amy, sitting between her parents on a couch, met with me in a conference room of Oberly's spacious ninth-floor office overlooking downtown Wilmington and out into Pennsylvania. Her attorneys would not let her discuss the case, and it lasted just a few minutes, but they knew it was a safe way to give the public a brief glimpse of a scared young girl. She sat quietly, leaning forward, her hands folded on her lap. She looked uncomfortable, almost dazed. Her voice was barely audible as she spoke.

"Of course I'm scared. Anyone would be," she said. She said she desperately "wanted to say a lot. But I can't."

She said she was disappointed in the judge's decision earlier but respected it. She talked about sleepless nights in prison and the burden of being monitored everywhere she went.

Her parents were visibly frustrated at being muzzled by the gag order, and they said so.

"Imagine you know something important, but you can't tell anyone," Alan said. "Wouldn't that drive you crazy?"

Then it was over, and the three of them went back to the office lobby, where Brian and his mother were waiting.

The M&M's were almost gone when all of the parents in unison seemed to glance at their watches and then at their children. It was nearing six P.M., the end of a long and disappointing day for both families. It was time to go. Not because they had a two-hour drive home to Wyckoff from Wilmington, but because they had to go. Curfew called. And their lawyers had work to do.

No matter how strong a case lawyers have, how much evidence they have accumulated, they know that the makeup of the jury can sometimes be the key to the verdict. And when the case is being tracked around the country by legal analysts and the public, the stakes are that much higher, the pressure that much greater, and both the prosecuting and defense attorneys in Amy's and Brian's case knew it.

The job of a jury consultant is to tell a lawyer what type of juror would probably best fit the case. Prosecutors want to know who would have the least sympathy for the defendant, whether a man, woman, thirtysomething person, or senior citizen would be most likely to vote for a conviction. Defense lawyers want the opposite. They want to know who would acquit.

On the afternoon of May 4, 1997, six months after Amy and Brian were arrested, their lawyers gathered in the spacious office of Litman's law firm, high above downtown Manhattan. Brian and Amy were there with their parents. Everyone listened as their jury consultant told them that their ideal juror was a white, middle-aged, middle-class woman with a daughter who was Amy's age. That juror would look at Amy, and how she feared disappointing her parents, and maybe understand why she kept her secret.

"We wanted people who see their own kids sitting on that chair," Russell Gioiella said. "We wanted people who saw that these were good kids who made bad, bad decisions."

That was not what Letang wanted, which was why the exact juror that Brian's and Amy's lawyers would seek was the one Letang wanted to avoid. He, too, hired a jury consultant, who told him he wanted either young mothers who had recently given birth or senior citizens with grown children and maybe even grandchildren. The older the better.

Trial was four months away, and everything was on track. For both sides.

# THE SPLIT

As summer approached, the defense lawyers were confident. They had clients who had been model citizens while free on bail. Brian had coached soccer briefly before having to stop, had worked at his mother's video business, and was about to begin a full load of classes at Felician College in Lodi, New Jersey, close enough to home that he didn't have to worry about missing his curfew. Amy had been volunteering at her temple, had returned to her job at the gourmet food store, and had restarted art sessions with her longtime mentor, Mary Guidetti, to update her portfolio.

The combination of Amy's severe illness in the hours leading up to, and after, her delivery and Brian's faithfulness in remaining by her side every minute gave them a sympathy their lawyers believed was crucial to go before a jury. There was a brain-damaged baby and an autopsy that, in their view, had been botched by an inexperienced assistant medical examiner. They had the failure by police to keep the trash in the Dumpster, raising even more doubt as to where and when the head injuries occurred. Showing reasonable doubt about whether it was a premeditated murder seemed highly possible. Their goal was simply to raise the possibility that Brian had thought he was disposing of a dead baby.

But Letang was equally confident. He and his co-pros-

ecutor, Paul Wallace, were exploring just how sick Amy
had been. Her lawyers kept saying she was in a near death
condition, but the picture the emergency room doctors had
painted for Letang was different. She was sick, no question, the doctors and nurses had told investigators. But she
was also alert and seemed to intentionally avoid their
questions about the baby. That, plus Brian's admission to
Gettysburg police that he had thrown the baby in a Dumpster, helped Letang believe in the strength of his case.

Then they had the mysterious skull fractures. Letang
envisioned putting gruesome picture after gruesome picture up in front of a jury. He wouldn't need to explain
what caused the injuries. He didn't know. The pictures
would speak for themselves.

Then, for an emotional cap, he was planning to parade
in children for the jury to see, active children, athletic
children, smiling, happy children from around the country. All of them born with schizencephaly.

"Our purpose was to show that the defect wasn't a
death knell," Letang would say later.

He found the children on the Internet, on a World Wide
Web site called Schiz Kidz Buddies, launched by parents
of children with the disease. They talk regularly about the
illness, the treatments and progress their kids are making.
The parents remember the births of their children vividly,
and not one of them recalls a doctor telling them their
newborn was sick. Only after a few months passed did
parents begin to notice their babies having motor skill and
speech problems. In its most severe form, schizencephaly
can cause physical deformities to an infant's nose, eyes,
and lips, but that is extremely rare.

"She had good color, she looked like the perfect baby,"
said Lynn Niedzwiecki of Winnipeg, Manitoba, in
Canada. Her daughter, Danika, was born in 1995, and like
the other babies of the parents she speaks with, she came
out screaming and crying, with ten fingers, ten toes, and
no immediately noticeable defects. That was exactly what
Letang wanted to hear.

The case reached its sixth month in early May, and for the defense attorneys things looked good. Until Sonye Grossberg got her three Delaware attorneys on the telephone for a conference call, the call that would ultimately change the entire face of the case.

Without telling her attorneys, she had begun listening in on telephone conversations between her daughter and Brian. She didn't like what she heard. She was suspicious that Brian's lawyers had asked him to try to learn what Amy's lawyers were plotting. Brian's lawyers wanted nothing more than to work with Amy's lawyers. But one phone call in particular from Brian had finally sent Sonye over the edge. Brian had asked about the case, and Sonye butted in on the two.

She yelled to Brian that it was none of his business.

It was the beginning of the end.

Over the next few weeks the calls between the two diminished and then stopped cold. A relationship that had taken Amy and Brian through high school into college, their first sexual experience, talk about marriage, an unwanted pregnancy, and both of their arrests was in its last days.

Sonye had been calling at least one of her lawyers every afternoon, sometimes two or three times a day, and they had reluctantly grown to accept it. She faxed them every newspaper clipping, called with strategy suggestions, pestered them endlessly. But she was the mother of the client. Obviously emotional and involved.

They knew that she disagreed with their approach that Amy did a lot of things wrong morally and socially, but not criminally. They knew that she was desperate to do a television interview to defend their daughter publicly. They also suspected in the back of their minds that a part of Alan and Sonye would be more comfortable with a Jewish lawyer defending Amy. They knew she wasn't happy, but they refused to tell her what she wanted to hear from them: *Amy did nothing wrong.* Still, they had no idea just how unhappy she was until she called on this afternoon.

"I've got some good news," she told the attorneys all at once. "I've added an attorney to the team. I know you're going to like him."

Before Slanina, Oberly, or Jennings could speak to express their shock, Robert Gottlieb was on the telephone. He had met with Amy and her parents for hours, talking about the case, hearing their concerns about the defense Amy was getting. He told her attorneys how excited he was to work with them and to vindicate Amy and said he would see them soon. The call was quick, and outrage immediately replaced shock for the Delaware lawyers as they talked to each other.

*What does this mean? How does our role change? Is he the lead lawyer? Who is Robert Gottlieb?*

There is no more obvious a vote of no confidence than to have your client tell you she has hired another lawyer to help out. And when that lawyer is from out of state, the pain is only worse.

The forty-seven-year-old Gottlieb, with his thinning hair, roundish glasses, and slight frame, looked more like a high school physics teacher than a criminal defense attorney. The father of two children, he bases his practice in Commack, Long Island, not far from where he was raised with his family. He started his career as an assistant district attorney in Manhattan, where he eventually became a respected homicide prosecutor. After turning to private practice in 1980, he lost in a bid for Suffolk County district attorney in 1989. But even in defeat he gained attention, and he used it to become a commentator for Court TV.

"Amy did not commit a crime," Gottlieb said after being hired by Amy's parents. "As emphatically as I can say this, Amy is not guilty of any crime whatsoever. And the jury will understand and realize that."

Finally the Grossbergs had someone who told them what they wanted to hear.

*Amy did nothing wrong.*

Brian had his New York lawyer, and now Amy had hers.

With Gottlieb suddenly in charge, Slanina, Oberly, and Jennings had no interest in running his errands, explaining the nuances of Delaware law to him, and filing the motions that he would write. When he told them he was driving down to pick up a copy of the case file, they explained the joint defense agreement to him, that he had to sign it and agree to share anything he found with Brian's lawyers.

Gottlieb refused. He wasn't signing anything. Amy was Amy. Brian was Brian. They could fend for themselves. His decision, in essence, turned the case from a team effort to "us against them."

Amy's Delaware lawyers were stunned and hurt that the Grossbergs had hired a new litigator without even discussing it with them. Over a span of two weeks in May, all three quit the case, forcing Gottlieb to hire a new local attorney, Eugene Maurer, the same attorney Slanina had been unable to reach early in the case when he was looking for help. With one sudden move Amy's new defense took shape.

There was never a plan to kill the baby. The baby was stillborn. Amy played no role whatsoever in disposing of the body. Brian did that. Amy was too weak and sick even to know what had happened. *Amy did nothing wrong.*

Amy and Brian were a couple no more.

Melissa Drexler walked into her senior prom on the evening of June 6, a slinky black dress on her back, her boyfriend on her arm in a tuxedo, and went straight into the headlines alongside Amy and Brian. She looked a little like Amy, with her long brown hair and pretty, fair skin. She came from a solid family with good parents. And she had a secret. A whopper.

After complaining of stomach cramps on her way to the prom in central New Jersey, she walked into the Garden Manor in Aberdeen Township and went straight to the women's bathroom with a friend. Drexler's friend saw blood drip onto the floor of the stall Drexler was in and heard banging on some sort of metal. Drexler told her friend she was having an extra heavy menstruation and would be out in twenty minutes.

Drexler did reappear on the dance floor, eating a salad, around seven-thirty P.M. But when a maintenance worker was called to clean up a mess found in the women's bathroom, he picked up the bag in the trash can and became alarmed at how heavy it was. The bag was opened and inside lay a newborn boy. Dead. Strangled and asphyxiated, prosecutors said, the umbilical cord severed on the serrated edge of the sanitary napkin dispenser.

School officials who had seen Drexler in the bathroom confronted her, and after first denying the baby was hers, she admitted it. She was charged with murder, released to her parents on $50,000 personal recognizance bond, and immediately thrust into the spotlight as "Prom Mom," every tabloid headline writer's dream, every parent's nightmare all over again. The detectives in her case contacted Letang in Delaware a few weeks later to talk about the similarities in their cases and the difficulties in prosecuting them. Drexler would eventually plead guilty to aggravated manslaughter and face up to fifteen years in prison. Every Drexler story made reference to Amy Grossberg. How could they not? The two were even born on the same date: July 10, 1978.

Two bright New Jersey girls, from strong families and close-knit communities, charged within seven months of each other with the same crime: killing their newborn sons. Even the babies were similar. Six pounds, six ounces, nineteen inches for Drexler. Six pounds, two ounces, twenty inches for Amy.

The same night Drexler walked into the headlines, Amy walked into living rooms around the country. In Robert Gottlieb, Barbara Walters finally got her man. The famed interviewer wanted Amy badly, and Gottlieb's first act as Amy's lead lawyer was to deliver her to ABC. The gag order was of little concern.

On the night of June 6, Walters's ABC program, *20/20*,

aired its talk with Amy and her parents, which had been shot a week earlier in the Grossbergs' town house. Everyone in Wyckoff had heard about the interview. ABC had teased it with advertisements all week, and those who didn't stay home to watch it taped it.

The piece opened with photographs from the family album, all of them glowing at family gatherings, followed by a videotape of the arrests of Amy and Brian. Sonye described Amy as "warm and sensitive and caring," a girl who always set the table for dinner, loved children, and never had a parking ticket.

A quick shot of Gottlieb followed.

"Amy should not have been charged. Amy is not guilty," he said. He said prosecutors should take a fresh look at the case and reconsider charging Amy.

Amy's father said a dozen words in the interview. Sonye did the talking. And the sobbing. She called Brian a "nice boy" and said she looked at Amy and Brian as a couple similar to her and Alan in high school. Hardly a ringing endorsement.

Gottlieb would claim after the interview that Amy and her family were not bound by the gag order and that no evidence had been discussed. He could not have been more wrong. Virtually the entire interview covered evidence.

When Sonye discussed her relationship with Amy, that was evidence. It was that relationship that prosecutors were planning to argue led Amy to hide her pregnancy. When Sonye said she knew why her daughter concealed her pregnancy, but refused to give the reason, that was evidence.

Amy's interview with Walters followed her parents' interview, with Amy sitting on a bed covered with stuffed animals, most of them gifts from Brian. She called Brian "a great kid" and said that their relationship was strained, but not without promise for the future. Then she discussed even more vital evidence than her parents had mentioned.

"During the summer, were you ever sick?" Walters asked. "Were you ever nauseous? Were you ever tired?"

"No, never. My summer was spent working at a summer camp."

"You didn't notice anything about your physical condition that was different?"

"No."

Prosecutors would eventually learn about the failed abortion attempts, which would directly prove that Amy lied when she indicated she didn't know she was pregnant.

Walters then asked if Amy's periods were irregular. It was an obvious setup question from Gottlieb. How else would Walters have known to phrase it that way? Wouldn't she have asked if Amy's periods were regular instead of irregular unless she knew the answer? Amy said her menstrual cycle has always been irregular. More evidence.

She went on to discuss her relationship with her mother, what she remembered from her hospitalization, and whether she mourned the loss of her baby, all of it evidence, all of it to come back later and bite her.

"Of course," she said when asked if she mourned her baby. "It was a part of me. My heart breaks. I would never hurt anything or anybody, especially something that could come from me."

Her words were interesting. The baby was not a "he" but an "it." Just like her dozens of letters to Brian, when she wrote, "Make it go away," over and over, she refused to talk about the pregnancy or the baby as a person. The interview was gushing, and most viewers saw right through it. The backlash was almost immediate. No one likes feeling duped, and the interview had been so soft and lacking any of the questions that people wanted to hear asked that they felt cheated.

Was Amy mourning her baby when she thrust her face into her hands at the end of the interview in apparent tears, or was she crying for the deep trouble she knew she faced?

Prosecutors didn't care. What they did care about was whether potential jurors had been swayed by the interview. The Monday after the interview aired, an angry Letang filed a motion asking that Gottlieb be removed from the case, calling the interview a "promo piece" and a blatant violation of Judge Ridgely's gag order. A hearing was set for July 3.

"We all agreed that this case would be tried in a courtroom, not in the media," Letang said.

What he didn't know was that the interview would land a jewel of a witness in his lap without his having to lift a finger. On Monday, June 9, Christian Jackson walked into Letang's office. The part-time student at UD who had given Amy a ride on campus the morning after she had secretly given birth had watched the *20/20* interview like so many others. And it had infuriated her. She recounted the entire semester for Letang, from her first asking Amy when her baby was due and Amy denying being pregnant, to her driving Amy to class the morning after the delivery and Amy again denying ever being pregnant. Jackson was a devastating potential witness.

Amy and her family had hoped the television interview would help them. In the end, it helped only Letang.

It was two weeks before Letang would argue to have Gottlieb thrown off Amy's case when he and Steve Fox flew out of Philadelphia to Chicago on June 23. If the defense lawyers were going to insist that the head injuries to the baby took place either during the toss into the Dumpster or while lying in the trash, Letang wanted to be ready to refute that. Armed with the torn gray plastic Hefty bag with yellow drawstrings in which the baby was found, along with a seemingly identical bag police had recovered from Amy's dormitory room, Letang and Fox visited McCrone Associates, Inc., a laboratory outside Chicago that specializes in testing forensic evidence. Letang asked scientists at McCrone to confirm that the plastic bag with the baby was from the same package as the bag Amy had in her dormitory room trash can. The scientists were also asked to examine the sections of the evidence bag that had been torn and stretched to try to determine what had caused the damage.

The first question was easy. The bag with the baby most likely came from the same box as the bag in Amy's room.

As for the damage, Scott Stoeffler, a senior research microscopist with McCrone, found it highly unlikely that the splits in the bag were caused by its being struck against another object or by random blows. He also put weights ranging from five to thirteen pounds in a similar bag and swung it around to see what happened to the bag.

Stoeffler told Letang in his report that the bag showed no sign of having been struck against something hard and no sign of stretching. In other words, he believed the skull fractures did not take place while the baby was in the bag. Where, then, did they take place?

That question continued to haunt Letang as July 3 approached. No one, not Letang, not Gottlieb, absolutely no one connected to the case truly believed the judge would toss Gottlieb from the case for the ABC interview. Letang expected, at the most, a fine, maybe a verbal warning, and that was it. That made what happened in the typically packed Wilmington courtroom all the more shocking. Despite receiving a letter from Amy that said Gottlieb was "the best person possible to defend me," Ridgely ruled that Gottlieb had in essence flaunted the gag order in his face.

"Mr. Gottlieb knew or should have known that the change in counsel, coupled with an interview of his client, would rekindle public interest and provide him a significant audience," Ridgely said. "The impact of his statements was maximized by the context of prime-time, national television only ninety-seven days before trial. Accordingly, the admission of Robert Gottlieb to practice before this court is revoked."

He banged his gavel and Amy shrieked in horror, jumping from her seat into Gottlieb's arms and then her mother's. No New York attorney was going to come to Delaware, into Ridgely's courtroom, and ignore his rules. Suddenly Eugene Maurer, the respected Delaware lawyer Gottlieb had hired only because he'd had to, was Amy's new lawyer.

Three attorneys had quit her case. A fourth had been thrown off after barely two months of work. Amy's defense was in turmoil, and she and her parents hadn't even left the courtroom on this afternoon when it got dramatically worse.

The courtroom was still buzzing as Letang discreetly walked past Amy sobbing with her parents and handed two slips of paper to Maurer. No one saw the exchange. Alan and Sonye Grossberg were not expecting anything from Letang, much less subpoenas. But that's what they got.

When Barbara Walters asked Amy's parents on national television why their daughter never told them she was pregnant, Sonye said: "I know the answer to that, but I'm not at liberty right now to give it."

By admitting that they knew the reason Amy had concealed her pregnancy, they had unknowingly opened a door for Letang. What they'd said was evidence. And Letang wanted it. The law is very clear in protecting spouses from testifying against each other. But no law protects parents from having to testify against their children. Letang ordered Amy's parents to tell him what they knew. They would not come without a fight.

The trial, scheduled to start in two months, was delayed until May 1998, as Amy's parents sought the next new attorney for their daughter.

Once deputy chief counsel to the Congressional Committee Investigation into the assassinations of President John F. Kennedy and Martin Luther King Jr., Robert K. Tanenbaum was a name the public knew. Not as a lawyer, not as the former mayor of Beverly Hills, California, not from his days as a New York City assistant district attorney, but as a best-selling author of seven novels and two true-crime books. His novels, courtroom thrillers, revolve around a feisty attorney named Butch Karp and his trials.

The Grossbergs' hiring of Tanenbaum baffled people following the case, and prosecutors. Although a prominent lawyer, he had long since concentrated primarily on his writing. He typically took one case a year, a case that would often provide him a framework for his next novel. Though he had worked in New York City with Gottlieb, through whom the Grossbergs found him, his involvement in the case—trekking three thousand miles across the country for meetings and hearings—seemed, if nothing else, peculiar.

Tanenbaum, a towering six feet five with a square face, slicked-back salt-and-pepper hair, and a powerful walk, picked up right where Gottlieb had left off. *Amy did nothing wrong.* And, like Gottlieb, Tanenbaum was from New York and Jewish. After Maurer quit, Tanenbaum hired two attorneys to work with him, John Malik, a young and respected Wilmington lawyer, and Jack Gruenstein of Philadelphia. The three of them launched an aggressive attack on the prosecutors. Tanenbaum began filing motions that read more like press releases than legal arguments. He released critical information about the disputed health of the baby, and his strong wording only served to anger Letang.

"Letang has been told by defense counsel that defense medical experts have concluded that the baby suffered extreme stress in utero; that it was stillborn; that there was, significantly, no blood found in the fracture lines of the baby's skull, which indicates, clearly, that the fractures occurred after the baby already was dead," Tanenbaum wrote in a motion on September 15. He wrote that the baby's heart had shifted from its normal position on the left side to the right center of the chest cavity and that Letang was ignoring all that critical evidence. And he said there was not one shred of evidence that Amy had participated in the disposal of the baby. He never said, "Brian did it," but he might as well have.

Letang had heard it all before. He knew what the defense experts had said. And he knew that his experts said otherwise, that the baby was born alive and full-term and was murdered. Brutally.

The case was more than a year old in early October when a television program caught the attention of everyone linked to Amy and Brian. NBC's *Law & Order,* a popular police drama based in New York City that boasts its plotlines are "ripped from the headlines," ripped out the story of Amy and Brian. The characters were chillingly accurate, from a cute, baby-faced couple in a motel room to a mother hell-bent on defending a daughter she saw as perfect. In the one hour of the episode called "Denial," NBC showed the birth, the recovery of the body, the arrests, the trial, and the verdict. Guilty.

If only the legal system moved so quickly.

In late October Tanenbaum finally said what had been suspected for months. The Grossbergs wanted a separate trial from Brian.

"That's a motion we will make," Tanenbaum said.

His promise showed just how far apart the two defendants had grown. They had stopped speaking months ago. What had started out as a joint defense with a plan to walk into court together had become a finger-pointing, "he said she said" affair. Amy's defense would be that Brian took her from her dormitory, Brian got the motel room, Brian took the baby without her knowing and threw him out, and Amy was deathly sick throughout each step and had no idea what had happened until she was told later by doctors and police.

*Amy did nothing wrong.*

As the one-year anniversary of the baby's death approached, the gravesite of the baby still had the same plastic metal stick with the name "Baby Boy Grossberg-Peterson" that had been there since the burial. No headstone. Jewish law says a headstone is supposed to be unveiled a year after death, sometimes ten months or eleven, but usually no more than a year.

Tanenbaum, when asked about a headstone, said: "It's on order."

Four weeks later, three weeks after the November 13 anniversary of the baby's death, a headstone finally appeared.

"Always in Our Hearts," it read above the Star of David.

Tanenbaum, meanwhile, was busy trying anything he could to get Amy's defense position into the court record, into the judge's office, and into prosecutors' heads. On November 19, a year and a day after Amy's arrest, Amy and her mother drove into midtown Manhattan, a block from Columbus Circle, to a business called Scientific Lie Detection, Inc. Founded in 1958 by the husband-and-wife team of Richard and Catherine Arther, it had administered more than twenty-six thousand polygraph examinations. Among the original founders of the American Polygraph Association, Richard Arther was one of the polygraph consultants assigned by Congress to look into the murders of President John F. Kennedy and Reverend Martin Luther King Jr.

Amy was wired up and questioned by Richard Arther.

"Did you and Brian go to the motel to give birth to a baby?"

"No."

"Before the baby was born, did you and Brian ever discuss killing the baby?"

"No."

"The entire time you were at the motel, did you believe you had a miscarriage?"

"Yes."

"At any time at the motel did you and Brian discuss killing the baby?"

"No."

"Did you ever see the baby?"

"No."

"At any time while at the motel did you know you had delivered a live baby?"

"No."

She passed. Every question. The next day Catherine Arther asked the same questions of Amy. Again she passed. Or did she?

The reason polygraph tests are never admitted as evidence in court cases is that they are considered unreliable. Lawyers know it. Judges know it. The science has not been proven to be foolproof. Convicted people have passed polygraphs. Innocent ones have failed. Even people who pleaded guilty have failed. The mere possibility that a person might be able to lie their way through a lie detector test has kept polygraphs out of the courts over the years. But that wouldn't stop Tanenbaum from trying. If he was going to file a motion to have the results admitted, he didn't want it to be a short story in a few newspapers. He wanted maximum publicity, so the whole country could see that Amy had passed. He would wait for the right moment.

The investigation had slowed by December 1997. Steve Fox had returned to police duty while also working the case, when the stress of a failing marriage along with a running feud he had been having with his superiors about working too much on the case overwhelmed him. He had been transferred back to the dreaded six P.M. to two A.M. shift, back to being a patrolman, and he was not happy.

To take out his anger, he often found himself practicing karate. A second-degree black belt, he was at a local school on December 14, working out with a series of jump kicks and feeling strong, when suddenly he began to sweat profusely. Nausea was followed by dizziness, and he barely made his way to the bathroom, where he threw water on his face as his chest pains became stronger. He was on his way outside to sit down when a doctor happened by and asked if he was okay.

He wasn't. Fox walked back inside the school and called 911 himself.

"I need an ambulance," he would remember saying later.

After four days at Christiana Hospital, and one major angioplasty to improve blood flow to his heart, Fox was released and told to relax. A lot. He would not return to work until February, but when he did, he wasted no time returning his attention to Amy and Brian.

On February 12, 1998, he drove to Wyckoff. It was a town he had heard so much about, and now he needed to see it, drive it, talk to its people, walk its shopping centers, try to learn about the environment that had surrounded Amy and Brian while they'd dated. His visit gave him a taste of what experts say is a problem not just in Wyckoff, but in upper-middle-class America.

"The parents are overprotective to a fault," Fox would say later. "These children grow up making no life decisions on their own."

The psychiatry of the crime, what might have driven Amy to do what she did, is what put Letang on a plane to California on February 15. Leaving behind the Wilmington winter for the California sun wasn't too difficult, but he hated traveling with the photographs of the dead baby in his briefcase. They made him queasy.

In Newport Beach, California, Letang met with Park Dietz, the longtime FBI consultant and widely renowned psychiatrist who had recently testified for prosecutors in the trial of the Menendez brothers charged with killing their parents. Letang knew from the first day of the case that Amy's state of mind would be critical for her lawyers, and he wanted to have his own expert ready. He had been talking to Dietz for months and had sent him a case file, including a videotape of the family's interview with Barbara Walters. For three hours Letang shared with Dietz everything he knew, focusing on the argument her lawyers were making that Amy was too weak to know what happened. Dietz, like Letang, believed Amy and Brian had

had no intention of walking out of that motel room carrying a live baby. That was what Letang wanted to hear, and he told Dietz before leaving to be prepared to testify.

Amy's parents, meanwhile, were desperate. For months Letang had been trying to enforce the subpoenas he'd served them in July 1997. The subpoenas ordered them to tell Letang what their daughter had told them about hiding her pregnancy. But they refused.

Their argument was simple: Jewish law protected them. They found a local rabbi who said that under Jewish law, a mother or father is not allowed to give testimony against her or his child in a court proceeding. Nobody bought it. Lawyers scoffed at them. So did Jewish scholars. And so did Judge Ridgely. He ruled quickly that the Grossbergs were dealing not in Jewish law, but in U.S. constitutional law, and that law said they had to talk.

On February 20 Alan and Sonye Grossberg drove to Delaware and met Letang, Paul Wallace, and a third prosecutor, Tom Brown, at their Wilmington office. Letang agreed he needed to talk only to Sonye. Her husband stood outside in the hallway with all three of Amy's lawyers. For four hours Letang and Sonye went at it. She was defiant, angry about being there, and whenever she didn't like a question, she stood up and walked out to consult the lawyers. She wrote down every question on a pad. Some of her answers left Letang speechless, particularly when he asked for her thoughts on Amy's relationship with Brian in high school.

"Did you think it would be appropriate for her to be having sexual relationships with Brian?"

"I didn't think about it."

"You didn't think about it?" Letang asked. How could she not think about it? he thought. Amy dated Brian for three years in high school. Isn't that what parents think about?

The interview touched everything, from the doctor's appointment in Wyckoff, to the phone call from the hospital, to the drive down to be with Amy. The doctor's appointment still puzzled the prosecutors as the interview was ending. Why did this woman not only go with her daughter to the doctor, but sit with her throughout the appointment?

"Did you normally always go in the examination room with her?" Wallace asked.

"Yes."

"So basically, in your prior experience, she would have expected that you would be going in with her and everything like that at that time?"

"Yes."

That told them all they needed to know about the mother-daughter relationship they were dealing with. The interview ended just after five P.M.

While Tanenbaum was filing a barrage of motions throughout the winter, Litman and the rest of Peterson's defense team were quiet. And with good reason. As confident as they were that they would be able to refute the medical examiner's claim that the baby was born alive and healthy and was brutally murdered, with testimony that the baby was, in fact, blue and probably stillborn, they had no solution for Brian's statement to Detective Wilson in Gettysburg.

Wilson had done such a thorough job of making sure Brian knew his legal rights, and telling him repeatedly that he could have an attorney present, that his lawyers had a weak argument to try to get the statement thrown out. As long as it was 'in, they had to deal with the hard truth that Brian, when asked what happened to his baby, said: "I got rid of it. I threw it out."

They tried to have the statement suppressed with the only argument they had. Joe Hurley filed a motion to suppress Brian's statement, arguing he had been "in the throes of emotional distress" when Wilson questioned him and was incapable of comprehending his situation and understanding his legal right to counsel. A hearing was scheduled for March 6 to hear arguments on that issue and on Tanenbaum's motion for separate trials.

If Litman could not get Brian's statement suppressed, his defense would become extremely difficult. Even if his lawyers could convincingly prove that the baby appeared to be stillborn to Brian, jurors would hardly be sympathetic after hearing that Brian said he just "threw it out."

Ultimately it was that statement that led Litman in February 1998 to initiate talks with Letang in Delaware about a plea bargain. It wasn't what Litman wanted. He liked his chances at trial, but only if Amy and Brian were together. He had always felt they were stronger as a couple than as individual defendants. But that was no longer possible. Brian was on his own.

Letang had made it clear from day one that he would not even consider a plea deal for Amy or Brian that did not include jail time. Amy and her parents and lawyers had refused even to consider jail. *Amy did nothing wrong.* But Litman accepted it, so his mission instead became to get as little jail time as possible for Brian. And he knew one way to do that was to make it clear to Letang that in order to get Amy, prosecutors needed Brian and the details he could give them.

Letang wasn't sold. He felt confident he could convict both of them at trial, at least of manslaughter. Murder would be difficult.

When Letang stepped back and examined his case, what he knew and what he could prove beyond any doubt were two different things. He could not prove with absolute certainty how the head injuries occurred. He had theories, Amy's heel for one, a chair for another. But no evidence. That left him with a brain-damaged baby. He was confident he would be able to prove the baby had not been stillborn, but he knew the defense experts would challenge that. A jury would be unpredictable, especially when the defendants looked like Amy and Brian.

Letang's plan was to try Amy first and then Brian. But the more he and Litman talked, the more it became apparent that Brian would plead guilty to manslaughter and accept the judge's sentence. Letang would make no recommendation. Manslaughter in Delaware was punishable by anywhere from zero to ten years, but most people convicted of it are sentenced to two and a half years. Letang could live with that. So could Brian.

On Thursday, March 5, the media once again converged on the steps of the courthouse. Amy's lawyers wanted to suppress the evidence police had found in her dormitory room, an argument Tanenbaum would lose. He also was ready to argue for separate trials for Amy and Brian.

But reporters were more interested in the relationship, or lack of one. It was one year since Amy and Brian had last been in court together, and so much had changed. In March 1997 they were cuddling with each other in open court, still very much in love. A year later they were not talking. Both were nineteen years old when they arrived separately for the hearing. Watching them was sad. The tension was so obvious. It was as if they desperately wanted to look at each other but could not. Their lawyers tried to shield them from any awkward glances toward each other, and for hours these two teenagers who had been through so much together sat less than ten feet apart and never even acknowledged each other's presence.

"There are many, many sad aspects to this case," Brian's attorney, Gioiella, said afterward.

For Tanenbaum, the media mob in town provided the ideal opportunity to file a new motion, one he had been holding for months, waiting for the right opportunity to get maximum publicity out of it. At last he filed with Judge Ridgely his request asking to admit Amy's polygraph results.

"The polygraph evidence is relevant since it has a tendency to make proof of Amy's lack of any criminal responsibility," the motion said.

*Amy did nothing wrong.*

When Letang saw the motion, he blew up. The mere mention of polygraph results has led to mistrials, and he wanted Tanenbaum sanctioned. Letang was prepared to do battle the next day when he heard that Tanenbaum was meeting in private with Judge Ridgely in the judge's chambers. Now Letang was livid not only with Tanenbaum, but with Ridgely for granting a private meeting with the defense. It was a highly unusual move, for a judge to meet with one side and keep out the other, and Letang suspected it could be about only one thing.

Tanenbaum had filed a motion to admit positive polygraph results. But if he knew of other lie detector tests Amy had taken and failed, and he had not included that in his motion, he would be in deep trouble with the judge. Amy's first polygraph had been given when Slanina, Oberly, and Jennings were her lawyers. Tanenbaum knew of the test.

Even though Letang didn't know for certain if there had been a previous test, he suspected there had been, and that Amy had probably failed. Letang let it be known to Tanenbaum that he knew as much, and within the week the favorable polygraph results that Tanenbaum wanted desperately to get in were out before they ever had a chance.

# GUILTY

B y Monday, word had spread. Brian was pleading.
The morning of March 9, 1998, was overcast. It
looked like rain but didn't feel like rain. A few people carried umbrellas, but most just wore raincoats. By eight A.M.
the usual contingent of reporters had saturated the sidewalk in front of the courthouse in downtown Wilmington.
Television news trucks occupied most of the parking
spaces, their cameramen holding their gear on their shoulders, turning left, then right, making sure not to miss anyone connected to the case walking past.

This had become the ritual for every court hearing in
the case. Police stood on the sidewalk with the news
crews, making sure no doorways were blocked and
passersby had no problems making their way through
the throng. People walking past who knew what the
commotion was about would snicker and moan,
annoyed that they had to weave their way through the
crowd of reporters and photographers, but still curious,
hoping to catch a glimpse of the defendants. People who
did not know whom the attention was for asked, and
when they were told Amy and Brian, that was all they
needed to hear.

"There, him, him!" shouted Marge Pala, a reporter for
KYW Channel 3 in Philadelphia. She yelled for her cameraman to get a shot of an older gentleman, dark suit,

heading up the few steps to the courthouse front door. Dutifully the cameraman got the man just as he entered the courthouse. He never glanced at the camera. Other cameramen also shot him, following the lead of their competitor. But reporters, both television and newspaper, stared at each other quizzically.

"Who was that?" one reporter asked a cameraman.

"I have no idea," said the cameraman.

And so it went.

The buzz all morning among the reporters was that instead of going through with the hearing that was scheduled, in which Brian's attorneys would try to have the interview he had given to Detective Wilson thrown out as evidence, Brian would plead guilty to manslaughter and agree to testify against Amy.

Even though Hurley had vehemently denied the stories, suspicions lingered that Brian would not go to trial. The case against him was strong. Prosecutors had him telling police he had taken his baby boy, not knowing if he was dead or alive, and throwing the body in the trash. When Hurley emerged from the courthouse at nine-fifteen A.M., reporters swarmed to him.

"Joe, will he plead today?"

"Joe, where is Brian?"

"Are you going to get him, Joe?"

"Yes, I'm going to go get him," Hurley said. "Short day. It will be a short day."

At nine forty-five a moving mass appeared a block away, walking from Hurley's office toward the courthouse. The cameramen backpedaled carefully, stumbling occasionally on their own cords, while the reporters shouted questions at Hurley and Russell Gioiella, as well as at Brian. When it became obvious they would not talk, the mass became hushed. It still moved, crossing the street slowly and walking in front of the courthouse.

The November day Brian had surrendered to police, in his blue fleece jacket and Villanova baseball cap, he'd looked thin to the point of gaunt, closer to fifteen years old than eighteen. He'd worn a frightened, almost dazed look, as his mother clutched his arm from behind. But now both of them looked different. Brian's preppy look was gone: no more khaki pants, sweater vests, and braided belts. No baseball hat. Walking between Hurley and Gioiella, Brian wore a sharp navy suit, and he filled it out. His chest was broader, his shoulders wider. But almost as a reminder of his youth, a small bit of acne had broken out on his chin. His mother, walking with her ex-husband, looked relaxed. Not at ease, but not scared.

Inside the courtroom, every seat was filled. Brian sat at his table, his mother in the first row behind him, and filled out paperwork. When he signed his signature to the plea agreement, he was saying he was guilty of recklessly causing his baby's death: manslaughter.

Letang stood before Ridgely and explained that an agreement had been reached for Brian to plead guilty to manslaughter and to agree to testify against his former girlfriend if she went to trial. Gioiella agreed that was the deal and then provided the public the first glimpse of what went on inside room 220 of the Comfort Inn early in the morning of November 12, 1996.

"After the baby was born, the infant did not show any sign of life, and he believed the baby was dead," Gioiella said. "He acknowledges great regret that they did not summon medical aid. He did not confirm it was dead. Amy is telling Brian, 'Get rid of it, get rid of it,' and Brian eventually puts the baby in a bag and throws it in a Dumpster outside the motel."

His guilty plea entered, Brian would quickly have his annoying electronic monitoring ankle bracelet removed until his sentencing.

Tanenbaum, Amy's lawyer, said he was not surprised by Brian's plea, but that Amy would not follow his lead.

"The only thing that matters to my client is that we get the truth out so she can get her life back," he told reporters outside the courthouse.

A week later Amy did get her life back. Sort of. Letang

dropped the death penalty from her case. Despite what the attorney general Jane Brady had said from the first day, that they would seek the death penalty, that was never true. She knew it. The defense lawyers knew it. But she dangled the mere possibility of it out there for Amy and Brian to think about. When Brian pleaded guilty, Amy's lawyers immediately argued for the charges against her to be dropped. Prosecutors had their man, Tanenbaum argued. And it was Brian. Brian did it. He admitted it. *Amy did nothing wrong.*

Brian would say otherwise.

On April 1 Brian drove to Delaware to meet with Steve Fox. The two had spent March 18 and 19 together in New Jersey after Brian had pleaded guilty. Brian took Fox around Wyckoff, showing him where he lived, where he went to high school, where Amy lived, what his life was like as a teenager. One of the terms of his plea deal was that Brian had to make a formal statement and tell all.

And he would. In tremendous detail. In one hour, with Gioiella and a court reporter in a small office on the sixth floor of the Delaware Attorney General's Office in Wilmington, Brian walked Fox through his three years with Amy.

"What kind of contact did you have with her parents?" Fox asked.

"It was pretty much, I guess, either on a week, during the week or weekend when I would go over to pick Amy up if we were going out. And, like, there were times when Amy's parents, if they were eating dinner, they would make me dinner and always be insistent upon me eating something when I was over. And if they were ordering out, to order me something. So I had pretty much regular contact with them."

"As your and Amy's relationship progressed, did you guys discuss any future plans?"

"Yes. Definitely. We discussed having a future together."

"Was marriage ever discussed in there?"

"Yes."

"Were children ever discussed?"

"Yes."

Brian said that by May or June of 1996 he and Amy were sure she was pregnant. He said they'd both accepted they were not ready for kids and that they had tried twice to have the baby aborted, but Amy had backed out both times.

"She was scared that her mother would find out about it. And if the place was dirty or she could get sick. And if she got sick, she would go to a hospital and her mother would find out about it. So it was a lot of, like, she didn't want to get sick and her sickness would cause her mother to find out, so her mother was, like, the big factor in everything that took place."

He told Fox about Amy's physical with Dr. Fenkart and how she had called him in Italy and told him about getting the chickenpox vaccine.

"She was saying, 'There was no way that I could say that I was pregnant and not get the shot because my mother was sitting right there, so I had to say that I wasn't pregnant and get the shot even though I was,'" Brian recalled.

He offered a concise account of the delivery and the day after, never blaming Amy for anything. Just giving his version. It would be the version Letang found most plausible, most believable. Everything that could be verified was verified, right down to the days that Brian said they attempted to have abortions. Fox was able to get the receipt for the $500 Brian took from his bank to pay for the abortion appointment on August 6, 1996.

With Brian's statement in hand, Letang knew there was only one thing to do with it. He had a hunch that Amy had not told her lawyers everything Brian had told Fox, so on Friday, April 17, Letang sent a copy of Brian's statement to John Malik, Amy's attorney in Wilmington, who immediately forwarded it to Tanenbaum in Beverly Hills.

"I thought, Let's hit them in the face with it and see what happens," Letang would say later.

It took only the weekend for Letang to see the fallout.

But he may have had some help. Many would speculate that the Grossbergs first began considering a plea six months earlier, after a Massachusetts jury found British au pair Louise Woodward guilty of second-degree murder in the death of an eight-month-old boy she was watching. The verdict, which was eventually reduced to manslaughter, followed a prolonged trial that revolved mostly on medical evidence about the baby's death.

Whether Woodward's case influenced the Grossbergs or not, Brian had done what his lawyers had promised. He'd given them Amy. Malik stopped Letang on the street on Monday and said it was time to talk. Amy's lawyers had been caught off guard by the details in Brian's statement, and Amy agreed enough was enough. The trial everyone wanted, a six-week trial that *Court TV* had anticipated covering from start to finish, was off.

The two families had spent more than $1 million combined on their defenses over twenty months, depleting most of what they had worked so hard for to raise their children. And they had achieved a result prosecutors had said was available to them more than a year earlier.

Amy arrived on April 22 for her hearing to plead guilty to manslaughter sharply dressed as usual, wearing a full-length black skirt, black sweater, and sky blue blouse. Walking alongside her parents, her brother, her maternal grandparents, and her aunt and uncle, she entered the courtroom sniffling, wrapped in the hulking right arm of Tanenbaum. She sat and cried in her parents' arms. Her mother stroked her hair, and then her grandmother whispered in her ear and kissed her forehead before she joined her lawyers at the defense table in the front of the courtroom.

"Amy has always taken personal responsibility for the consequences of what occurred," Tanenbaum told Judge Ridgely in the standing-room-only courtroom. "Now she wants to step forward and take public responsibility. She is the girl next door, the girl we ask to baby-sit our children."

In answering a series of questions from Ridgely, Amy remained composed as Tanenbaum rested his hands on her shoulders.

"Are you in fact guilty of this charge?" Ridgely asked.

"Yes, Your Honor."

Ridgely set sentencing for July 9, the same day as Brian's. Amy turned and rushed to her mother, who joined her in a group hug with two of her best friends who had come to the sentencing and sat quietly amid the reporters, dabbing their eyes with tissues as Amy spoke. Tanenbaum said Amy's decision to plead was "hers and hers alone," trying to deflect attention from Amy's parents, who had been so adamant that their daughter should not have to serve jail time.

Outside the courthouse afterward, Letang said he hoped other teenagers facing unwanted pregnancies would learn from Amy and Brian that options are available other than abandonment.

"A baby's dead," he said into a bank of a dozen microphones. "This child has nobody to talk for him. Our responsibility is to be the proxy for this child. This is a tragedy. Nothing that we do in this world is going to bring that kid back, and hopefully somebody somewhere down the road is maybe going to look at this and decide that this could have been prevented."

Letang's co-prosecutor, Paul Wallace, summarized the prosecution's case that would have been offered at trial had Amy not pleaded guilty.

"This child had a separate existence; it was born alive. Amy Grossberg, through her actions or inactions, caused the death. And she showed a chilling indifference toward its life."

All that was left was the punishment.

# SENTENCING

**July 9, 1998**

First Amy, then Brian. That was how Judge Ridgely had said he would sentence them on this day. Separately, for a crime they had committed together.

For almost four years they had been a couple. For their junior prom they had been a couple. For their senior prom they had been a couple. For high school graduation they had been a couple. For the duration of a full-term pregnancy they had been a couple. For the birth of their son they had been a couple. For the disposal of their son they had been a couple. For their arrests they had been a couple.

But for their punishments they were no longer a couple, no longer that smiling, cheek-to-cheek pair in the yearbook photograph that the world had come to know. Brian had filled out, with wider shoulders and a broader chest, and his hair was longer, parted in the middle. Amy had changed, too. She was cute, and her face was rounder, her hair a lighter shade of brown. But the innocence was gone. They were guilty.

On June 18 Letang had sent a letter to the state presentence office, which had prepared individual reports on Amy and Brian and interviewed them both. He left no doubt as to whom he believed and whom he did not.

"Grossberg denied pregnancy, denied delivery, and subsequently blamed Peterson for the disposal of this child,"

Letang wrote. "Conversely, Peterson advised Simonds, Parker, and the Gettysburg police that he disposed of a child in a Dumpster, and he subsequently cooperated with the authorities."

Long before the courthouse doors opened, reporters began lining up outside for their press passes, which were given out first come, first serve. In a courtroom that seats ninety, fourteen passes were reserved for the local media, the Delaware reporters, and eighteen more were set aside for out-of-state media. *The New York Times, People* magazine, *The Washington Post,* NBC's *Dateline,* and ABC's *Good Morning America* were all there as early as five A.M. Without a press pass, reporters would have to try to get in with the general public for the remaining fifty-eight seats.

The courthouse opened at eight-thirty, and almost immediately the line began forming behind the metal detector in front of Courtroom 301: ten, twenty, thirty people, most of them Amy's aunts, uncles, and friends from home, in addition to the dozens of reporters. They stood quietly, looking straight ahead with sad eyes. Amy arrived first at nine-thirty, wearing a lilac blouse and long black skirt. She walked quickly through the mass of people there to watch her be sentenced, her head leaning on Tanenbaum as they moved ahead of her parents. Inside the courtroom, Brian arrived a few minutes later with his mother, father, and stepfather. He took his seat to the right of the podium alongside Hurley, Litman, and Gioiella, while Amy, after hugging her parents, sat to the left, ten feet apart from Brian but divided by so much more.

The ringing bell broke the courtroom silence, and in walked Ridgely. Letang had agreed with the defense lawyers and had not offered a recommendation to the judge as far as how much jail time Amy and Brian should receive. So Ridgely was on his own. The most a person convicted of manslaughter in Delaware can get is ten years, but the state's presumptive guidelines recommend just two and a half years. The judge could set them free, put them away until 2008, or find some sort of middle ground.

Tanenbaum stood at the podium and began his last plea for leniency from the judge.

"She lives in agony," he said, looking down at Amy, who was sitting with her head down, crying softly. "She visits the baby's grave. She prays. She is in agony, filled with self-criticism."

When a person pleads guilty, a judge wants to hear remorse, sorrow, regret. He does not want to hear remorse followed by excuses. Guilty means guilty. Say you did it, say you're sorry, say you've learned a valuable lesson. Otherwise, don't plead guilty and save the explanations for trial. Ridgely had seen everything there was to see in the case, from the dispute over the baby's health, to the concerns for Amy's sickness, to the mystery over the skull fractures. That was why Tanenbaum's approach with the judge stunned so many of the courtroom observers, among them her first lawyers from Delaware.

He criticized the autopsy on the baby, he criticized the Delaware Attorney General's Office for its rush to judgment in announcing it would seek the death penalty, he restated his claim that Amy was suffering from "a disease that almost took her life," he denied that Amy had manipulated anyone at her July 1996 doctor's appointment when her pregnancy was missed, he went so far as to say that by seeking no prenatal care, Amy had not, in fact, violated any law. He was right.

In essence he gave the judge an abbreviated version of his case all over again. Only at the very end did he say what the judge had come to hear.

"Amy's agony is real, and remorse is without question. Tomorrow is Amy's birthday; she'll be twenty. Please find a way to let her help others avoid wrecking their lives. She has shattered her own."

Brian sat quietly as Tanenbaum talked, and Litman rubbed his shoulders softly. Behind them, a sketch artist furiously outlined the characters in court for the art that would be photographed afterward and shown on the evening news and in the morning newspapers. Amy stood to talk next to Tanenbaum, her sobs and sniffles coming clearly through the microphone and bouncing loudly around the courtroom.

"I don't know where to begin. I only can tell you that so much has been said about my family and me."

Brian reached up with his left hand and wiped a tear from his eye. This was the girl he had loved, still loved in some ways.

"I'm extremely sorry for what happened to my baby," Amy said. "I have no one to blame but myself. I know I could have prevented this from happening by talking to my parents or seeing a doctor."

She paused to take a deep breath. Every word was a struggle. Her parents and brother sat a few feet behind her in the first row of the courtroom, her mother convulsing in tears. "The pain inside will be with me for the rest of my life. When I'm at home, we all feel the pain. I want to help others. I want the opportunity to make a difference. I will never be able to forgive myself for what happened."

Letang was not about to forgive her, either. This was his day to shine, to show the world that this was not a case to be brushed off lightly as two scared kids who made an error in judgment. He described how the baby had been found, in a plastic bag in a Dumpster on a cold night, with serious head trauma. He would not try to speculate about what caused the injuries. He left that for people to decide on their own.

"We will not know ever what transpired in that motel room," he said, the built-up passion of twenty months coming out in his voice. "Three people were in that room. One is dead, and the two others are co-defendants of this homicide."

Forced to answer Tanenbaum's argument that the baby was stillborn, Letang said simply that the "baby was not compromised." The defense, he said, knows that, because if they could prove otherwise, they would have gone to trial and not pleaded guilty.

He left the judge a nugget of curiosity, that Amy had

been alone with her baby for ninety seconds while Brian had left the room for the plastic bag.

"We do not know what happened in that room," Letang said. "Mr. Peterson has spoken to us. Ms. Grossberg has not."

Armed with Amy's letters to Brian, Letang started reading them.

"All I want is for it to go away. I can't get caught. Can't."

He told of the chickenpox vaccine that Amy had been willing to receive, knowing it could harm her fetus.

"Amy Grossberg sacrificed that baby to hide the truth. Her secret was more important than the life of her child."

Letang looked straight at Ridgely. "Jail is plainly the right thing to do," he told the judge. "We're also telling people, 'You cannot do this.' If there is anything positive to come out of this process, the public has got to know this is not what we do."

He turned to Amy. "I trust that she's a bright and intelligent person. She's also self-absorbed and selfish, and for that she goes to jail."

Amy cried.

Paul Wallace stood up. For the entire case he had been in Letang's shadow, the second prosecutor on a major case, an expert in child abuse cases, more soft-spoken, a balding Irish Catholic from a family of six siblings, a thirty-three-year-old father of two young children. An hour before the sentencing he had read Letang a letter he said he wanted to read aloud in court. Letang listened and was not so sure about it. He found it to be uncomfortable and unorthodox. At every sentencing in criminal cases, the victim is always allowed to speak in court. The victim may have been robbed, raped, stabbed, or simply deceived. But Amy and Brian's victim would never speak, and Wallace wanted the judge to remember why as he stood at the podium.

*I was born on November 12, 1996. My mother was artistic and my father was a good athlete. While my* parents weren't married when I was born, they had more than sufficient financial and family support to care for me.

Before I was born my mother continually denied I was coming. She never sought a doctor's help to make sure I was okay. The only doctor she saw when she was expecting me, she lied to so he wouldn't know I was coming. The only thing she would say about me were things like: I was the worst thing that could happen to her; why won't it just go away; she'd do anything to have it just leave; and I just want it to go away and it will all be over with. Even after I was born and people knew about me, she would go on national TV—just so people thought better of her—and call me "something that came from" her.

When I was born, I was 6.2 pounds and was twenty inches long. I had blue eyes and brown curly hair. I did not live very long after I was born. My parents had me in a motel room because they didn't want anyone to know about me. The doctors say if I had been born in a hospital, and didn't suffer terrible head trauma and the cold and suffocation of being put in a plastic bag and thrown away like trash, I'd be alive today. Although I may have eventually developed cerebral palsy, I may have been epileptic or may have even been mentally retarded.

Nobody knows exactly what my parents did before I died, but I know it was because they simply didn't care if I lived or died. My mom especially just didn't want to get caught. She just cared much more about herself than me so she did absolutely nothing to make sure I'd be here today, but she did everything to make sure nobody ever knew I existed.

I am the only victim in this case.

There were few dry eyes in the courtroom as Wallace sat and Ridgely told Amy to rise. She moved toward the podium, but just as the judge was about to start talking Amy turned around, her face crinkled up in tears, and looked at her mother.

"The court clearly recognizes your exemplary background. Your family worked hard, you have been loyal to your synagogue. I received one hundred and forty character reference letters. But there is a disturbing aspect of your character as the time of the childbirth neared. You showed this thorough resistance only that your parents not be told. Many young mothers have faced challenges you did with much less support. The combined recklessness of the two of you caused the death of a defenseless infant whose life is no less important than anyone else in this courtroom."

Ending the suspense, he read his sentence. The first words out of his mouth were eight years, causing a gasp to go up. But Ridgely quickly explained that he was suspending all but two and a half years, giving her credit for the two months she served after her arrest, and ordering her to serve three hundred hours of community service by speaking to pregnant teenagers. Ridgely had stuck by the guidelines. Thirty months. With good behavior and her credit for time served, Amy could be free by September 2000.

As she was being led away by sheriff's officers, Amy turned to her mother, who was crying as she stood leaning on the oak railing that separated them.

"I love you," Amy said through tears as she disappeared through the side door.

"Don't worry. We'll appeal," Sonye said back to her. Defiant to the end, even though there was absolutely no grounds for an appeal. *Amy did nothing wrong.*

Afterward Letang would say why he never believed that argument.

"This homicide was completed during a few hours' duration on November 12, 1996, but was the product of many months of acknowledgment, contemplation, fear, obfuscation, manipulation, and deceit. Although there may not have been a preconceived plan regarding the disposal of this child, it cannot realistically be controverted that the events that unfolded on November twelfth came as a surprise to either defendant. A defenseless baby was discarded in the trash like so much refuse."

With Amy gone, Brian's attorneys would take a vastly different tack with Ridgely than had Tanenbaum. It was obvious to Litman and Gioiella that the judge probably had his mind made up and was clearly uninterested in hearing the evidence argued all over again, as it had been for months. Gioiella stood and bluntly told the judge that he would attempt to show that Brian deserved less time than Amy.

At the outset of the case in November 1996, legal experts predicted that Amy would clearly get off lighter than Brian because she had suffered through a traumatic delivery, she had been hospitalized with seizures, she was the mother. Brian had confessed to throwing the baby in the trash. Any sympathy for him was minimal. Of course Amy would get off lighter.

As Gioiella and, later, Litman spoke, though, it became clear that the perceptions of Amy and Brian had reversed.

"He did what he did not out of selfishness," Gioiella said, "but out of love for Amy. He didn't do what he should have done. He should have forced her to have more concern for her child."

But when Gioiella began to say that Brian could not convince Amy to go to the hospital early in the morning when he picked her up at her dorm, the judge cut him off.

"He was driving the car, wasn't he?" Ridgely asked firmly. Brian's mother brought her hands up and covered her face.

"That is correct, Your Honor," Gioiella answered. "He didn't take control and do the right thing. And that is why we are here today. His feelings for Amy overwhelmed his judgment."

Litman stood up and continued to pour on the sentiment that Brian was nothing more than a teenager in love, determined to stand by his girl. No matter what.

"Brian's remorse, Brian's contrition, is completely sincere," Litman said, a slight dig at Amy and her interview on national television. "It was not done in public. It is private. It is real."

He told of how Amy had threatened to take her life and that Brian believed she would have if he betrayed her and revealed their secret. He told how Brian made one last attempt in the car to change Amy's mind.

"He didn't want to go to a motel. He wanted to go to a hospital."

Litman disputed, as he had for months, that Amy was near unconsciousness as she gave birth and said she played just as much a role in the disposal as did Brian.

"Amy said, 'Get rid of it,' and against better judgment, he did," Litman said in his slow, deep voice.

Brian, in his business suit and sharp dark blue shirt and gray tie, stood next to Litman, stoic and expressionless, and looked squarely at the judge, leaning slightly to his left.

"I have written to you expressing my sorrow for the loss of the life of my son. All I can say is I am so sorry for what has happened." And he sat down. No tears.

When Letang stood last, he was visibly less animated than he had been for Amy's sentencing. He had felt that Amy's tears were for herself and her punishment, not for her baby, and that irked him. Brian, Letang believed, was sincerely sorry for what he did. But that didn't excuse his actions.

"Brian Peterson should go to jail," Letang told Ridgely. "He showed a callous disrespect for life. He threw a baby in the trash."

Then Letang softened. He said Brian was clearly not out to commit a crime on the night the baby was born. He said Brian had had a fake license in his wallet when he'd checked into the motel but he'd used his real one.

"To a fault, he did what he did out of chivalry, being a

gentleman. He told me he didn't want to violate the trust Amy had in him. With all due respect, that's stupid."

Letang was done and had just sat down when Litman asked Ridgely for a minute to speak with the prosecutor. He whispered in Letang's ear, and Letang stood again.

"I do believe Mr. Peterson has expressed genuine remorse," Letang said.

He explained that Brian, after his release from jail in January 1997, had begun visiting his baby's grave without telling anyone, not his lawyers, his mother, his friends. Ridgely nodded his head.

"I agree with defense counsel that you have accepted your role in this," the judge said. "You, like Amy, should not have kept this pregnancy secret. You should have protected him from an unassisted childbirth."

One hour after sending Amy away for thirty months, Ridgely sentenced Brian to six months less than his high school sweetheart. In twenty-four months, and possibly sixteen if he got time off for good behavior, Brian could be free.

"I was hoping for a little more jail time," Letang would admit later. "But I'm satisfied with the sentences."

As Brian stood, a sheriff's officer on either side of him, his mother crept through the wood gate to where the lawyers' tables were. She stood a foot from her son, her only child, crying softly. They were not allowed to touch, but he looked at her as he was led away. No words were necessary. As he disappeared, his mother stood alone, her hand over her mouth, desperate for someone to hug. Her knees buckled, and she was caught by her ex-husband.

As he walked into his house at six P.M., after all of his interviews, receiving congratulations from lawyers he passed on the street, and after sharing a beer with his co-workers, Pete Letang bent down to pick up his "Manth" and to hug Nick.

"Daddy, Daddy, we saw you on TV!" they shouted as they ran into his arms.

Nothing would have made his night more than to just slouch in front of the television and watch *Rug Rats* with his kids on Nickelodeon. Debbie, limping from a leg injury she had suffered while exercising that morning, winced with every step she took through the kitchen but could not hide her immense relief.

For twenty months her husband had been going to work and spending his days studying photographs of a dead baby, talking to doctors about the dead baby, flying around the country to talk to psychiatrists about who killed the baby, and preparing a case against the parents of the dead baby. Debbie never grew comfortable talking about this case, but it had invaded their home. The media calls came at all hours. They never changed their listed telephone number, even after reporters called her husband at midnight, but they did get a caller identification box.

Now, as Samantha climbed on his lap, Letang was reminded of how old the case was. Manth was born on November 3, 1996. Baby Boy Grossberg-Peterson came nine days later. Manth was now at that age where her every move, her every expression, captivated anyone in the room. She understood, she communicated, she cried, she cooed. As she sat on his legs, Letang whispered the word "eyes" to Manth, a game they played, and he watched as his daughter crinkled up her eyes in the cutest of faces. He said "cold" and watched her put her fists up by her side and do a pretend shiver.

Amy and Brian's baby might have been doing all of those things today. Maybe not. Maybe he would have been retarded. He would not be dead, Letang thought. He would have been cute. That's certain, with blue eyes like Brian's and Amy's dark hair.

Letang went to his study and collected a cluster of files from the case to throw out. After changing out of his suit into a baggy T-shirt and gray shorts, he settled into a chair at the kitchen table and turned on the small color television that sits on the window ledge overlooking his front lawn. The floor was covered with crumbs and toys. The sentencing was the lead story on every news channel. There were the pictures of Amy arriving at court, sobbing in Tanenbaum's arm. There was Brian, stoic, no tears.

There was Letang, on his big day, with his parents in court to watch him, on the steps of the courthouse afterward, speaking into a cluster of microphones to a hundred reporters, finally able to talk freely with the gag order lifted and the case done. There was Steve Fox, off to the side, seven months after his heart almost failed him, eventually leading to his early retirement.

"How would you characterize what was done to this baby?" was shouted at Letang.

"Horrible." He paused and then again. Louder. "Horrible!"

Next question.

"The public does not understand two and a half years for the killing of a poor little innocent newborn. How do you explain that to the public?"

"We know there's a baby in the trash who has substantial head trauma. We have a proof problem. How that child got killed is the problem. You've got to prove that beyond a reasonable doubt. This is a very difficult case. We're very comfortable that they pleaded to manslaughter. We think it's appropriate, and we think the sentence is appropriate."

Click. Every channel, there he was. His fifteen minutes. The next morning he would do the *Today* show and *Good Morning America*, but for now he was tired of it all.

Click. No escaping it. There were Hurley and Tanenbaum on CNN's *Larry King Live*, arguing over why Brian got less time than Amy.

Click. Ah, the Chicago Cubs. Baseball. He put down the remote and watched as Debbie carried twenty-month-old Samantha away to bed.

# EPILOGUE

From the courtroom, Amy and Brian went their separate ways. Amy was taken back to the Delores J. Baylor Women's Correctional Institute, where she was kept isolated from the general population for her protection. Brian was taken first to Gander Hill Prison, but his lawyers were able to have him transferred immediately to a minimum-security jail called the John E. Morris Correctional Institution in Dover, Delaware, an hour south of Wilmington. Though the inmates there were less violent, mostly drug offenders and tax cheats, Brian, like Amy, was isolated for his protection.

Public opinion was predictably mixed about Ridgely's sentencings, but a majority seemed to believe that Amy and Brian got off easy. America Online provided a forum for users of the service to voice their thoughts. In barely a week more than 18,000 messages were posted, many of them by high schoolers and young adults. More than 14,000, or roughly 75 percent, said the sentences were too lenient. Roughly 2,500 said just right, and the remaining 1,500 said too harsh.

The families of the two teenagers, who had become cordial over the course of their relationship during high school, no longer spoke with each other. The entire town of Wyckoff seemed to breathe a sigh of relief after the sentencing. No more reporters knocking on their doors, stopping them in parking lots to ask their opinion, showing their town on the evening news for the whole world to see.

On October 29, 1998, Melissa Drexler, the "Prom Mom" who gave birth in a bathroom stall at her New Jersey high school prom, was sentenced. Though the judge said Drexler deserved public sympathy, and she sobbed throughout the hearing, he called her actions "explainable, but not excusable" and sentenced her to fifteen years in prison. Her lawyer said she would probably serve two and a half years before being moved to a halfway house and she could be released in just under three years when her first parole hearing arrives.

Not long after Brian and Amy began serving their sentences, their lawyers filed motions asking for their jail time to be reduced, a common move but one that's rarely granted. Amy's motion said that she had been working as a janitor in prison, had enrolled in college correspondence classes, and was helping to develop an interactive computer game that would allow teenagers to experience the consequences of their actions and choices in life. In a letter to Judge Ridgely, Amy wrote that she has been tutoring other inmates and helping them make beaded jewelry. She said she has helped with the computer game because "I not only give my opinion from a young person's perspective, but also through what I have experienced."

Steve Fox, the police detective on whom the case took its toll both physically and emotionally, left home on a hike just days after the sentencing. The prosecutors returned to their daily grind.

Every so often a small stone appears on the gravesite of the baby in Union, New Jersey. While most people like to place cut flowers at a grave, the flowers inevitably wither and die in a few days. Jewish tradition says that a small piece of the earth, such as a rock, is a way of saying to the deceased that our memory of them is eternal and will last as long as the earth.

# AFTERWORD

*They felt like they only had each other.*
      —Neil S. Kaye, psychiatrist

The people in Wyckoff, New Jersey, had been whisper-ing for three days about Amy Grossberg and Brian Peterson before I first heard their names. Word had quietly spread through their small hometown starting on Novem-ber 14, 1996, that the police in Delaware were investigat-ing a dead baby found in a trash bin. Disbelief spread quickly through the streets, the schools, the homes, the temples, and the churches. No one could believe the baby was Amy's, as the police said. Amy had everything, like so many of the teenagers in town: the best clothes, a new car, her college bills paid, loving parents, the best friends. Girls like Amy wouldn't get pregnant. Girls like Amy wouldn't keep secrets. And girls like Amy certainly wouldn't toss away a baby like day-old trash.

In truth, alarmingly, it is girls exactly like Amy who are doing all of those things more and more frequently. The crime of neonaticide has long been viewed as a problem only of young, poor, inner city, minority women with no money and no support system. But in recent years, the crime has taken on a new face. Amy's face: young, middle class, and white. These children have tremendous support sys-tems, from their parents, to their teachers, to their friends, to their clergy, yet they choose to ignore all of them and protect their secret. Why? I interviewed teenagers, parents, rabbis and priests, lawyers, police, and prosecutors. No one has the answer. But this is a question that needs to be explored.

I hope by doing that in this book, parents with Amys and Brians in their homes will be forced to look in the mirror and ask themselves if they know their children. Not their grade-point average, their after-school activities, and their career track, but their habits, their friends, their sexual maturity, and their experiences with drugs.

Wyckoff is no different from any affluent, American suburb in that image counts. They are towns that loathe having their dirt unearthed for the whole world to see. The town leaders want to protect the image that attracts newcomers, and keeps property values high. The police prefer to keep incidents, particularly those involving children, to themselves rather than risk harming the community's identity. The sight of a television news truck in Wyckoff, or a reporter with a pad, makes residents cringe, knowing that their world, their glass bubble, has probably been scratched. Or worse, shattered.

There is no tougher job in life than parenting. And it's no less challenging in suburbs such as Wyckoff than it is in cities such as New York. As parents everywhere have now seen with Amy and Brian, money is meaningless when it comes to parenting. It does not instill values. It does not make life simpler. It does not allow parents to do less parenting. It does not teach children the difference between right and wrong. It does not teach responsibility.

Money does, however, unlock doors. But it doesn't open those doors. Money buys a lot of things, but it doesn't buy a guarantee of success. Nothing does. Too many parents today in these affluent suburbs like Wyckoff fail to recognize that, and they assume that if they raise their children in safe neighborhoods, educate them in the best schools, buy them a car, and provide them with almost anything money can buy, that their children are sure to shine. How can they not?

When studies on teen pregnancy and pregnancy rates come out, the people in Wyckoff hardly blink. When the Alan Guttmacher Institute reports that only 70 percent of women who give birth as teenagers finish high school, compared to 90 percent who give birth later, Wyckoff shrugs it off. Towns like Wyckoff ignore the news that a teenage mother is two and a half times less likely to own a home and 50 percent less likely to have accumulated any savings than mothers who do not give birth until after they turn twenty-four. Those are someone else's problems. Not my kid.

One parent in Wyckoff told me that parenting is a "crapshoot." I understood what she meant. At some point, children must be responsible for their own actions. The parents can only hold their hands for so long. But that mother must also acknowledge that some parents do it better than others, some parents do sit down with their children long before they reach the age of eighteen and make it clear that it's okay to fail once in a while. Even to fail horribly, as Amy and Brian did.

"This has been a crushing reality of what could happen," Diane Dobrow, the teacher at the high school Amy and Brian attended who is a close family friend of the Grossbergs, told me months into the case. "Lines of communication have been opened and will remain open. That's the only positive to come of this nightmare."

But that type of change doesn't happen overnight. One dinner table conversation won't change the culture in these towns. The children in Wyckoff see what their parents have provided for them, and they see almost unattainable goals for themselves.

The teenagers in town use the word "cutthroat" to describe their high school and the principal smiles and the parents smile and everyone looks the other way. "Cutthroat" is good, they surmise. But "cutthroat" is the reason why some of the brightest students in Wyckoff sometimes feel the need to slip a cheat sheet into their baseball caps for the next test. Better to cheat and bring home the A than not cheat and bring home the B.

When I showed up for work at *The Record* in Hackensack on Sunday, November 17, 1996, a pretty fall day, I was expecting a quiet afternoon. Instead, the editor that day, Robin Phillips, sent me two hours south to the University of Delaware to ask students what they knew about this freshman from New Jersey who had been charged along with her boyfriend with killing their newborn son. The very first girl I interviewed on the Delaware campus that afternoon was watching friends play football when she asked what many would echo in the weeks and months to follow.

"How could somebody take a brand new infant and throw it in the trash when thousands of people out there want new babies?" said Renae Miller, a senior at the time.

Amy's pregnancy tortured her. And Brian. They were hardly alone. More than half of all pregnancies in the United States are unintended, and half of those—almost one and a half million a year—end in abortion. Amy's parents undoubtedly would have been crushed if she had told them about it. But they probably would have recovered and dealt with it as most parents do. The problem is Amy didn't believe that.

No one had told her.

That's why she behaved like a junkie who had pulled a stick-up at a local convenience store. I can't get caught.

In Wyckoff, the people who saw Brian and Amy as the boy and girl next door were the same ones who looked at the decisions they had made, and then at their own teenagers, and were quick to insist: Not my kid. My kid looks and acts just like Amy and Brian; but my kid wouldn't do that.

It's easy to say. But are they so sure?

For as long as they want, parents of smart, suburban teenagers can continue looking at the secrets kept by these two from New Jersey and go right on saying it: Not my kid.

Just remember. Amy's parents, and Brian's, used to say it, too.

Doug Most
*October 1998*

# POSTSCRIPT—
# JANUARY 2000

Their time in prisons just a few miles apart passed quietly, with neither of them having any problems with prison staff or fellow inmates. Their lawyers tried repeatedly to have them released early, only to hear Letang argue that it would look like two young inmates from affluent families catching a break. In late November 1999, Hurley asked to have Brian released Christmas Eve so he could spend the holiday with his family. Letang was not sympathetic. Neither was Judge Ridgely.

"The court took into account all of the information provided for sentencing, including Peterson's cooperation with the authorities, his proven reckless conduct at the time of the offense, his background and lack of criminal record, and his anticipated good behavior while incarcerated," Ridgely wrote in his ruling. "When a reduction of sentence application is made more than ninety days after sentencing, it may be granted only upon showing extraordinary circumstances. None of the reasons cited by Peterson's counsel meet that standard."

Letang was relieved, and reminded the public why Brian was in prison.

"This sentence was not for rehabilitation. This is for punishment. He should serve his full sentence."

Both Brian and Amy kept busy in prison. Amy tutored other women. Brian worked in the kitchen, policed the prison grounds, and did laundry.

Brian was released from prison on January 4, 2000, walking out of prison with his arm around his mother and his stepfather walking in front of them. They returned home to Wyckoff to a throng of reporters. With Litman and Gioiella by his side, along with his mother, Brian said on his front lawn he was sorry for his role in his baby's death. He spoke firmly and looked tired and pale, but otherwise stronger and more mature, with a hint of a goatee on his chin.

"I want everyone to know how sorry I am for my part in the tragic events that occurred three years ago," he said reading from a typed statement. "I am very happy to be home with my family and loved ones, and I look forward to resuming my life. I cannot adequately express my appreciation for the sympathy and support I received from so many people during these trying times. I can assure everyone that I will reward their confidence in me, and make them proud of me in the future."

Brian's freedom no doubt irked Amy and her family, who never accepted why she received a longer sentence. Amy, who like Brian, was a model prisoner, was due out in late May. The two of them never corresponded while in jail, and when Brian was asked whether he might contact her, he said nothing.

"He has no plans to speak with her," Gioiella said.

The rift that developed between the two reached the national media a few days later, when Tanenbaum and Hurley went on CNN's "Larry King Live" and feuded over who was more to blame for the baby's death. Tanenbaum continued insisting that Amy was near-comatose during the pregnancy and did nothing while Brian disposed of the baby, and later lied about Amy's role. Hurley said Brian only did what he did because Amy told him to "get rid of it."

"He and I have a philosophical difference about allocating blame," Hurley told King about Tanenbaum. "I think

Bob likes to say my client sold his soul to the devil, and I could say that his client seems to think that she's a fairy-tale princess who did nothing wrong."

Letang, who found himself impressed with Brian even while he prosecuted him, visited him in jail and saw a young man instead of a teenage boy. Weightlifting bulked up Brian's outside, but Letang said he also had grown on the inside.

"He's a different human being," Letang said. "I saw tremendous growth in him. His outlook on life has changed."

Still, even while he had grown to respect Brian more, Letang's opinion on the sentence handed down by Ridgely never changed.

"They both should have received more time."

# RESEARCH METHODS

**O**ne advantage I had in writing this book was that when I started, I already knew the case cold. From the arrests of Amy Grossberg and Brian Peterson in November 1996 to their sentencings in July 1998, I was there for every step, every court proceeding. For my newspaper, *The Record*, I wrote more than 150 articles on this case. I never had to catch up with any development or familiarize myself with any proceeding that had happened by asking participants to describe it for me. I was there. Always.

Throughout the case the lawyers were not allowed to discuss what was happening and why because of a gag order imposed by the judge that kept many details from being released. However, as soon as the two teenagers were sentenced, the gag order was lifted. It was only then that I was allowed to read portions of the case file of the Delaware prosecutors to learn what they had learned. Much of this story came directly from the case file. The lead police detective walked me through every minute of the search for the baby and the arrests of the defendants, as well as his twenty months investigating. No one knew the case better than he did.

To understand what the night of November 12, 1996, was like when Amy and Brian delivered their baby in a Newark, Delaware, motel, I stayed at the same motel on a

Monday night, the same weeknight they were there. The motel would not allow reporters to stay in the same room Amy and Brian had, though I did see the room. I went outside into the parking lot at the same time Brian did with the baby in a bag, and I drove the streets at the same hour they had. I stood and watched as a garbage truck picked up the Dumpster behind the motel a few minutes after five A.M.

Although both defendants and their families declined to be interviewed for this book, many of the questions I would have asked them were asked by police and prosecutors.

When the prosecutors interviewed Amy Grossberg's mother about the case, a court reporter was present. Her transcript of that interview, 140 pages of questions and answers, provided insight into the relationship between Amy and her mother as well as facts about the case.

Also, before Brian was sentenced, his lawyers filed a memorandum with the court seeking leniency from the judge. That hundred-plus-page brief contained vivid details of Brian's first few hours in police custody, including his meeting with a college counselor. The counselor recalled not only what Brian said word for word, but also his emotional state.

Two other documents that proved invaluable were a fifty-page statement that Brian made to police after agreeing to plead guilty and a report that Amy's family had prepared by a professional firm in an attempt to sway the judge toward leniency. Those documents provided information straight from the mouths of Amy, Brian, and Amy's family.

Without question, it is a difficult task to reconstruct a crime when the facts are in dispute as they were in this case. Ultimately I had to rely on what my own interviews told me and what seemed most plausible.

In describing life in the town of Wyckoff and the pressures on the children to succeed, I relied on dozens of interviews with town officials, school officials, clergy, students, parents, and the local weekly newspaper, the *Wyckoff Gazette*. I spent more than a month in the town, sometimes simply standing on street corners for hours, walking through parking lots, reading in the town library, watching children, watching their parents, and watching them together.

To help me understand the values and issues in Wyckoff, and towns just like it, I read books and studies and consulted the experts who wrote many of those books and studies. Most helpful were Robert Fishman, the author of *Bourgeois Utopias: The Rise and Fall of Suburbia,* and Harriet Porton, who co-edited the book *Adolescent Behavior and Society: A Book of Reading.*

I spent a substantial amount of time researching the crime of neonaticide to understand not only who most often commits such a horrific act, but why. I interviewed leading authorities on neonaticide including Phillip Resnick, the Ohio doctor who coined the word almost thirty years ago. He, along with Delaware psychiatrist Neil S. Kaye, was immensely helpful.

Unquestionably, the most significant dispute in this case was between prosecutors and defense attorneys over the health of this baby when he was born and the head injuries he was found with inside the Dumpster.

Only two people will ever know how this baby looked when he was born and if he cried or appeared not to be breathing. Only two people will know if the head injuries were intentionally inflicted or took place after the baby was abandoned. I did not speculate about what happened to the baby. I simply laid out the arguments that were offered by the medical experts for the prosecutors and the defense and will leave it to readers to decide for themselves. I talked to more than two dozen doctors about the health of this baby—doctors who were connected to the case and those who were not. While they helped me draw some conclusions, they, like everyone else, will never know for certain what crushed this baby's skull and whether this baby appeared to be stillborn or was alive and kicking.

Lastly, I visited the grave of this baby half a dozen times.

# NOTES

1. *New York* magazine, Melanie Thernstrom, July 13, 1998. "Child's Play," p. 20.
2. National Center on Institutions and Alternatives, "Sentencing Report for Amy Suzanne Grossberg," submitted to Dover, Delaware, Superior Court President Judge Henry duPont Ridgely, June 1998.
3. *People* magazine, March 23, 1998. "His Way Out," p. 48.
4. National Center on Institutions and Alternatives, p. 2.
5. National Center on Institutions and Alternatives, p. 3.
6. National Center on Institutions and Alternatives, p. 5.
7. ABC-TV, *20/20*. Transcript of June 6 program, interview with Alan, Sonye, and Amy Grossberg.
8. National Center on Institutions and Alternatives, p. 7.
9. *New York* magazine, Melanie Thernstrom, p. 21.
10. National Center on Institutions and Alternatives, p. 10.
11. National Center on Institutions and Alternatives, p. 10.
12. National Center on Institutions and Alternatives, p. 10.

# INDEX